THE GREAT BRITISH
VEGETABLE
COOKBOOK

THE GREAT BRITISH
VEGETABLE
COOKBOOK

SYBIL KAPOOR

National Trust

Author Sybil Kapoor

For Raju, with love

First published in the United Kingdom in 2013 by
National Trust Books
10 Southcombe Street
London W14 0RA

An imprint of Anova Books Ltd

ISBN: 9781907892622

A CIP catalogue record for this book is available from the
British Library.

20 19 18 17 16 15 14 13
10 9 8 7 6 5 4 3 2 1

Reproduction by Mission Productions Ltd, Hong Kong
Printed by 1010 Printing International, China

Senior Commissioning Editor: Cathy Gosling
Project Editor: Lucy Smith
Copy Editor: Heather Thomas
Designer: Lee-May Lim
Proofreader: Katie Hewett
Photography: Karen Thomas
Photography Assistant: Laura Urschel
Food Styling: Bridget Sargeson, Jack Sargeson
Prop Styling: Cynthia Inions

This book can be ordered direct from the publisher
at the website: www.anovabooks.com, or try your local
bookshop. Also available at National Trust shops or
www.shop.nationaltrust.org.uk.

CONTENTS

INTRODUCTION

As you might guess from the title, this is a book about vegetables. I've written it as a labour of love for both omnivores and vegetarians, who, like me, are fascinated by the incredible array of vegetables that we have at our disposal in Britain throughout the year.

It is a book that can be used on three levels. First and foremost, it is designed to be a source of delicious vegetable recipes that you can dip into whenever you're seeking inspiration. I've divided the book into the four seasons and organised the vegetables in such a way that they appear in their peak season, when they're at their best and cheapest. Thus, cauliflowers are in the autumn section, although you can buy British-grown ones throughout much of the year.

Within each season, the vegetables are organised roughly in order of their appearance. Spring, for example, which officially runs from March to May, begins with purple sprouting broccoli and ends with the arrival of the first Jersey Royal new potatoes. At the end of each vegetable section, you'll find a list of recipes that use the vegetable elsewhere in the book. You will also find a seasonal chart on page 12.

Secondly, *The Great British Vegetable Cookbook* can be read as an unusual manual to develop your cooking skills. I wanted to give further insight into how best to enhance your chosen vegetable. Each vegetable section includes practical tips and culinary suggestions, but if you turn to the seasonal introductions you will find all sorts of thought-provoking ideas that may influence how you cook. Many of them lie at the heart of my philosophy of cooking and are not commonly discussed in cookbooks. In the introduction to spring, for example, I explore the power of suggestion, discuss how to make vegetables more attractive and appetising to people who dislike them, and look at sources of inspiration when trying to create a spring dish. My aim, as always, is to stimulate both thought and pleasure.

Lastly, but equally importantly, the book is an informal guide, which can lead you into sourcing interesting and sustainably grown British vegetables. The National Trust is heavily involved in this area with their own restaurants, kitchen gardens, farms and a myriad of different community

ABOVE The kitchen garden at Wordsworth House, Cumbria, in July.

projects, all designed to enhance the many special places it cares for. These range from farming the now-rare Formby asparagus near Liverpool to developing allotments for urban areas, such as Minnowburn community allotments in South Belfast.

I've worked closely with the National Trust to highlight some of the different ways in which you can access home-grown produce, from farmers' markets and sourcing heritage seeds, to school plots, family allotments and community-supported agriculture schemes. I suggest a different way of sourcing vegetables in each of the seasonal introductions. I've only scratched the surface by mentioning a few of the many exciting projects the National Trust is undertaking, but I hope that it will inspire you to investigate further in your local area.

As always with cooking, inspiration can come in many forms. For me, having grown up in the country, rambling old vegetable gardens are still a great source of culinary ideas. Just wandering around the lovely eighteenth-century kitchen garden at Attingham Park in Shropshire, for example, sets my mind humming. What might I do with the old-fashioned purple carrots they've set out for sale? Stepping into their pretty, restored 1922 greenhouse, there are crystal apple cucumbers and Hungarian hot wax peppers to tempt me – perhaps they are also for sale?

ABOVE LEFT Onions dug from the kitchen garden at Knightshayes Court, Devon.

ABOVE RIGHT Squash growing in the walled kitchen garden at Clumber Park, Nottinghamshire.

Cooking with lots of seasonal vegetables has always represented an ideal way of life in Britain. Deep within our national psyche, consuming vegetables symbolises an almost spiritual sense of oneness with the natural world. It's as though every time you buy a floppy lettuce from your local farmers' market for salad, or pull up some leeks from your garden for a pie, you're working in harmony with your surroundings. Eating British vegetables is imbued with positive values, ranging from good health to thriftiness – it's like taking a bite of positivity every time you munch a radish!

Nevertheless, over the years, there have been surprisingly few books dedicated to the pleasures of cooking with British vegetables, especially for omnivores. I should add here that vegetarians can easily adapt many of the meat or fish recipes in this book, so don't be discouraged. My primary aim throughout the book has been to create recipes that bring out the very best of each vegetable. A naturally sweet onion, for example, tastes even better with a hint of sourness, whether it is soaked in buttermilk before being coated in semolina and deep-fried to make ultra-crispy onion rings, or baked in a tart with soured cream.

Perhaps the most influential British vegetable cookbook is Jane Grigson's *Vegetable Book*, which was first published in 1978. She listed her vegetables alphabetically, placed each within its broad historic context and gave a wide variety of recipes. Her book included pulses and supermarket exotics, such as sweet potato, bean shoots and okra, and it reflects our culture at that time.

My criteria are slightly different insofar as I want to encourage cooks to use more local produce within its natural season, which means only selecting British-grown vegetables. I also explore how each vegetable sits within our culture – after all, we don't regard chillies as being British, despite the fact that we started to grow them here in the seventeenth century and have cultivated them commercially since the eighteenth century. Are peas more British than potatoes?

As I started to research the book, I quickly realised that our attitude towards vegetables and how to cook them has been shaped by our national self-image and our changing attitude towards the world. Over the centuries, we have avidly collected vegetables from far and wide, our desire for new and interesting foods fed by our natural curiosity. Once the said plants were safely home, we set about trying to improve their flavour and productivity. Such work continues today: British plantsmen and women still travel to the wilds of China and South America to find new and interesting vegetables. Meanwhile, farmers are seeking to improve their produce from growing ever-sweeter cabbages, sprouts and spring greens to the perfect British tomato.

As we travelled and sampled foreign vegetable dishes, so our culinary repertoire changed. We may have first been introduced to aubergines in the sixteenth century, but it was only after the advent of package holidays in the late twentieth century that they became popular. After all, aubergines don't suit being prepared in the classic British manner, namely boiled, and buttered or tossed in a sauce, but once Mediterranean dishes, such as ratatouille and moussaka, had been sampled, it was only a matter of time before the supermarkets started to sell home-grown aubergines. Incidentally, you won't find either recipe in this book – instead you will discover the likes of fried spiced aubergine with yoghurt dip, and aubergine noodles.

Today, we are still experimenting with different ways of cooking vegetables. Our national confidence enables us to apply the best methods from around the world to our chosen vegetable. This may be a book about British vegetables, but you will find an internationally inspired selection of recipes, albeit shaped to our taste. I also make full use of imported ingredients, such as olive oil and soy sauce. I am, after all, following in the footsteps of my ancestors, who kept a well-stocked larder full of exotic flavourings to enhance their cooking.

All of which leads me on to older varieties of vegetables. Over the centuries, vegetables and vegetable varieties have fallen in and out of fashion, and it is well worth seeking out such unfamiliar vegetables as some of them taste amazing while yet others look fabulous. One of the easiest ways to discover them is to wander around some of the kitchen gardens of National Trust properties. Many nurture forgotten plants, such as Clayworth Prize Pink celery at Clumber

Park in Nottinghamshire, Cottager's kale at Knightshayes Court in Devon, and scorzonera in the seventeenth-century inspired kitchen bed at Ham House in Surrey. Hence, you will find a section for salsify and scorzonera in this book, despite the fact that, unless you grow it, it's not easy to find – both taste gorgeous. Sadly, lack of space has meant that I've had to be quite ruthless in my selection, so you won't find kohlrabi or sea kale. Please forgive any such omissions on my part.

Lastly, when you turn to the end of the book, you will see a section entitled 'In a Perfect Kitchen', which includes recipes for everything from pastry to pasta. Like so much of this book, it represents an ideal. In a perfect world, there are certain foods that are good to have to hand, whether they're home-made stock or pizza dough – home made tastes so much better than shop bought. However, many cooks suffer from lack of time and, as always in life, it's a fine balance. If you're someone who enjoys cooking as a form of relaxation, then you will take great pleasure in making everything from scratch and freezing some of it for future use, but if you are pressurised, it's better to be pragmatic and buy what you need. I have no wish to engender guilt, quite the reverse; my hope is that you will find endless hours of enjoyment from this book.

ABOVE LEFT The kitchen garden at Knightshayes Court, Devon.

ABOVE RIGHT The Victorian-style kitchen garden at Avebury Manor, Wiltshire.

SEASONAL CHART FOR VEGETABLES

	January	February	March	April	May	June	July	August	September	October	November	December
Artichokes, globe					■	■	■	■	■	■		
Artichokes, Jerusalem	■	■	■							■	■	■
Asparagus				■	■	■						
Aubergines							■	■	■	■		
Beans, borlotti								■	■	■	■	
Beans, broad					■	■	■	■				
Beans, French & green								■	■	■		
Beans, runner								■	■	■		
Beetroot	■	■					■	■	■	■	■	■
Broccoli, calabrese							■	■	■	■	■	
Broccoli, purple sprouting	■	■	■	■	■							■
Brussels sprouts	■	■	■								■	■
Brussels tops	■	■									■	■
Cabbage, green	■	■	■	■	■	■	■	■	■	■	■	■
Cabbage, red	■	■								■	■	■
Cabbage, white	■	■	■							■	■	■
Carrots	■				■	■	■	■	■	■	■	■
Cauliflower			■	■	■	■	■	■	■	■	■	■
Celeriac	■									■	■	■
Celery	■	■						■	■	■	■	■
Chard	■	■	■	■	■	■	■					
Chicory	■	■	■	■						■	■	■
Courgettes							■	■	■	■		
Cucumber							■	■	■			
Endive	■	■	■	■						■	■	■
Fennel							■	■	■	■		
Garlic						■	■	■	■	■		
Greens, spring & winter	■	■	■	■	■						■	■

■ In Season   ■ Peak Season

	January	February	March	April	May	June	July	August	September	October	November	December
Kale	■	■	■	■					■	■	■	■
Leeks	■	■	■	■				■	■	■	■	■
Lettuce	■	■	■	■	■	■	■	■	■	■	■	■
Lettuce, lamb's					■	■	■	■	■	■	■	
Lovage						■	■	■	■	■		
Mushrooms, ceps								■	■	■	■	
Mushrooms, chanterelles							■	■	■	■	■	
Mushrooms, field							■	■	■	■		
Nettles		■	■	■	■							
Onions	■	■	■	■	■	■	■	■	■	■	■	■
Onions, spring	■	■	■	■	■	■	■	■	■	■	■	■
Parsnips	■	■	■						■	■	■	■
Peas, sugar snap & mangetout					■	■	■	■	■	■		
Peppers & chillies								■	■	■	■	
Potatoes	■	■	■	■	■	■	■	■	■	■	■	■
Potatoes, new				■	■	■	■	■				
Pumpkins & squashes								■	■	■	■	■
Radishes					■	■	■	■	■	■		
Rocket	■	■	■	■	■	■	■	■	■	■	■	■
Scorzonera & salsify	■	■						■	■	■	■	■
Shallots	■	■	■	■	■	■	■	■	■	■	■	■
Sorrel		■	■	■	■	■	■	■	■	■	■	
Spinach	■	■	■	■	■	■	■	■	■	■	■	■
Swede	■	■	■						■	■	■	■
Sweetcorn								■	■	■	■	
Tomatoes						■	■	■	■	■	■	
Turnips	■	■						■	■	■	■	■
Watercress	■	■	■	■	■	■	■	■	■	■	■	■

■ In Season   ■ Peak Season

SPRING

SPRING

In early March, the scent of spring fills the air. Sweet, fresh and dewy, it carries the promise of green growth and gentle showers. As the days grow longer, blackthorn bursts into flower and stinging nettles carpet neglected spaces. It is a time when all British cooks yearn for fresh new foods that will mark the end of winter – there is a desire for lighter, vegetable-based dishes to replace the calorific comfort eating of cold days.

Yet, as any gardener knows, spring is a sparse time for home-grown produce in Britain. In March, there are purple sprouting broccoli, spring greens and, if the weather is mild, bunches of watercress for sale. To source locally grown vegetables, you have to continue, much as your ancestors did, with the cabbages, onions and stored roots that fed you through the winter months.

It takes time for the soil to warm: the first tender leaves of sorrel appear in gardens in April; asparagus soon follows, pushing its tightly furled buds through the bare beds in readiness for St George's Day on 23 April. At the same time, pretty bunches of English radishes and the first Jersey Royals start to appear in the shops, along with early spinach and glasshouse cucumbers and aubergines.

IMAGINATION

It requires imagination – a quality that Britons possess in abundance – to conjure up seasonal spring dishes every day. It demands focusing on the new season's vegetables while changing the style of your recipes, so they evoke the soft colours and fresh flavours of spring. The emerald green of stir-fried greens hints at spring, as does the frill of watercress bursting out of a crusty sandwich, and the zingy flavour of orange in a soy dip for purple sprouting broccoli.

Begin by using your chosen vegetable as a focal point within a meal. Who can fail to feel delight at the sight of breakfast radishes arranged around a minty yoghurt dip, or gain pleasure from the aroma of a pale green asparagus risotto?

As the days lengthen, seek out inspiration from your surroundings. A wild March day instigates a warming potato, bacon and greens cheesy bake; a bank of primroses conjures up the tastes and colours of a sorrel omelette; and a misty walk at dusk in May suggests a dish of buttered radishes.

ABOVE Spring blossom at Acorn Bank in Cumbria.

THE POWER OF SUGGESTION

Remember that everyone is susceptible to the power of suggestion. Serve a creamy nettle soup and your diners will find themselves recalling childhood escapades as they sup the delicious liquid. Offer your guests a beautiful plate of new potatoes with smoked salmon, watercress sprigs and horseradish cream, and they'll instantly dream of balmy spring days.

One of the principal reasons people enjoy eating certain foods is that they associate an ingredient with something good. Asparagus is a classic example: on one level, there's a general association with an ingredient, but on another level, there's each individual's personal experience. Asparagus is commonly linked to the idea of luxury, easy summer living or romance, yet, for me, it will always be associated with my early catering experiences, when we had to use what were then regarded as very expensive cans of asparagus to make rolls and tarts for parties.

In contrast, rocket is forever linked in my mind with the sophistication and excitement of restaurant kitchens. I was introduced to it as a chef in the mid-1980s. It seemed a wondrous salad leaf with its peppery taste, dark colour and bouncy structure – perfect for adding flavour, colour and structure to a new style of salad-based appetiser. At that time, however, I had no idea that it had been grown in Britain for centuries.

CHALLENGING NEGATIVE ASSOCIATIONS

Of course, the cook must also counter negative associations, especially when it comes to certain vegetables. There are many people who can't countenance the idea of eating spring greens, so strongly do they associate them with nasty, over-cooked school dinners. The challenge is to create a new positive association that converts the eater into loving such vegetables.

The best way to tackle such a problem is to acknowledge which factors triggered the initial dislike and then to remove them. Over-cooked greens, for example, smell horrible, look unpleasant and are slimy and bitter when eaten. However, by stripping away their bitter outer leaves and cooking them in the lightest way possible, they will look pretty and taste sweet and crunchy. You also need to adopt a level of cunning, whereby you slip them on to a plate as a tiny garnish to accompany a favourite complementary dish, such as crispy roast chicken. Little by little, the phobia will be overcome.

SOURCING SEASONAL VEGETABLES

Shoppers are equally susceptible to the power of the suggestion. The supermarkets play on our desire to cook spring ingredients by arranging an alluring selection of vegetables that carry the promise of summer, but look a little closer. You will find that before the start of each British vegetable season, imported vegetables take pride of place. Thus, Spanish asparagus will appear a month before the British season begins, and once it ends, imported asparagus will reappear from as far afield as Peru. Unless you read the label, it's not always easy to realise that the country of origin has changed. Supermarket marketing believes that this policy encourages sales of the British crop – you can draw your own conclusions.

Farmers' markets are a good way to get a sense of which vegetables are in season within your area. Alongside the winter roots in March and April will be early spinach, spring greens and wonderful salad mixes, including sorrel, rocket and watercress. In May, many markets will have special stalls dedicated exclusively to asparagus.

However, one of the best ways for urbanites to gain a true sense of our vegetable seasons is to wander around the kitchen gardens of their nearest National Trust properties or even to become involved in one of their gardening groups. Tucked away in quiet places of many National Trust gardens are simple plots that are lent out to local groups or schools. Were you to walk behind the Orangery at Ham House in Surrey in late spring, for example, you would see two large neatly hoed vegetable plots, each carefully marked out with seed labels. One might be sown with radishes, pumpkins and suchlike by Year Three at The Russell Junior and Infant School. There might even be a strip of intense green Paragon wheat seedlings, which the children will later harvest, grind into a flour and bake into bread. The other plot might be sown with beans, salad leaves, peas and mint by the Ham Multi-cultural Women's Group, who are learning about English gardening behind the protective walls of Ham House's kitchen garden.

The long daylight hours will soon warm the soil and yield intensely flavoured vegetables for us to pick in the coming months. Who cannot share that sense of wonder each spring that our mild northern climate can nurture so many delicious vegetables throughout the year? It's time to get creative and start cooking.

PURPLE SPROUTING BROCCOLI

Broccoli comes in two forms: sprouting and heading. The former is made up of a loose cluster of flower heads on one or several branches, as opposed to a single head. Both were introduced to British cooks in the eighteenth century. The latter can be found on page 160.

Sprouting broccoli, or Italian asparagus as it was sometimes called, came in many different colours, including white, green, purple and black. It was quickly regarded as a luxurious vegetable, due in part to its novelty and in part to the fact that it's at its best in March and April – a sparse time for home-grown vegetables.

Indeed, so novel was it that Hannah Glasse takes the unusual step of explaining how to prepare its stem for cooking in *The Art of Cookery Made Plain and Easy* (1747). She then suggests, amongst other things, serving it boiled like asparagus and dressing it in a salad with some oil and vinegar, garnished with pickled nasturtium buds.

It remains an early spring favourite today, although modern cooks are more likely to season it with soy sauce and sesame seeds than pickled nasturtium buds, oil and vinegar.

PRACTICALITIES

■ To prepare: strip away the small side leaves and buds of each head and use a potato peeler to finely pare the tough skin from the stalks.

■ Blanching lessens the bitterness of purple sprouting broccoli. Drop it in unsalted boiling water for a few seconds, then drain and cool under cold running water. Add to cooked dishes, such as spiced coconut broth, and reheat.

■ Like all brassicas, purple sprouting broccoli develops a lovely, slightly nutty flavour when stir-fried from raw.

■ To steam or to boil? It's best steamed to prevent the fragile heads from becoming soggy.

CULINARY NOTES

■ Strong flavours, used with a light hand, work well with purple sprouting broccoli – for example, ginger, chilli, garlic, soy sauce, orange zest, lemon zest, black or white toasted sesame seeds, toasted sesame oil and tahini (sesame paste).

■ Slow-cooked broccoli is often partnered with strong-flavoured cheeses, such as Pecorino or Parmesan. See two ways with slow-cooked broccoli on page 168.

■ Anchovy lovers might favour seasoning their purple sprouting broccoli with a little chopped salted anchovy.

PURPLE SPROUTING BROCCOLI WITH HOLLANDAISE SAUCE

In *The Art of Cookery Made Plain and Easy* (1747), Hannah Glasse recommends serving purple sprouting broccoli, boiled like asparagus, with butter in a cup. By the twentieth century, Hollandaise and Maltaise sauces had become fashionable accompaniments. The latter is a Hollandaise sauce flavoured with the zest and juice of blood oranges.

SERVES 4

450g/1lb purple sprouting broccoli
1 tablespoon white wine vinegar
3 tablespoons water
3 peppercorns

a pinch of salt
3 egg yolks, strained
250g/9oz unsalted butter, diced
juice of ½ lemon

1 Prepare the purple sprouting broccoli, as described on page 20. Heat a Thermos flask with boiling water. Tip out the water and seal – you want a warm, not hot, flask. Warm 6 plates in an oven set to fan 100°C/gas ¼.

2 To make the sauce, put the vinegar in a small saucepan with 2 tablespoons water. Roughly crush the peppercorns and add to the vinegar with a pinch of salt. Set over a medium heat and reduce the liquid to one tablespoon. Strain into a double saucepan or a pan that can sit in a larger pan of barely simmering hot water.

3 Add a tablespoon of cold water and the egg yolks to the vinegar. Set over the pan of barely simmering water and whisk continuously, gradually adding the butter, so that the mixture forms a thick emulsion. Be careful not to over-heat or the mixture will separate – if worried, keep removing the pan from the heat and continue whisking. Finally, mix in the lemon juice. Adjust the seasoning to taste and pour into the Thermos flask and seal. It will be quite runny.

4 Steam or boil the purple sprouting broccoli (see page 20) for 4–5 minutes, or until tender. Divide between 6 warm plates. Add a small bowl of Hollandaise sauce to each plate, so that your guests can dip their stems into the sauce. Serve immediately.

TAHINI DRESSED PURPLE SPROUTING BROCCOLI

The simplicity of this spring dish belies its sophisticated flavour. Tahini paste is made from ground sesame seeds and adds a complex nutty taste, which makes you want to keep eating the fresh-tasting broccoli.

SERVES 4

450g/1lb purple sprouting broccoli
2 tablespoons tahini paste
2 teaspoons caster sugar

2 teaspoons lemon juice
1 tablespoon naturally brewed soy sauce
1 tablespoon sake

1 Trim and pare the purple sprouting broccoli, as described on page 20. Cut each stem into even-sized pieces.

2 Drop half the broccoli into a saucepan of boiling unsalted water. Cook for 3 minutes, or until bright green and just cooked. Remove from the water, place in a colander and cool under cold running water. Repeat the process with the remaining broccoli, and then dry on kitchen paper.

3 Put the tahini paste into a small bowl. Using a wooden spoon, beat in the caster sugar, lemon juice, soy sauce, sake and 3 tablespoons of cold water.

4 Divide the broccoli between 4 plates, drizzle with the tahini sauce and serve.

ORIENTAL PURPLE SPROUTING BROCCOLI

This can be served warm or cold. For the latter, cool under cold running water and pat dry on kitchen paper. You can use a dry sherry if you can't source any sake.

SERVES 4

4 tablespoons naturally brewed soy sauce

4 tablespoons sake

2 teaspoons honey

2 teaspoons finely shredded peeled ginger

½ small red Thai chilli, or to taste,
    finely sliced (optional)

finely grated zest of 1 orange + 6 tablespoons juice

2 tablespoons toasted sesame oil

450g/1lb purple sprouting broccoli

1 Place the soy sauce, sake, honey, ginger, chilli and orange zest in a small non-corrosive saucepan, and set over a low heat. Simmer gently for 5 minutes or until slightly reduced. Add the orange juice and remove from the heat. Set aside to cool a little, then whisk in the toasted sesame oil.

2 Trim the sprouting broccoli, as described on page 20, making sure that each stem is cut into even-sized pieces. Pour some boiling water into the bottom of a steamer. Once it comes back to the boil, add the broccoli

in single layers in the steam pans. Cover and cook for 3–5 minutes, or until tender. Otherwise, cook in a large saucepan of boiling water for 3–5 minutes, or until tender. Drain, then dry on kitchen paper.

3 Divide the tepid or cold sauce between 4 small ramekins or dipping bowls. Place each on a plate and arrange the broccoli stems beside each small bowl. Serve with napkins and let your guests dip their stems into the aromatic sauce.

SEE ALSO

- Two ways with slow-cooked broccoli on page 168.

SPRING GREENS

Beautiful, purple-tinged greens are sold in the early spring. These seasonal loose-leafed cabbages are closely related to the stronger-flavoured, hardy winter greens and kales. Spring greens are a vegetable that tests the metal of any cook. In sensitive hands, they can be turned into an exquisite dish, whereas in the wrong hands, they can become something horrid.

Two factors determine success. First, it's essential to adopt a wasteful disposition towards spring greens: use only their tender bright green hearts. The tougher outer leaves are often too strong for a simple vegetable accompaniment. Second, you must always cook them very lightly at the last minute – this ensures that they taste sweet. Over-cooking releases the sulphurous compounds in their leaves and will remind unfortunates of the horrors of badly-cooked school dinners.

Our past habit of over-cooking our greens is believed by some people to originate from a time when our native wild cabbage would have required long or repeated cooking to rid it of its intrinsic bitterness. In recent years, both farmers and scientists have striven to cultivate ever sweeter-tasting brassicas, so if you have always eschewed spring greens, now is a good time to try them once more – you will be pleasantly surprised at how delicious they taste.

PRACTICALITIES

■ Allow around 600g/1lb 5oz uncleaned greens to serve 4 people.

■ To prepare: wash the greens and strip away and discard any damaged or tough outer leaves. Pull out their pale hearts and set aside. Taste the outer leaves; if they are sweet enough to eat, cut away their tough stalks and add to the hearts or reserve for a late addition to a slow-cooked chunky vegetable soup (see page 292).

■ To ensure sweetness, lightly steam, boil or stir-fry your greens. Over-cooking brings out their sulphurous notes.

CULINARY NOTES

■ Spring greens benefit from a simple approach and few ingredients. They are delicious eaten with meaty dishes, white fish, scallops and prawns. The inner hearts can replace green cabbage in recipes: see Cabbage and Kale on page 286 and Brussels Sprouts on page 280 for further inspiration.

■ Stir-frying brings out the nutty flavour of brassicas; choose between seasoning them with sesame, mustard or caraway seeds, or a hint of ginger or chilli.

■ All greens work well with creamy-textured foods, such as coconut milk, butter, cream and Taleggio cheese.

CRISPY CHICKEN WITH GREENS

For centuries, boiled 'greens' have accompanied every conceivable British dish. Eaten with a good gravy, lightly cooked spring greens are a heavenly combination. Try serving this with the salt-baked celeriac (see page 271) or celeriac and potato fluff (see page 273).

SERVES 4

4 tablespoons extra virgin olive oil
sea salt
4 boned chicken breasts with skin
3 tablespoons dry white wine

500ml/18fl oz good chicken stock (see page 307)
30g/1oz chilled unsalted butter, diced
450g/1lb cleaned spring greens (see page 26)

1 Preheat the oven to fan 200°C/gas 7. Rub the salt, followed by 1 tablespoon olive oil, into the chicken breasts, especially the skin. Set a large non-stick frying pan over a high heat. Add the remaining olive oil to the pan and, as soon as it is hot, add the chicken breasts, skin-side down. Fry briskly for 2 minutes, then turn them over and fry for 2 minutes on the other side.

2 Transfer to a non-stick roasting pan, skin-side up, along with the oil from the frying pan. Roast for 15 minutes or until cooked. They are done when their juices run clear when a skewer is inserted into the thickest part of the breast. Allow to rest in a warm place while you make the gravy.

3 Discard any excess oil from the roasting tray, then set it on the hob over a medium-high heat. Add the wine and bubble vigorously while you scrape any sediment off the bottom of the tray with a wooden spoon, then add the chicken stock and boil vigorously until it reduces to a syrupy gravy. Tip in any juices from the chicken breasts. Season to taste, remove from the heat and whisk in the butter. Strain into a warm sauce boat.

4 While the gravy is cooking, drop the greens into a large pan of boiling unsalted water. Cook for 2–3 minutes, or until tender, then drain and serve piping hot. Serve immediately with the roast chicken breasts and gravy.

STIR-FRIED GREENS WITH MUSTARD SEEDS

Spring greens take on a fragrant nutty flavour in this recipe, but it's important to cook this dish at the last minute. You can use sprout tops or green cabbage instead of spring greens, if wished.

SERVES 4

600g/1lb 5oz whole spring greens
3 tablespoons sunflower oil
1 clove garlic, finely sliced

1 tablespoon yellow mustard seeds
sea salt

1 Thoroughly wash the spring greens to remove any dirt. Remove the tough, dark green outer leaves, and cut off and discard the bottom stems. Slice the fresh-looking hearts into wide strips.

2 Set a large non-stick frying pan over a high heat until hot. Add the oil and, as soon as it's hot, add the garlic and mustard seeds – the latter will immediately start jumping out. Quickly add the greens, lightly salt and stir-fry briskly. Within seconds, the leaves will turn a brilliant green and wilt slightly. Serve immediately.

ABOVE The bluebells that carpet woodland floors are a welcome sign of spring.

POTATO, BACON AND GREENS CHEESY BAKE

This hearty supper dish fills you up and keeps out the cold. You can replace the spring greens in this recipe with any variety of green cabbage. Vegetarians can omit the bacon.

SERVES 4

680g/1½ lb potatoes, peeled
650g/1lb 7oz spring greens, cleaned and
    roughly chopped
3 tablespoons extra virgin olive oil
185g/6½ oz sliced back bacon, diced
1 large onion, finely sliced

1 clove garlic, finely diced
1 teaspoon caraway seeds
30g/1oz finely grated Parmesan + 3 tablespoons
salt and freshly ground black pepper
250g/9oz Taleggio, rind removed and diced

1 Preheat the oven to fan 200°C/gas 7 and lightly oil a 5cm/2in deep gratin dish. Peel the potatoes and cut them into 2cm/¾in thick chunks. Place in a saucepan of cold unsalted water. Bring up to the boil and cook for 15–20 minutes, or until tender. Drain into a colander.

2 Clean the spring greens, so that you are left with their hearts. Roughly slice the hearts.

3 Set a non-stick frying pan over a medium-high heat. Add 3 tablespoons oil and, once hot, add the bacon and fry for 3 minutes, or until it begins to colour. Reduce the heat to low and add the onion and garlic. Fry gently for 8 minutes, then add the caraway seeds and cook for a few minutes until the onion is soft and golden.

4 Increase the heat and stir in the greens – you may need to add them in two batches. Add a tiny bit of water, if necessary, to prevent them from catching. As soon as they've wilted, mix in the potatoes, followed by 30g/1oz Parmesan. Season to taste.

5 Spoon half the warm mixture into the bottom of the oiled dish. Dot with half of the diced Taleggio, then cover with the remaining potato mixture and strew the top with the remaining Taleggio. Sprinkle with the remaining Parmesan. Bake immediately in the centre of the preheated oven for 15–20 minutes, or until the vegetables are piping hot and the cheese is bubbling and flecked gold.

NETTLES

The soft emerald leaves of common or stinging nettles (*Urtica dioica*) emerge in early March, carpeting the hedgerows, banks and forgotten corners in a mass of fuzzy green leaves. For centuries, they were irresistible to country cooks who were short of fresh greens after the long winter. Children were sent out to gather their young shoots, so that their mothers could strip their leaves to add to simple nourishing broths, or cook them in butter to serve as a green vegetable. As the nettles grew larger, stalks and all were turned into nettle beer.

During the Second World War, people were encouraged to eat nettles. In *Wild Food* (1984), Roger Phillips recalls being sent out from his village school to pick nettles, which the school cook would 'cook into a most unsavoury pulp. Then when it was time for the babies' lunch, the long-suffering six [Phillips and his schoolmates] had to attempt to push it down the babies' gullets – the babies, quite rightly, explosively rejected it, usually into the face of the feeder… believe it or not, I love them now!'

As with all greens, nettles need light cooking. Handled with care, they can be used in place of spinach in pasta, soup and tarts, or mixed into mashed potato with wild garlic to make colcannon (see page 298).

PRACTICALITIES

■ Nettle tops should be picked when the plants are still small and tender, just a few inches high. This can be from late February to late May, depending on where you live. Don't pick for eating from early June onwards – the leaves undergo a chemical change, making them unpleasantly bitter and fibrous, as well as a powerful laxative.

■ Always use thick gloves when picking nettles, and rubber gloves when preparing them.

■ Wash the nettles in several changes of cold water, then strip the leaves from their stems and discard the stems. The leaves should be cooked.

CULINARY NOTES

■ Nettles have an unusual slightly woolly texture once cooked. For this reason, I prefer to combine them with other ingredients rather than eat them simply wilted in butter like spinach.

■ They soak up creamy foods, such as butter, cream and soft cheeses, and thus work well in some traditional British dishes, including leek soup and bubble and squeak, especially when partnered with potatoes.

■ Flavour them with spring onions, wild garlic or leeks, perhaps with a touch of lemon zest, mace or grated nutmeg.

NETTLE AND LEEK SOUP

As you make this elegant, delicately flavoured soup, marvel over the fact that you are following in the footsteps of your primitive farming ancestors who added nettles and other wild greens to their grain-rich pottages in the lean times of early spring. You can serve this soup hot or chilled.

SERVES 4

55g/2oz young stinging nettle leaves
4 leeks, trimmed and finely diced
3 tablespoons extra virgin olive oil
1 medium potato, peeled and finely diced

425ml/¾ pint chicken (or vegetable) stock
200ml/7fl oz double cream
salt and freshly ground black pepper
a handful of snipped chives or a few wild
   garlic flowers

1 Wearing rubber gloves, thoroughly wash the stinging nettles in plenty of cold water. Strip the leaves from their stems, discarding any damaged or eaten ones. Wash the leaves once more, then spin dry in a salad spinner and weigh them.

2 Trim the leeks of their roots and darker green leaves. Remove the tough outer leaves and cut a cross through the centre of the green-coloured section of leaves. Wash thoroughly in a sink of cold water, shake dry, finely slice and place in a colander.

3 Set a heavy-bottomed pan over a low heat. Once hot, add the oil, followed by the potato. Gently fry for about 3–5 minutes, stirring regularly to prevent them catching.

4 Mix the leeks into the potato and continue to fry gently for 5 minutes, or until softened and wilted. Stir in the stock, bring up to the boil and simmer for 20 minutes, or until the vegetables are meltingly soft.

5 Stir in the nettle leaves and cook for a minute. Remove from the heat and immediately liquidise – otherwise it will turn a nasty green. Add 150ml/5fl oz cream, then strain and season to taste. If serving chilled, refrigerate the soup once tepid.

6 If serving hot, reheat the soup at the last minute. Hot or cold, divide between 4 bowls. Add a swirl of the remaining cream to each bowl, then scatter with chives or wild garlic flowers and serve immediately.

NETTLE RAVIOLI

Don't be put off by the length of this recipe – it takes time, but it is easy to make. You can make the ravioli ahead and then keep it chilled until ready to cook. You can also adapt it to spinach.

SERVES 6

300g/10½ oz (flour weight) home-made pasta
    (see page 313)
beaten egg yolk, for brushing

1 tablespoon extra virgin olive oil
4 spring onions, finely chopped
salt and freshly ground black pepper

Filling
115g/4oz tender young stinging nettle leaves
300g/10½ oz ricotta
3 medium egg yolks
finely grated zest of 2 lemons

Dressing
55g/2oz unsalted butter
55g/2oz extra finely grated Parmesan

1 Begin by making the pasta, as instructed on page 313.

2 Prepare the nettles, as described on page 34. Drop them into a saucepan of boiling unsalted water. Cook briskly for 2 minutes, or until wilted, then drain and cool under cold running water. Squeeze dry and finely chop. Place them in a bowl with the ricotta, egg yolks and lemon zest. Heat the oil in a small frying pan over a medium heat. Add the spring onions and fry for 3 minutes, or until just cooked. Beat into the ricotta and season to taste.

3 Cut the pasta sheets into easy-to-work lengths. Cut the first in half lengthways and lay it out on a lightly floured surface. Place about 5 spoonfuls of nettle filling at regular intervals down its length. Lightly brush with egg yolk around the filling and then lay the second pasta half over the filling. Using your fingertips, gently press

down, before firmly pressing the 2 sheets together. Cut into squares and trim the edges. Arrange on a tray covered with greaseproof paper. Repeat with the remaining pasta until you have 24 ravioli. Cover with a clean tea towel and chill until you are ready to serve.

4 Warm 6 wide soup bowls in the oven, fan 100°C/ gas ¼. Bring 2 wide saucepans of salted water to the boil. Slide a few ravioli at a time into each pan, and once they've returned to the boil, cook for 2–3 minutes. You will have to cook them in batches. Once tender, remove with a slotted spoon and transfer immediately to the warm bowls.

5 Melt the butter in a small saucepan, pour over the hot ravioli, season with a little black pepper and serve with grated Parmesan. Eat immediately.

ASPARAGUS

On a warm April day, you can almost see the soil moving as the asparagus shoots push their way up into the sunlight of the walled kitchen garden at Knightshayes Court in Devon. The spears are cut and bunched according to the thickness of their stems, although the 'wild' varieties are always thin, before being sent to the kitchen or to Tiverton Pannier market. They are an irresistible temptation to lovers of butter-dipped asparagus tips.

There was a time when asparagus was widely cultivated across England. In Formby, near Liverpool, for example, the sandy back dunes were enriched with night soil from Liverpool to grow a unique variety of asparagus that was bought by the great shipping lines to serve on their transatlantic crossings. You can still stroll past Formby asparagus growing behind the dunes as part of a National Trust walk.

Many people believe that British asparagus has a particularly intense flavour, due to our long daylight hours and cool growing temperatures. Freshness, however, is also an important factor – the sooner you eat asparagus after picking, the more intense it will taste.

Traditional British varieties are green with mauve-tinged spears, but you can find sweet-tasting purple varieties and even white 'blanched' asparagus. Asparagus recipes, meanwhile, have become ever more adventurous, ranging from finely sliced raw asparagus to deep-fried tempura.

PRACTICALITIES

■ Asparagus comes in various sizes from fat (jumbo) to thin (sprue) stems. Choose straight, unblemished stems with tightly furled, dry buds. Avoid soft, bendy, dry, wrinkled or slimy ones.

■ To prepare: wash the stems in plenty of cold water to loosen any sand from their tips. Trim them, cut off any woody inedible parts and, using a potato peeler, pare the lower part of the stems.

■ To boil: drop into a large pan of boiling water. Cook until *al dente*, about 3–5 minutes. Dry on kitchen paper, so as not to dilute the sauce.

■ It is fashionable to grill asparagus (see page 106). Very tender asparagus can be griddled from raw, but I prefer to lightly blanch it first.

CULINARY NOTES

■ Unctuous textured foods, such as butter, eggs and cream, have an affinity with asparagus. As they cling to the tips, you can add further flavourings through such ingredients as vermouth, lemon or Parmesan.

■ Tarragon, chervil and basil all taste good with asparagus, as do morels, carrots, mustard and chicken. In fact, there are endless delicious combinations for you to try.

■ For maximum flavour for cold asparagus, drain the boiled asparagus and spread out to cool on a plate, rather than cooling it under cold water. Dry with kitchen paper.

POACHED EGG AND ASPARAGUS ON CLYSTON MILL TOAST

During the asparagus season, this is a very popular brunch dish at the Kitchen restaurant at Killerton House in Devon. You will need to get everything ready before you start cooking.

SERVES 2

170g/6oz asparagus tips
40g/1½ oz unsalted butter
salt and freshly ground black pepper

2 medium eggs
a dash of vinegar
2 thick slices of Clyston Mill bread (see page 312)

1 Wash the asparagus tips and drop them into a saucepan of boiling unsalted water. Return to the boil and cook for 3 minutes, or until just tender, then drain and pat dry on kitchen paper. Over a low heat, melt just under half the butter in the asparagus pan. Add the drained asparagus, season to taste and toss thoroughly in the melted butter. Keep warm.

2 You now need to toast the bread and poach the eggs at the same time. Poach the eggs: bring a saucepan of water to a rolling boil, add a dash of vinegar to stiffen the egg white, stir the water and then carefully break each egg into the water. Cook for 3 minutes.

3 Meanwhile toast the bread and spread with the remaining butter. Divide the buttery asparagus between the two slices.

4 Remove the poached eggs, draining carefully, and place on top of the warm asparagus. Season with cracked black pepper and sea salt. Serve immediately.

CREAM OF ASPARAGUS SOUP

I created this elegant recipe to maximise end-of season asparagus. If you want a slightly lighter flavour, use two-thirds of the stock and replace the remaining third with water. This soup freezes well.

SERVES 6

3 tablespoons extra virgin olive oil
1 onion, roughly diced
1 large clove garlic, roughly diced
1 litre/1¾ pints good chicken stock (see page 307)

1kg/2lb 3oz asparagus
salt and freshly ground black pepper
3 tablespoons double cream

1 Set a large saucepan over a low heat. Add the olive oil and, once hot, stir in the diced onion and garlic. Fry gently for 8 minutes, or until soft and golden. Add the stock, then increase the heat and bring up to a full boil.

2 Meanwhile, trim the asparagus. Tip it into a sink, which has been filled with cold water, and wash thoroughly, then drain and finely slice. Add to the boiling stock and, as soon as it returns to a full boil, in about 5 minutes, reduce the heat and simmer for 25 minutes, or until the asparagus is meltingly soft.

3 Season and liquidise the soup. If the asparagus is fibrous, you may need to pass it through a sieve. Adjust the seasoning to taste. You can either add the cream at this stage, or save it until you are ready to serve, then add a swirl to each bowl of soup.

ASPARAGUS RISOTTO

This simple dish is a good way to extend asparagus. Don't be put off by the length of the method – it's very easy to make and well worth the effort. Serve the risotto with a pretty salad of mixed leaves.

SERVES 4

450g/1lb bunch asparagus, washed
30g/1oz unsalted butter
1 onion, finely chopped
1 litre/1¾ pints good chicken or vegetable stock
    (see pages 306–7)

310g/11oz Arborio or Carnaroli rice
15g/½ oz Parmesan, freshly grated + extra
    for serving
salt and freshly ground black pepper

1 Wash the asparagus. Cut off and discard the tough end of the stalks. Cut off the tips and set aside. Working from the tender tip end of each asparagus stalk, cut a 2.5cm/1in length of the stalk into pea-sized slices. Add these to the tips. Then roughly slice the remaining (slightly tougher) length of each stem and set aside in another bowl.

2 Set a wide heavy-bottomed saucepan over a medium-low heat. Add the butter, and, once melted, mix in the onion. Fry gently for 10 minutes, or until soft and golden.

3 While the onion is cooking, divide the stock between 2 small saucepans. Bring both to the boil. Add the second batch of roughly sliced asparagus stems to one of the pans. Cover and once it has returned to the boil,

simmer for 10 minutes, or until the asparagus is very soft. Liquidise and, if fibrous, strain through a fine sieve and return the asparagus stock to the pan.

4 Stir the asparagus tips and pea-sized sliced stems into the softened onion. Fry for 2 minutes, then stir in the rice. Fry for a further minute, then mix in 2–3 ladles of plain hot stock. Stir regularly, gradually adding more stock as the simmering stock is absorbed. Gradually add both the plain stock and the green asparagus stock until all the stock is used up.

5 After 25–30 minutes, the rice should have cooked into a fluffy, slightly sloppy *al dente* risotto. Stir in the Parmesan and season to taste. Serve immediately.

SEE ALSO

- Griddled asparagus, spring onion and Feta salad on page 106.
- Prawn and spring onion tempura on page 107.

SORREL

Both common (wild) sorrel (*Rumex acetosa*) and the more recently introduced French sorrel (*R. scutatus*) grow like weeds in Britain. For centuries, sorrel was much favoured for its fresh lemony sourness, which is due to the oxalic acid in its leaves, and many cooks would think nothing of using its tart leaves to enliven a spring soup, sauce or salad.

Over time, sorrel drifted out of our national consciousness until it began to assume an almost foreign identity, aided by the fact that it was used in French recipes. Jane Grigson tried to revive its use in her cookbooks, including *English Food* (1974) and her *Vegetable Book* (1978). As she writes in the latter: 'Do not be irritated by the "handful" measurement. Sorrel is rarely, if ever, on sale: one always has to go into the garden or yard to pick for oneself. So "handful" is more useful than weight. However, as a general guide I find my handful varies between 125 and 150g (4–5oz), and that for most occasions a couple of handfuls is enough'. Worse still, once cooked, sorrel quickly discolours to a khaki green, which is not the most appetising colour to nervous English eaters! Luckily its delicious taste is unaffected, so I urge you to put aside any reservations and try this exquisite vegetable.

PRACTICALITIES

■ Wild sorrel is at its best before it flowers, but cultivated French sorrel will last until the hard frosts of November if you keep it well picked to promote young growth.

■ Wild sorrel is more acidic than cultivated sorrel, so use less.

■ To prepare: wash and dry the sorrel leaves. Strip away their stems by folding together each leaf (at the top of each stem – glossy side in) and pulling the stem down towards its tip and then away from the leaf, so that you are left with two pieces of stalkless leaf. These can be piled up in a stack, then rolled and finely sliced to create a 'chiffonade'.

CULINARY NOTES

■ There are two methods of cooking sorrel: the first entails cooking the sorrel first, in butter, bacon fat or olive oil, then adding it your chosen dish, such as omelette or soup; the second adds the sorrel at the last moment, so that it is barely cooked, for example, in the sorrel sauce on page 44, or the spring omelette on page 45. The latter method imbues the dish with a lighter, sharper flavour and a brighter colour.

■ Sorrel tastes wonderful in soup with chicken stock, cream and potatoes. It's delicious as a sauce, made with butter, cream, gooseberry or apple, served with chicken, pork, veal or fish.

■ Sorrel can also be combined with apples or gooseberries and sugar in pies, tarts and fritters.

SORREL SAUCE

In the seventeenth century, sorrel was widely eaten in England, particularly in dishes in which its acidity could be used in place of lemon or orange juice. Sorrel sauce is best made at the last moment as it turns a khaki green if it is left to sit for too long, although it will still taste excellent.

SERVES 6

1 bunch spring onions, trimmed
285ml/½ pint double cream

a large bunch of sorrel
salt and freshly ground black pepper

1 Finely slice the spring onions and place in a small non-corrosive saucepan with the cream. Set over a low heat and slowly bring to the boil, then reduce the heat and simmer for 5 minutes.

2 Wash the sorrel, discarding any tough stems. Finely slice the leaves and mix two-thirds of the shredded sorrel into the simmering cream. As soon as the sorrel wilts, remove it from the heat and liquidise. Immediately add the remaining sorrel, and process once again. Return to the pan and season to taste. Once ready to serve, reheat over a medium heat and serve immediately.

APPLE AND SORREL SAUCE

This traditional English style of sorrel sauce comes from my first book, *Modern British Food* (1995). The combination of apple and sorrel is wonderful and works well with roast pork.

SERVES 4–6

225g/8oz dessert apples, such as Braeburn
150ml/5fl oz white wine vinegar
55g/2oz granulated sugar

115g/4oz sorrel leaves, washed
30g/1oz unsalted butter

1 Peel, core and dice the apples. Place in a non-corrosive saucepan with the vinegar and sugar. Simmer gently until very soft. Add the sorrel and cook for 5 minutes, then purée and beat in the butter. Serve warm or cold.

SPRING OMELETTE

Sorrel tastes very good with eggs, cream and cheese. I've combined them here in a simple omelette, which you might serve for lunch with some crusty bread and unsalted butter. You can vary the cheese to your taste.

SERVES 1

15g/½ oz unsalted butter
1 shallot, diced
2 tablespoons finely chopped sorrel
½ tablespoon finely sliced chives

2 medium eggs
salt and freshly ground black pepper
1 tablespoon finely grated Lancashire cheese

1 Place a non-stick omelette pan over a low heat. Melt the butter and gently fry the shallot for about 5 minutes, or until softened.

2 Put the sorrel, chives and eggs in a bowl. Lightly season and roughly beat the mixture with a fork.

3 Increase the heat to medium-high and pour the beaten eggs into the pan. Draw a wooden spoon through the eggs towards the centre of the pan, letting the liquid egg refill the channels. As soon as the omelette shows the first sign of setting, sprinkle on the cheese. Once it begins to set, but is still soft, tilt the pan. Using a spatula, either flip over one edge, if you like soft-cooked egg, or flip over the entire omelette if you prefer it well cooked. Once the omelette is cooked to your liking, slide it out on to a warm plate.

ENGLISH SORREL SALAD

In *Modern Cookery for Private Families* (1845), Eliza Acton recommends serving a sorrel salad with lamb cutlets, veal cutlets, or roast lamb – all of which are delicious. Here is my interpretation of her salad. She uses equal quantities of tender lettuces to sorrel, but I prefer a slightly less tart combination.

SERVES 4

a generous handful of young sorrel leaves

3 soft round lettuces

3 sprigs tarragon

4 spring onions, trimmed

1 tablespoon tarragon vinegar

3 tablespoons extra virgin olive oil

salt and freshly ground black pepper

1 Wash and dry the sorrel leaves. Strip away their stems by folding together each leaf (at the top of each stem – glossy side in) and pulling the stem down towards its tip and then away from the leaf, so that you are left with two pieces of stalkless leaf. Rip these into slightly smaller pieces and place in your salad bowl.

2 Twist out the hearts of the lettuces – the outer leaves can be used in soup (see page 96) – and separate the heart leaves before washing and drying them. Mix them into the sorrel leaves.

3 Strip the tarragon stems of their leaves and sprinkle these leaves over the salad. Finely slice the spring onions at a slight angle and add to the salad.

4 In a small bowl, whisk together the vinegar with the olive oil. Season to taste. Once you are ready to serve, pour the dressing over the salad leaves and lightly toss before serving.

RADISHES

With names like China Rose, Icicle and Sparkler, radishes take on a romance of their own. Wild radishes are indigenous to Britain, but they first appear in English books in the sixteenth century. They belong to the *Cruciferae* (*Brassicaceae*) family and come in many different forms, from mild pink and white breakfast radishes to peppery white-fleshed black Spanish long radishes. The latter is a winter radish, which takes time to grow and can be stored through the winter months without turning hollow.

Their heat has caused some writers, such as Mrs Beeton, to warn against the dangers of eating them in excess. Others, however, understood exactly how a radish should be consumed. In *Kettner's Book of the Table* (1877), E.S. Dallas writes: 'Not a word against the radish. Still it may be lawful to record that it is not of much use in cookery, whatever it may be in eating. May I also venture to say that it is a mistake in a salad – an intrusion; and that the only way to eat it is to nibble it by itself while waiting for the feast, or in any convenient interlude.' How true, nothing is nicer than a radish dipped in salt.

PRACTICALITIES

■ Always choose perky, fresh-looking radishes. Soft, bendy or limp-looking ones should be avoided. Prepare radishes at the last minute for maximum flavour.

■ Larger radishes require peeling as they have thicker skins, for example, Japanese Shogoin types, mouli, China Rose and round black Spanish. The skin is also more pungent.

■ Radish sprouts, leaves and young seed can also be eaten. The latter can be pickled when the seeds are soft.

CULINARY NOTES

■ Raw radish is always best seasoned with few ingredients, namely, salt, pepper, cayenne pepper and/or citrus juice. The finer you slice your radish, the less you will taste it.

■ Small radishes and their leaves can be lightly cooked, either blanched in water before being tossed in butter or sautéed from raw in the roasting juices of duck or goose. Always add the leaves at the last minute.

■ Stronger-flavoured winter radish can also be cooked and treated like turnips. If you're using Japanese 'daikon' radish, the peeled, sliced root must be simmered in water until tender before cooking in a flavoursome savoury broth.

RADISHES WITH YOGHURT HERB DIP

This is perfect for serving with spring drinks. Use any pretty small radishes. You can add other nibbles, such as hard-boiled quail's eggs, celery sticks or small slices of toasted pitta bread.

SERVES 4

2 tablespoons finely sliced chives
1 tablespoon finely chopped mint
finely grated zest of 1 lemon

200g/7oz Greek natural yoghurt
salt and freshly ground black pepper
2 bunches breakfast radishes

1 Mix together the finely sliced chives, mint, lemon zest and yoghurt. Season to taste and transfer to a small bowl. Chill, covered, until needed.

2 Wash the radishes and trim their roots. Remove most of their leaves, leaving a few pretty stems. Arrange on a plate with the dip.

ABOVE Collecting radishes from the vegetable garden at Sissinghurst Castle, Kent.

CUCUMBER, PEAR AND RADISH SALAD

You can also use mouli or any other tender radish in this recipe. You can vary this salad to include different fruits such as apples or grapes. The idea is that it should be sweet and sour, salty and crunchy. It is particularly good eaten with spicy grills such as Tandoori-marinated lamb and paprika-spiced fish.

SERVES 4

1 bunch radishes, trimmed
½ cucumber, peeled
2 ripe pears, such as Concorde or Comice

juice of 1 lime
salt and freshly ground black pepper

1 Halve or quarter the radishes. Place them in a mixing bowl. Dice the cucumber roughly the same size as the radish pieces, and add to the radishes.

2 Quarter and core the pears. Cut into medium-sized slices across the width of each pear quarter. Add the pears to the cucumber and radishes, and mix in the lime juice. Season to taste and set aside until needed.

BUTTERED RADISHES

It might seem counter-intuitive, but cooked radishes make a peppery side dish, which is similar to turnips. They cut the richness of meat dishes, such as roast duck or slow-cooked shin of beef, by adding a light mustard flavour.

SERVES 4

3 bunches radishes, trimmed
30g/1oz unsalted butter
salt and freshly ground black pepper

1 Trim the radishes by slicing off their roots and cutting off all but 1cm/½ in of their leaves. Scrub them clean and then set aside.

2 When you're nearly ready to serve, drop the radishes into a large saucepan of unsalted boiling water. Return to the boil and cook briskly for 2–3 minutes, until pale pink but still crunchy, then drain into a colander. Return the pan to a low heat and add the butter. As soon as it has melted, add the radishes. Season to taste and quickly toss in the butter, until all the radishes are coated and glazed. Serve immediately.

SEE ALSO
- Broad bean, dill and rice salad on page 79.

WATERCRESS AND ROCKET

Imagine living in a world where pepper was very expensive, chilli had barely been discovered and lemons were a luxury that only the rich enjoyed. Your palate would seek out excitement from where it could, which in sixteenth-century England would have been from vinegary pickles, alliums, mustard and strong-flavoured peppery greens, such as wild watercress and garden rocket.

Such greens were regarded as both flavoursome and beneficial to health. The poor would have added them to their humble pottages of simmered oats or grain with seasonal root vegetables and leeks or onions. Nowadays, it's almost impossible to imagine how intense such greens would have tasted to a restricted palate. Today, we take both rocket and watercress for granted, yet nibble them plain and your mouth will explode with flavour.

It is time to re-evaluate their role in our cooking. Both benefit from last-minute preparation and both lose their heat once subjected to heat. Try serving them simply prepared: plain watercress sprigs with roast chicken, chips and a lovely jus, or rocket mixed into a simple pink grapefruit and feta cheese salad.

PRACTICALITIES

■ Rocket and watercress are at their best before they flower. A pretty bronze tinge on watercress leaves indicates a stronger flavour. Avoid any with limp or yellowing leaves.

■ Store rocket and watercress wrapped in damp kitchen paper in an inflated plastic bag in the salad drawer of the fridge.

■ Always wash both watercress and rocket thoroughly in water before drying in a salad spinner. Never eat wild watercress as it can host liver fluke larvae.

CULINARY NOTES

■ Rocket and watercress work well with tarragon, chervil, parsley, chives or wild garlic, as well as citrus fruit and lemony spices, such as nutmeg and mace.

■ Both make good soups and sauces – cooked or raw. They have a tendency to bitterness, so are often combined with other sweeter ingredients, such as soft cheeses, eggs, butter and cream, to dilute their intense flavour.

■ The bitterness of watercress can be lessened by blanching – drop into boiling water, refresh under cold running water and squeeze dry. Blanched watercress can be served cold as a relish or hot as a vegetable. The former works well when seasoned with soy, sesame oil, lemon and honey.

A PEPPERY ROAST BEEF AND WATERCRESS SANDWICH

This sandwich is equally good made with rocket, but, in either case, assemble it at the last minute for maximum flavour and texture. It's lovely eaten for lunch with some potato crisps. If you have access to fresh horseradish, peel and finely grate; otherwise, some supermarkets sell jars of freshly grated horseradish alongside the mustard.

SERVES 2

½ tablespoon finely grated fresh horseradish
1½ tablespoons crème fraîche
salt and freshly ground black pepper
15g/½ oz softened unsalted butter

½ teaspoon English mustard powder
½ bunch watercress, washed
4–6 thin slices rare roast beef
4 slices good-quality crusty white bread

1 In a small bowl, mix together the horseradish and crème fraîche. Season to taste. In a separate bowl, beat together the softened butter and mustard powder. Season to taste with salt and pepper.

2 Dry the watercress and trim into sprigs. Trim the meat of any fat, unless you like eating beef fat. Cut the bread and spread one side of each slice with the mustard butter. Cover 2 slices of buttered bread with the beef. Season lightly, then top with the horseradish cream and watercress sprigs. Press each of the remaining 2 slices of bread, buttered-side down, on to the watercress. Firmly squash and cut each sandwich in half.

WATERCRESS MAYONNAISE

Blanching lessens the natural bitterness of watercress in this pretty mayonnaise. Try serving it with crudités and quail's eggs or as a sauce for griddled salmon or chicken.

SERVES 6

85g/3oz watercress sprigs, washed
2 medium egg yolks
1 teaspoon smooth Dijon mustard
salt and freshly ground black pepper

juice of 1 lemon
100ml/3½ fl oz sunflower oil
100ml/3½ fl oz extra virgin olive oil
120ml/4fl oz double cream, softly whisked

1 Drop the watercress sprigs into a small saucepan of boiling unsalted water. Wait for 3 seconds until they have just wilted, then drain and cool under cold running water. Dry on kitchen paper.

2 Place the watercress in a food processor. Add the egg yolks, mustard, salt and pepper. Whizz until puréed. Add half the lemon juice and continue to process, slowly adding a stream of sunflower oil. Once that is finished, slowly add a stream of olive oil, until all the oil is finished and you have a thick emulsion in the food processor.

3 Scrape the emulsion into a mixing bowl and gently fold in the softly whipped cream. Adjust the seasoning to taste – adding more lemon, salt or pepper as you deem necessary.

WATERCRESS BUTTER

Watercress butter can be used in sandwiches or melted over grilled fish or meat – you can even use it in sandwiches. Mrs Leyel and Miss Hartley recommend spreading it on toast and topping with caviar to make Russian Sandwiches in their wonderful book *The Gentle Art of Cookery* (1929).

SERVES 6

85g/3oz softened unsalted butter
1 teaspoon lemon juice
3 tablespoons finely chopped watercress leaves

a pinch of cayenne pepper
a pinch of ground mace
salt and freshly ground black pepper

1 Beat together the butter, lemon juice and chopped watercress. Season to taste with the cayenne pepper, mace, salt and freshly ground black pepper.

2 Spoon the mixture onto some wet greaseproof paper in the shape of a sausage. Wrap up and then gently roll under your fingertips until it forms a smooth cylinder. Chill until needed, then slice as required.

PAPAYA, MINT AND WATERCRESS SALAD

This refreshing salad brings the promise of spring. I love eating this as a starter but it's also good served as a main course with seared prawns.

SERVES 6

3 ripe papayas
4½ tablespoons lime juice
1 small bunch mint
400g/14oz white Belgian endive (chicory),
        roughly sliced

2 bunches watercress, trimmed and washed
3 tablespoons extra virgin olive oil
salt and freshly ground black pepper

1 Peel the papayas. Cut them in half lengthways and scoop out and discard the seeds. Cut the papaya flesh into chunks and place in a large mixing bowl. Lightly season in 3 tablespoons lime juice.

2 Strip the mint leaves from their stems and roughly slice. Add to the papaya with the sliced Belgian endive and watercress sprigs. Add the remaining lime juice with the olive oil. Season to taste and gently mix together. Serve immediately.

ROCKET DIP

This is reminiscent of pesto in texture. You can vary the herbs to taste but take care as rocket is bitter – don't combine with other bitter herbs, such as parsley. Use a very mild olive oil or mix half extra virgin olive oil with sunflower oil.

SERVES 4 as a dip

55g/2oz rocket leaves
30g/1oz mint leaves
1 clove garlic, roughly chopped
finely grated zest of 2 lemons

30g/1oz shelled unsalted pistachios
30g/1oz barrel-cured Feta
4 tablespoons mild olive oil

1 Strip the rocket and mint leaves from their stalks. Place in a food processor with the chopped garlic and lemon zest. Whizz in short bursts until the leaves are finely chopped. Add the pistachios and briefly process until the mixture forms a rough paste.

2 Add the Feta, and continue to blend before gradually adding the oil until the mixture forms a purée. Adjust the seasoning to taste. Cover and chill until needed.

ROCKET, ROAST PEAR AND BLUE CHEESE SALAD

British-grown pears, such as Doyenne du Comice, Concorde and Conference, store well throughout the winter months and taste lovely in the spring, if left to ripen in the kitchen. They are delicious with either rocket or watercress. Serve as a starter or in place of a cheese course.

SERVES 4

2 tablespoons walnut oil + extra for oiling
170g/6oz ripe creamy British blue cheese,
    such as Stichelton
salt and freshly ground black pepper
4 ripe pears

2½ tablespoons lemon juice
55g/2oz rocket leaves
55g/2oz red beet leaves
55g/2oz walnut kernels

1 Preheat the oven to fan 200°C/gas 7. Lightly oil a small baking dish with the walnut oil. Remove the rind from the cheese and place in a bowl. Mash vigorously and season to taste with freshly ground black pepper.

2 Peel the first pear. Cut in half lengthways and, using a small sharp knife, cut out the core and seeds from each half so you have a neat cavity, removing the calyx and if wished, the stem as you do so. Place 2 tablespoons lemon juice in a small bowl, and toss the prepared pear halves in the juice. Repeat with the remaining pears.

3 Arrange the pear halves in the baking dish, cut-side up, and stuff their cavities with the mashed cheese. Bake in the preheated oven for 15–20 minutes, or until the pears are lightly cooked and covered in bubbling cheese.

4 Place the salad leaves and walnut kernels in a mixing bowl. Once the pears are ready, add ½ tablespoon lemon juice, 2 tablespoons walnut oil and season to taste.

5 Divide the cooked pears between 4 plates. Add an airy pile of salad to each plate and serve immediately.

SEE ALSO

- Chicory, crab and avocado salad on page 256.
- Grilled aubergine with green beans and leeks on page 134.
- Prawn and Jersusalem artichoke salad on page 277.
- Salad leaves, saffron lamb and pitta bread on page 94.
- Smoked salmon and new potato salad with horseradish cream on page 65.
- Twice-baked sweetcorn soufflés on page 150.

NEW POTATOES

The sight of Jersey Royals in April sends a thrill through most cooks. Their appearance marks the beginning of the British new potato season and they will be followed by a succession of delicious small waxy potatoes, such as Pink Fir Apple, Ratte and Charlotte potatoes.

Jersey Royals first appeared on our tables in around 1879, although they were then called the International Kidney potato. Robert Fenn of Sulhampsted in Berkshire, a part-time potato breeder, is credited with having bred them. They were greeted with mixed acclaim, some people disliking their waxy texture. Nevertheless, they became popular and were grown as a commercial crop in England until 1900. However, it is thought that a certain Hugh De La Haye introduced them to Jersey, changing their name to the more appealing Jersey Royals. As such, they were sent to the London markets in the 1880s. Today, they are protected by European law and have to be grown in Jersey.

As the Jersey Royal season ends in June, Charlottes appear. The French developed them in 1981 for their potato salad market. Knobbly Pink Fir Apple (1850) potatoes soon follow in July, while the wonderful chestnut-flavoured La Ratte (1872) potatoes appear in August – all perfect for summer dishes.

PRACTICALITIES

■ Ideally, store 'muddy' paper-skinned potatoes like Jersey Royals, as the mud will help retain their moisture. However, don't contaminate other foodstuffs with their mud and wash thoroughly before cooking.

■ Many new potatoes, such as Jersey Royals, need only to be scrubbed vigorously to remove their thin, papery skin. However, thicker-skinned or knobbly salad potatoes are best peeled after boiling, unless being used for a dish that requires peeling in advance, in which case use a potato peeler.

■ New potatoes and salad potatoes can be baked in their jackets and served split-open as a canapé with crème fraiche and other goodies.

CULINARY NOTES

■ Boiled new potatoes need only mint, butter and salt to taste sublime. For maximum flavour, dress your potatoes warm, so that they can absorb the different tastes. A spoonful of mayonnaise or a drizzle of olive oil is wonderful, especially when accompanied with chives or finely sliced spring onion. Once you tire of such luxuries, try a mustard- or herb-based vinaigrette.

■ Crispy bacon, chorizo, cold salmon, quail's, hen's or duck's eggs, olives, capers and cornichons all taste good in potato salad.

■ Left-over boiled new potatoes are lovely sautéed, cooked in a Spanish omelette or mixed into a salad the following day.

SPICED NEW POTATOES

You can change the tone of this dish subtly by altering the spice – cumin seeds will imbue it with a slightly smoky flavour whereas black mustard seeds will add a fresher note.

SERVES 4

600g/1lb 5oz new potatoes
2 tablespoons sunflower oil
30g/1oz unsalted butter
1 tablespoon peeled and finely shredded ginger
1 teaspoon cumin seeds or black mustard seeds

1 teaspoon ground turmeric
1 teaspoon garam masala
¼ teaspoon (or to taste) ground chilli
salt

1 Scrub the skin off the potatoes. If they're thick-skinned salad potatoes, you will need to use a potato peeler. Cut the potatoes into even-sized chunks or quarters.

2 Set a wide pan over a low heat. Add the oil and butter. Once the butter starts to melt, stir in the shredded ginger and your chosen spices. Sizzle for a minute, but don't let the ginger burn. Stir in the potatoes, liberally salt and make sure that the potatoes are thoroughly coated in the spice mixture. Fry for a couple of minutes, then cover the pan and reduce the heat to medium low.

3 Cook for 10 minutes, stirring regularly, so that the potatoes steam cook, then remove the lid and continue to fry for a further 15–20 minutes, or until the potatoes are soft inside and crusty on the outside. You may need to increase the heat slightly.

SMOKED SALMON AND NEW POTATO SALAD WITH HORSERADISH CREAM

You need waxy potatoes, such as Jersey Royals or Charlotte potatoes, for this starter together with a lovely fruity olive oil. This is a very simple dish, which tastes wonderful. If you have access to fresh horseradish, peel and finely grate; otherwise, some supermarkets sell jars of freshly grated horseradish alongside the mustard.

SERVES 4

500g/1lb 2oz Jersey Royals or Charlotte potatoes, scrubbed clean
5 tablespoons extra virgin olive oil
salt and freshly ground black pepper
1 bunch chives, roughly snipped

1 tablespoon finely grated fresh horseradish
3 tablespoons crème fraîche
1 large bunch watercress, washed
½ tablespoon lemon juice
340g/12oz finely sliced smoked salmon

1 Place the potatoes in a saucepan and cover with boiling water. Return to the boil, cover the pan and cook briskly for 15–20 minutes, or until tender. Drain. Once cool enough to handle, peel and thickly slice into rounds.

2 Place the potatoes in a mixing bowl, then toss them in 4 tablespoons of really good olive oil and season to taste. Add the chives and set aside.

3 Beat the horseradish into the crème fraîche. Thin it with 2 teaspoons cold water and season to taste. Set aside. Wash the watercress, then break it into small pretty sprigs and dry.

4 Divide the potatoes between 4 plates. Place the watercress in the potato bowl and then dress with ½ tablespoon lemon juice and the remaining olive oil. Season to taste.

5 Rip the sliced smoked salmon into 2.5cm/1in wide, long strips. Gently weave into the potatoes. Follow by lightly tucking in the dressed watercress sprigs. Drizzle the smoked salmon with the horseradish sauce. Serve immediately.

NEW POTATOES IN PAPER PARCELS

This recipe is perfect for Jersey Royals, but you can adapt it to other new potatoes, such as Charlottes or Rattes
– the latter two can be peeled or not, as you wish. You can also adapt the flavouring to your own taste, for example,
by adding rosemary and a little lemon zest.

SERVES 4

500g/1lb 2oz small Jersey Royals
55g/2oz unsalted butter, very softened
sea salt and freshly ground black pepper

Optional Flavourings
2 teaspoons lemon thyme leaves
4 unpeeled garlic cloves, one per portion

1 Preheat the oven to fan 200°C/gas 7. Cut out
4 heart-shaped pieces of baking paper, each about
30 x 30cm/12 x 12in.

2 Scrub the potatoes, so that you remove their papery
skin and are left with creamy white potatoes. Wash and
pat dry on kitchen paper.

3 Place the softened butter in a bowl. Add the potatoes,
seasoning and your chosen flavouring, such as the thyme
or garlic cloves. Mix thoroughly, so that the potatoes are
coated in butter.

4 Divide the potatoes equally between the 4 paper
hearts, placing them on one side of each heart. Fold the
other half of each heart over the potatoes and seal by
twisting the edges of the 2 halves together, beginning
from the pointed end of the heart. Press the twisted
edges down to hold them together as you work your
way around the edge of the paper.

5 Place the parcels on a baking sheet and bake in the
preheated oven for 30 minutes. The paper parcels will
turn brown and puff up as they cook. Serve the paper
parcels so that each guest captures the incredible aroma
and juice from the potatoes.

SEE ALSO

- Baby artichoke, new potato and Parmesan salad
  on page 119.
- Seared salmon salad on page 82.

SUMMER

SUMMER

The warm days of summer bring with them myriad different vegetables. From June until the end of August it is impossible not to feel a sense of delight at being bombarded with so many delicious home-grown vegetables. Each and every one suggests an Arcadian vision of British life, from a curl of cucumber peel in a glass of Pimm's to sweetcorn grilled on a late summer barbecue.

For me, summer begins when I pod my first broad beans of the year. As I unwrap their fuzzy-lined pods and release their beans into a bowl, I dream of the long lazy days that lie ahead. I think with pleasure of all the dishes I'll make, from a picnic broad bean salad with rice, dill and radishes to a late summer corn and scallop chowder.

BRINGING OUT THE BEST

Such musings often lead me to consider how to bring out the best of a particular summer vegetable. I have a tendency to cook my favourite dishes over and over again – although these well-loved familiar recipes will themselves be subject to phases. Thus, when green beans come into season, if the weather is hot, I'll go through a period of serving them in French-influenced salads with new potatoes and grilled fish, or if it's cool, I'll stew them Middle Eastern-style with tomato and cumin.

Over the years, I have come to the conclusion that there are only a limited number of ways to enhance any given vegetable. Obviously, there are countless different means of preparing it, but, in my view, only a few methods will make a vegetable taste superb, subject, of course, to cultural taste – and my very British taste is for simplicity. Why use three flavourings when one works perfectly?

The key to cooking delicious summer food is to consider your chosen vegetable's taste, texture, aroma and colour. You need to draw out what is good and negate what is bad. If your cucumber is bitter, salting will remove its bitter juices, just as blanching will capture the colour of spinach in a cooked dish, and raw tomatoes will add greater fragrance to a dish than cooked ones. Do you want to emphasise the sweet succulence of capsicums by roasting them for a salsa or bring out the crunchiness of padron peppers by stir-frying them with salt?

Above all, try not to over-complicate a dish by introducing too many different elements. There are few things as lovely on a summer's day as a simple artichoke vinaigrette or a pea frittata flavoured with a hint of Parmesan.

FOREIGN INFLUENCES

As I researched this book, I realised that our habit of adapting foreign recipes to cook our vegetables sits very naturally with the fact that the majority of the ones we grow originated from elsewhere. This is particularly true in relation to summer vegetables.

Aubergines may have been introduced into Britain in the sixteenth century, but they only became popular here in the mid-twentieth century. The aubergine originated in Asia before spreading, via the silk route, through Persia, Africa, Arab Spain and mainland Europe. No wonder then that so many of our culinary methods embrace recipes from well-established aubergine-growing nations – they've had centuries to perfect their recipes. It is hard to better the delicate Indian-influenced spice of fried aubergine slices served with a cooling yoghurt dip, or the sweet and sour taste of an Italian-inspired aubergine salad.

Strangely, we still consider many of these vegetables to be new and therefore alien to our culinary culture, despite the fact that many have been established in Britain for centuries. Globe artichokes, green beans and tomatoes, for example, have been cultivated in England since the sixteenth century. The chilli family has been grown here since the seventeenth century, and chillies were being widely cultivated in London market gardens by the nineteenth century.

NEW SOURCES FOR HOME-GROWN VEGETABLES

As the summer progresses, many gardenless cooks become acutely aware of the amazing range and quality of vegetables available to those with gardens or allotments: freshly harvested peas that taste as sweet as sugar, basketfuls of just-picked exotic salad leaves, and intensely flavoured tomatoes that smell of summer. Many people haunt their local farmers' market or farm shop to compensate for their loss, or sign up to box schemes, whereas others will wander around National

Trust gardens, such as Knightshayes Court in Devon or Greys Court in Oxfordshire, dreaming of how they'd live if they had access to such grounds, before buying some freshly picked garden produce on their way out.

Such excursions are enjoyable but not quite the same as having that direct contact with the soil and what is grown in it. There is, however, a new and interesting alternative that is focused around the idea of producing sustainable food for everyone – a concept in which many National Trust properties are involved. It's called Community Supported Agriculture, or CSA for short, and it's based on the idea of a partnership between farmers and their local community, whereby the two enter an agreement into how and what is grown for the local group of 'shareholders'.

CSAs can take many different forms. Any local community can set one up, provided they can access the land to grow their produce, and all rely on a small subscription to cover the costs of a weekly delivery of vegetables. Some involve members voting on which crops they'd like grown by their farmer, while others include manual work from members to cut down the costs of production. Most cover their initial costs with start-up grants and local sponsorship.

Broadclyst Community Farm in Devon, for example, leases its land from the National Trust and is run by volunteers. It was set up in 2010 with the aim of enabling people, especially those who are disadvantaged, to grow their own food in a sustainable way by providing land, shared expertise, shared equipment and co-operative working. They harvested their first vegetables in 2011.

As with many other CSA schemes, they're taking on land that was originally used for mono-culture farming. It takes time to naturally enrich the soil for an organic style of vegetable growing, but already they're producing a wide variety of vegetables, ranging from broad beans and lettuce to tomatoes, peppers and sweetcorn. They're helping to fund their project by selling some of their produce to the National Trust kitchens at nearby Killerton House.

SUMMER DAYS

In the long, drowsy days of summer it's worth gently daydreaming about how to live the perfect life. Cooking with beautiful produce is part of that vision. In the cool of your kitchen, you can conjure up an idealised world as you turn cucumbers into a delicately flavoured ginger-spiced Victorian ice cream, or bake a fluffy pizza with those long sweet green peppers that appear in August. As the days grow ever hotter, relish the luxury of having so many wonderful vegetables at your fingertips.

ABOVE Courgette 'Parador' growing in the kitchen garden at Knightshayes Court, Devon.

BROAD BEANS

The honeyed smell of broad bean flowers in the vegetable patch evoke long summer evenings. We've been growing broad beans in Britain since at least the mid-sixth century BC, and have cooked them in soups and pottages ever since. Such was their importance in our diet that they were listed in 1270 in the Westminster Abbey Customary as one of the staples that the Abbey's gardener monks must grow. At that time, much of the crop would have been dried for storage.

Gradually, our image of broad beans has changed from hearty peasant fare to a summer delicacy. As Dorothy Hartley wrote in *Food in England* (1954): 'The broad bean is for early summer use, and duck and green beans are a special English delicacy. When young, the green beans are as delicious as peas, and should be cooked as simply and speedily, and served with nothing but a pat of butter. Older beans will need a little longer cooking and may be improved by a polish of hot, buttery parsley sauce.'

Today, broad beans are added to all manner of modern British dishes, from salads to pastas, and their jade kernels have become a fashionable garnish in many a Michelin-starred restaurant.

PRACTICALITIES

■ 450g/1lb fresh broad beans (in their pods) yield about 90g/3¼ oz podded beans. They freeze well, so you can use frozen beans out of season.

■ As broad beans age, they develop a tough, slightly mealy texture. If tough, boil the podded beans in unsalted water, then drain, cool and pop them out of their tough husks, so you are left with tender, bright green kernels.

■ Gardeners can cook the immature whole pods of broad beans when they're 5–7cm/2–3in long. Top, tail and remove the string down their sides. Serve raw as part of a plate of crudités, or cook by dropping into boiling water for a few minutes until tender, then toss in butter.

CULINARY NOTES

■ Broad beans, young or husked, are delicious in soups, salads, pastas, risottos, custards and dips, seasoned with sage, summer savory, parsley, mint, tarragon or chives; and/or garlic, spring onions or sautéed shallots.

■ They taste good with fresh-tasting dairy products, such as Feta cheese, soft goat's cheese, yoghurt and crème fraîche, especially with a hint of lemon zest.

■ Ingredients rich in umami, such as Parmesan, bacon, chicken stock, prawns, scallops and roast meat, add extra savour to broad beans.

SAGE AND BROAD BEAN CUSTARDS

These make a simple but delicious summer lunch. Try serving them with crusty bread and a pretty leaf salad.

SERVES 6

extra virgin olive oil for greasing
250ml/9fl oz double cream
2 leaves sage, roughly sliced
1 clove garlic, finely chopped

370g/13oz fresh or frozen (podded) broad beans
5 medium eggs
salt and freshly ground black pepper

1 Preheat the oven to fan 180°C/gas 5. Lightly oil six 150ml/5fl oz ramekin dishes and place on some kitchen paper in a deep roasting pan.

2 Put the cream, sage and garlic into a saucepan. Set over a medium heat and bring slowly up to the boil, then remove from the heat and set aside for 15 minutes, or until tepid.

3 Drop the broad beans into a pan of unsalted boiling water, return to the boil, cover and reduce to a simmer. Cook for 7 minutes, or until meltingly tender, then drain and tip into a food processor.

4 Add the tepid cream, and process until they form a purée. Add the eggs and process until they are thoroughly mixed into the purée, then push through a medium sieve into a bowl or jug. Discard the debris. Season to taste and divide the mixture evenly between the ramekin dishes, being careful to keep the lip of each dish clean.

5 Pour enough boiling water into the roasting pan to come halfway up the sides of the dishes and cover the roasting pan with foil. Bake in the preheated oven for 25 minutes, or until just set. Serve warm.

MINT, LITTLE GEM AND BROAD BEAN SALAD

This salad looks beautiful if you scatter a few chive flowers over it. I normally serve it with some grilled lamb or fish, but if you wanted to serve it as a starter, crumble in some Feta cheese.

SERVES 6

340g/12oz podded broad beans
1 small bunch chives, roughly snipped
a large handful of mint leaves, ripped
1 tablespoon roughly ripped tarragon leaves

8 fat little gem lettuce hearts
2 tablespoons white wine vinegar
6 tablespoons extra virgin olive oil
salt and freshly ground black pepper

1 Drop the broad beans into a saucepan of boiling unsalted water. Return to the boil and simmer, covered, for about 3–4 minutes, or until tender, then drain and cool under cold running water. Shell each bean by popping the bright green inner kernel out of its paler, thick-skinned casing. Place in a salad bowl.

2 Add the snipped chives and ripped mint and tarragon leaves. Trim the lettuces. Separate out the hearts, wash, dry and rip the leaves before mixing them into the broad beans.

3 In a small bowl, whisk together the vinegar and oil. Season to taste. Use to dress the salad when you're ready to serve.

BROAD BEAN, DILL AND RICE SALAD

This summery salad is perfect for picnics and barbecues. If your broad beans are young, simply pod and cook them; if mature, slip them out of their casings after cooking.

SERVES 4

250g/9oz mixed basmati and wild rice
115g/4oz podded and shelled broad beans
3 inner sticks celery, finely sliced
½ cucumber, peeled and diced
1 bunch radishes, trimmed and cut into chunks

1 tablespoon roughly snipped dill
3 tablespoons finely sliced chives
1 tablespoon white wine vinegar
3 tablespoons extra virgin olive oil
salt and freshly ground black pepper

1 Put the rice in a saucepan with 500ml/18 fl oz water. Bring up to the boil, cover and simmer for 15 minutes, or until tender and the water has all evaporated. Tip on to a plate and leave to cool.

2 Drop the broad beans into a saucepan of boiling unsalted water. Return to the boil and simmer, covered, for about 3–4 minutes, or until tender, then drain and cool under cold running water. Pat dry with kitchen paper. Place in a salad bowl with the celery, cucumber, radishes and chopped herbs. Mix in the cool rice.

3 In a small bowl, whisk together the vinegar and olive oil. Season to taste and mix into the salad. Adjust the seasoning to taste and serve.

GREEN BEANS

Only the English would eat an ornamental green bean, namely the scarlet runner bean (*Phaseolus coccineus*). Introduced from South America via Europe in the sixteenth century, along with its green bean cousin (*Phaseolus vulgaris*), we initially grew our scarlet runners to create shady arbours of brilliant red, white and pink flowers. However, by the eighteenth century, the temptation had grown too great and we'd started to eat their young pods, boiled and buttered.

It has to be said that these are an acquired taste, unlike 'green beans', which quickly became a popular vegetable in seventeenth-century Britain. Over time, countless varieties of both types of green beans have been cultivated. Wander around the gardens at Clumber Park in Nottinghamshire, for example, and you might come across Major Cook's bean, a pretty violet-flowered, purple-flecked, stringless climbing French bean. It's thought to date back to the 1900s, but like so many green and runner beans, it was not commercially produced.

Even today, British culinary opinion is divided on how best to cook green beans. Some advocate light cooking, so that the bean retains a squeak when eaten; others advise cooking the bean until it is meltingly soft. The latter produces a more flavoursome bean, but the former is good for some oriental dishes.

PRACTICALITIES

■ Green beans (climbing and dwarf) come in various shapes, colours and sizes but all belong to the *Phaseolus* genus and taste very similar. Young green beans are the sweetest. As beans mature and dry out, they develop a slightly mealy texture. Once past their best, they ripen further on the vine until they dry out inside their pod; use semi-dried (see Borlotti Beans on page 214).

■ I prefer to top and tail green beans, although some cooks leave the tails attached.

■ Top and tail scarlet runner beans when tiny; with bigger ones, run a potato peeler or small knife down each side to remove the stringy fibre. Slice at an angle, or cut into 2.5cm/1in lengths. Allow 450g/1lb runner beans for four people.

CULINARY NOTES

■ Runner beans taste best cooked simply and served with roast meat, baby beetroot and a really good home-made gravy. Otherwise, a little butter is all they need.

■ Green, as in French, beans are wonderful in curries: both dry North Indian-style – flavoured with mustard seeds, cumin or ginger and garam masala and turmeric; and stir-fried Thai-style with other crunchy vegetables, chilli, soy sauce and coconut.

■ Sesame seeds, sesame paste and nut oils also taste good with green beans, as do parsley, shallots and garlic.

SEARED SALMON SALAD

Fine green beans make fantastic salads. This dish is perfect for a summer supper, especially if you'd like to barbecue the salmon, as you can make up the salads and assemble everything at the last minute. You can serve the salmon whole or roughly broken into chunks.

SERVES 4

12 quail's eggs
340g/12oz new potatoes
4 tablespoons mayonnaise
½ bunch chives, finely sliced
salt and freshly ground black pepper
340g/12oz green beans, topped and tailed
1 small shallot, finely diced

1 tablespoon white wine vinegar
5 tablespoons extra virgin olive oil
8 green olives, stoned and sliced
4 x 150g/5½ oz salmon fillets
2 cos lettuce hearts, separated
1 lemon, quartered

1 Cover the eggs with cold water and bring to the boil. Simmer for 3 minutes, drain, cool and then peel under cold running water.

2 Drop the potatoes into a saucepan of boiling water. Cook for 15 minutes, or until tender, then drain. Once cool, peel, dice and mix into the mayonnaise and chives. Season to taste.

3 Drop the beans into a saucepan of boiling water. Cook for 6 minutes, or until tender. Drain and cool. In a large mixing bowl, whisk together the shallot, vinegar and 3 tablespoons olive oil. Season to taste, then mix in the beans and sliced olives.

4 Set a griddle pan over a medium-high heat. Rub the salmon fillets with the remaining olive oil and season. Place them, flesh-side down, on the griddle and cook for 4 minutes. Then lift and carefully reposition so that the flesh is seared with golden, diamond, criss-cross grill lines. After 4 minutes, turn them, skin-side down, and cook for 4 minutes, or until just rosy inside.

5 Halve the quail's eggs and gently mix into the beans with the cos lettuce leaves. Divide between 4 plates. Add the potatoes, so that they nestle into the salad, then top with the salmon. Garnish with lemon and serve.

RUNNER BEAN PICKLE

Runner beans are an acquired British taste, but for those who love them, there are few things as delicious as runner bean pickle. This recipe comes from *National Trust Good Old-Fashioned Jams, Preserves and Chutneys* by Sara Paston-Williams. Be sure to follow her advice and only use young and tender beans.

MAKES ABOUT 2.3kg/5lb

900g/2lb young runner beans, prepared weight
1½ tablespoons English mustard powder
1½ tablespoons ground turmeric
1½ tablespoons cornflour
850ml/1½ pints malt vinegar

4 medium onions, finely sliced
4 cloves garlic, finely sliced
1 tablespoon fine sea salt
680g/1½ lb Demerara sugar
6 dried red chillies

1 Snap the top and bottom of each runner bean and neatly remove any stringy fibres by finely slicing down the length of each side-seam of the bean. Finely slice by cutting at a slight angle across the width of each bean.

2 In a small bowl, mix the mustard, turmeric and cornflour with a little of the vinegar to make a smooth paste. Place the sliced beans, onions, garlic and salt in a non-corrodible pan and add the remaining vinegar. Simmer until the beans are tender. Stir in the spicy paste, sugar and chillies and heat gently, stirring frequently until the sugar dissolves. Bring to the boil, stirring, then simmer for 20–30 minutes, or until thick.

3 Sterilise your jam jars by washing them in hot soapy water, rinsing in very hot water, and then placing them in a cool oven, fan 130°C/gas 1, to dry. Alternatively, wash in the dishwasher, then leave to dry with the dishwasher door partially open.

4 Spoon the pickle into the warmed sterilised jars, then cover with a vinegar-proof lid. Label, date and store the pickle for 2–3 months before eating.

GREEN BEANS WITH TOMATO AND CUMIN

This is one of my favourite ways of preparing green beans. It can be served hot, warm or cold. I love it barely warm, accompanied by hummus, tabbouleh (see page 125) and home-made pitta bread (see page 311).

SERVES 4

4 tablespoons extra virgin olive oil

1 onion, finely diced

1 clove garlic, finely diced

2 teaspoons cumin seeds

400g/14oz ripe tomatoes

salt and freshly ground black pepper

450g/1lb French beans, topped and tailed

1 Set a wide pan over a low heat. Once hot, add the oil, followed by the onion, garlic and cumin seeds. Gently fry for 12 minutes, or until soft and golden.

2 Put the tomatoes in a large bowl. Cover with boiling water and lightly stab each one with a sharp knife so that you just pierce the skin. Leave for a minute, then drain and peel. Roughly chop the tomatoes and mix into the softened onion. Season lightly and then fry briskly for 8 minutes or until they form a thick paste and you can see the oil coming out of the sauce.

3 If the beans are quite long, cut in half. Mix into the tomato paste and fry briskly for 3 minutes, then add 345ml/12fl oz water, bring up to the boil and simmer gently for 30–45 minutes, or until the beans are soft and the water has evaporated into a thick tomato dressing. The cooking time will vary according to the plumpness of the beans. Season to taste and serve warm, cold or hot.

SEE ALSO

- Another bean salad on page 217.
- Grilled aubergine with green beans and leeks on page 134.
- Roast beef salad with radicchio and red onions on page 257.
- Tamarind chilli seared beef on page 145.

PEAS

One of the great pleasures of childhood is raiding the pea patch. Few things taste as good as illicitly picked garden peas on a hot summer's day. Bending down amongst the rustling plants, the stems squeak as you snap off plump, succulent pods. Under the nets, such peas taste sweeter than sugar and far better than any cooked meal.

The flavour of garden peas defines British culinary taste – pure, simple and sweet, peas need little work to make them taste heavenly: a pat of butter, a hint of mint or a little bacon. Our modern idea of peas is based on tender garden peas, which can be round or wrinkled, the latter being sweeter but less hardy. Yet, for 2,500 years, we've grown countless different types – field peas were found at an early Iron Age site in Glastonbury. Our ancestors grew starchy peas that could be dried for the winter months, hence pea soup, pease pudding and mushy peas.

Fresh (climbing) garden peas were grown in Tudor times, but only became widely available to cooks in the seventeenth century. Imagine the social torture of being served such delicacies and being unable to spear them on your two pronged fork!

PRACTICALITIES

■ 450g/1lb fresh peas (in their pods) yield about 185g/6½ oz shelled peas – depending on their size. Allow 400g/14oz shelled peas for four people, or about 1kg/2lb 3oz peas in their pods.

■ As soon as peas are picked they start to convert their sugar into starch, becoming less sweet and more mealy, so use quickly after picking or purchase.

■ Mangetout (snow peas) and sugar snap peas are pea cultivators that have not developed the stiff papery inner parchment of their pods, so can be eaten whole. Top and tail as required.

■ Pea shoots are pea sprouts snipped from their seed. They add a sweet pea-like flavour to salads and stir-fries.

CULINARY NOTES

■ The intense sweetness of peas is increased when they're combined with umami-tasting ingredients, such as bacon, caramelised onion, strong hard cheese, prawns, scallops, lobster, stock, tomato-based sauces, roast fowl and meat.

■ Peas benefit from the addition of herbs and spices, particularly ginger, garlic, chilli, coriander, mint and basil, as well as turmeric, cumin and dried coriander.

■ They are particularly delicious when combined with cream, crème fraîche and/or eggs – for example, puréed into a soufflé or baked whole in a savoury cheese tart or frittata.

SPICED PEA RAGOÛT

This dish is lovely eaten with rice or with the spiced new potatoes on page 64. It can be made in advance and freezes well. If you are sensitive to chilli, then use just a small pinch instead.

SERVES 4

3 tablespoons sunflower oil

1 onion, finely diced

1 clove garlic, finely diced

½ teaspoon finely diced peeled ginger root

¼ teaspoon chilli powder, or to taste

½ teaspoon ground turmeric

2 generous handfuls coriander leaves

450g/1lb ripe tomatoes, peeled and roughly chopped

salt and freshly ground black pepper

85ml/3fl oz double cream

370g/13oz shelled fresh peas

1 Set a saucepan over a low heat. Add the oil and, once hot, stir in the onion, garlic and ginger. Fry for 10 minutes, or until golden and soft.

2 Mix the chilli (to taste) and turmeric powder into the softened onions. Cook for 1 minute. Roughly chop half the coriander leaves, then stir into the onions and cook for 1 minute. Stir in the tomatoes, salt and freshly ground black pepper. Cook briskly for 10 minutes, or until the tomatoes reduce to a thick paste and start to release a little oil.

3 Stir in the cream and 200ml/7fl oz water. Bring up to the boil and add the peas. Return to the boil and simmer for 20 minutes, or until the peas are very tender. To serve: reheat, roughly chop the remaining coriander and mix into the ragoût.

PEA, BACON AND CREAM SPAGHETTI

This is one of my favourite suppers for when I feel like something quick and easy. You can add more or less of any of the ingredients, depending on what is in the fridge. If you're vegetarian, just omit the bacon and add the finely grated zest of one lemon with the cream.

SERVES 2

200g/7oz spaghetti
salt and freshly ground black pepper
5 medium thick slices back bacon, trimmed of fat
2 tablespoons extra virgin olive oil
2 shallots, halved and finely sliced

1 clove garlic, finely chopped
120ml/4fl oz double cream
140g/5oz fresh shelled (or frozen) peas
30g/1oz finely grated Parmesan

1 Drop the spaghetti into a large saucepan of boiling salted water. Cook the pasta until *al dente*, according to the packet instructions – usually 12–15 minutes.

2 Cut the lean bacon into short matchsticks. Set a shallow saucepan or frying pan over a high heat. Once hot, add the oil, followed by the bacon. Stir-fry briskly for 3 minutes, or until the bacon starts to colour and turn slightly crispy, then reduce the heat and add the shallots and garlic. Fry gently for 5 minutes, or until soft and golden.

3 Add the cream and 3 tablespoons water. Increase the heat slightly. As soon as it comes up to the boil, add the peas. Allow to come back up to the boil, then reduce the heat, cover and simmer for 5–7 minutes (less if using frozen petits pois), or until tender. Mix in half the Parmesan and season with black pepper to taste. It's quite salty with the bacon and cheese, so be careful about adding more salt.

4 Drain the cooked spaghetti and stir it into the pea and cream mix. Toss thoroughly and divide between 2 shallow bowls. Sprinkle with the remaining cheese and serve immediately.

PEA FRITTATA

This frittata makes a tempting summer lunch. You can, if wished, add some herbs, such as coriander or basil, or even a hint of chilli. Serve with crusty bread and a salad.

SERVES 2

3 tablespoons extra virgin olive oil
1 small onion, finely diced
1 clove garlic, finely chopped
¼ teaspoon finely diced peeled ginger root

85g/3oz shelled peas
4 medium eggs
salt and freshly ground black pepper
2 tablespoons finely grated Parmesan

1 Set an omelette pan or round hob-proof gratin dish over a low heat. Add the olive oil and, once hot, add the onion, garlic and ginger and fry gently, stirring occasionally, for about 10 minutes, or until soft and golden.

2 Add the peas to the onion and continue cooking for about 3 minutes, or until cooked tender. Meanwhile, break the eggs into a bowl, season with salt and pepper, and roughly beat with a fork.

3 Increase the heat to medium and pour in the eggs. Sprinkle on the cheese and stir briefly to distribute the peas. Cook for 2 minutes, then reduce the heat slightly and cook gently for 3–4 minutes. As soon as the frittata begins to set, loosen it a little around the edges with a spatula or palette knife. Then carefully slip it on to a plate, invert and return to the pan. Cook the underside for a further 4 minutes. Eat hot, warm or cold.

SEE ALSO
■ Stir-fried rice on page 247.

LETTUCE AND ORIENTAL SALAD LEAVES

We tend to think of eating different salad leaves as a modern convention, yet English cooks have always had an incredible array of salad leaves at their disposal. John Evelyn lists leaves as varied as purslane, orache, sorrel, oak leaf and cos lettuce in his wonderful *Acetaria: A Discourse of Sallets* in 1699.

Within the pages of old cookery books you will discover all sorts of interesting recipes for salad leaves. In *A Complete System of Cookery* (1759), for example, William Verral recommends stuffing blanched lettuce with forcemeat and simmering it in broth, before finishing the dish with egg yolks and cream. Evelyn preferred to dress his leaves raw with sour orange or lemon, sugar and pepper. Eliza Acton stewed her lettuces before saucing them in a thickened stock seasoned with lemon in *Modern Cookery for Private Families* (1845).

With specialist salad growers at farmers' markets, modern cooks have an extraordinary range of leaves to play with, ranging from oriental leaves, such as mustard leaves, mizuna and tatsoi, to traditional leaves, including land cress, lamb's lettuce and bibb lettuce. Our lettuce recipes have become even more varied than those of our ancestors. I'm sure Mrs Acton would have approved of lettuce stir-fries, soups and wraps as being highly nutritious.

PRACTICALITIES

■ Lettuce, *Lactuca sativa*, is commonly divided into two categories: 'cabbage', which have round or slightly flat heads of leaves, and 'cos', which have longer-leaved, elongated heads. They can range from pale green to flushed pink in colour.

■ Remove and discard damaged leaves before use. Save the tough outer leaves for soup or slice and stir-fry as a vegetable with the inner leaves.

■ Oriental salad leaves, like lettuces, should be thoroughly washed before eating. Store in the salad drawer in the fridge, wrapped in damp kitchen paper in a plastic bag. Always use as soon as possible after purchase or picking.

CULINARY NOTES

■ Salad leaves should be balanced for texture, flavour and colour if creating a salad. Dressings should be light to enhance your chosen leaves.

■ Large lettuce leaves can be blanched and used to wrap ingredients such as brill fillets prior to poaching, or they may be used raw as a cup for hot dishes, such as sweet and sour chicken or minced pork with Chinese yellow beans.

■ Salad leaves are inherently bitter, so cream, crème fraîche and eggs all sweeten them when cooked, as does stock or a hint of chilli, soy, bacon, mustard, anchovy or Parmesan. Fresh-tasting herbs bring out their peppery notes.

SALAD LEAVES, SAFFRON LAMB AND PITTA BREAD

One of the most delicious ways to eat mixed salad leaves is dressed in lemon and oil and stuffed into warm fluffy pitta bread with all manner of goodies. Try my recipe for home-made pitta bread on page 311 – it's in a different league to shop-bought pitta. It's easy to make and freezes well.

SERVES 4

Marinated Lamb

1 onion, roughly grated
565g/1¼ lb lean lamb fillet, diced
2 tablespoons extra virgin olive oil
juice of 1 lemon
black pepper to taste
a large pinch of saffron threads
a pinch of sea salt

Final Dish

200ml/7fl oz natural Greek yoghurt
½ teaspoon cumin seeds
150g/5½ oz mixed salad leaves, such as mizuna,
    rocket, baby chard, land cress and claytonia
1 cucumber, peeled
2 red onions, thickly sliced into rings
4 tablespoons extra virgin olive oil
8 home-made pitta breads (see page 311)
1 tablespoon lemon juice (or to taste)

1 Put the grated onion in a bowl with the lamb, olive oil, lemon juice and black pepper. Grind the saffron and salt with a pestle and mortar or in a small bowl with a teaspoon, and mix into the lamb. Cover and chill for a minimum of 30 minutes or up to 3 hours.

2 Preheat an oven-top grill-pan or a barbecue to a high heat. Put the yoghurt in a mixing bowl. Using a fork, beat in 5 tablespoons cold water. Season to taste. Place the cumin seeds in a small dry frying pan. Set over a high heat and toast them, giving the pan an occasional shake. As soon as the cumin seeds smell delicious, grind to a powder, either with a pestle and mortar or under a small rolling pin. Sprinkle over the yoghurt.

3 Wash and dry the salad leaves. Rip into easy-to-eat lengths and place in a large mixing bowl. Slice the cucumber into half moons and mix into the leaves.

4 Place the red onion rings on a plate, coat in 2 tablespoons olive oil and season. Place on the hot griddle or barbecue and cook for 2 minutes on each side, or until golden. Tip into the salad.

5 Place the lamb chunks on the hot griddle pan. If you are using a barbecue, you may need to thread the meat on to skewers to stop it slipping through the grill bars. To serve medium rare, cook for 3 minutes, then turn and cook for a further 2–3 minutes, or until grilled to your liking. Then mix into the salad.

6 Meanwhile, warm the pitta breads in a toaster or on the edges of the barbecue. Toss the salad in the lemon juice and 2 tablespoons olive oil and season to taste. Split open the pitta breads, stuff with the lamb salad mixture and drizzle with some of the yoghurt. Serve immediately with plenty of napkins.

LETTUCE SOUP

This refreshing summer soup is made from the tough outer leaves of green lettuces, such as cos, butterhead, little gem and soft round lettuces. It's one of those amenable soups that freezes well and makes you feel good because you're not wasting anything. You can vary it by adding rocket, watercress, leeks or peas.

SERVES 4

3 tablespoons extra virgin olive oil
2 onions, diced
1 clove garlic, diced
1 large potato, peeled and diced
850ml/1½ pints good chicken stock
salt and freshly ground black pepper

500g/1lb 2oz outer lettuce leaves, washed and
    finely sliced
120ml/4fl oz double cream
2 tablespoons finely sliced chives or a few sprigs
    of chervil

1 Set a heavy-bottomed saucepan over a low heat and add the olive oil. Once hot, stir in the onions and garlic. Fry gently for 10 minutes, or until soft and golden.

2 Mix in the diced potato and fry gently for 5 minutes. Add the stock, increase the heat and bring up to the boil, then season to taste. Cook briskly for 10 minutes, or until the potatoes are soft, then stir in the sliced lettuce and boil for 10 minutes, or until the lettuce is soft.

3 Liquidise the soup, stir in two-thirds of the cream and, if necessary, adjust the seasoning to taste. Serve hot or chilled. Add a swirl of cream to each bowl and garnish with chives or chervil.

ROAST LITTLE GEM LETTUCE

This simple dish depends on a good-quality stock for the sauce and plump fresh lettuce. It needs no extra flavouring and is particularly good with roast chicken and peas.

SERVES 4

4 fat little gem lettuces

2 tablespoons extra virgin olive oil

15g/½ oz unsalted butter

1 tablespoon dry vermouth

salt and freshly ground black pepper

120ml/4 fl oz good chicken stock

3 tablespoons double cream

1 Preheat the oven to fan 140°C/gas 2. Trim and quarter the lettuces. Set a wide ovenproof pan over a medium heat. Add the olive oil and the butter. Once hot, add the lettuce quarters, cut-side down. As soon as they start to sizzle, add the vermouth and season. Turn the lettuces to ensure that they're lightly coated in the butter. Bake in the oven for 10–15 minutes, or until tender.

2 Transfer the dish to the hob and remove the lettuce to a plate. Add the stock to the pan and set over a high heat. Boil briskly until it has reduced to a syrup, then add the cream and continue to boil until it forms a syrupy sauce. Return the lettuce, toss in the sauce and heat through before serving immediately,

SEE ALSO

- English sorrel salad on page 46.
- Griddled asparagus, spring onion and Feta salad on page 106.
- Mint, little gem and broad bean salad on page 77.
- Rocket, roast pear and blue cheese salad on page 60.
- Seared salmon salad on page 82.
- Warm artichoke mousse with dried ceps on page 278.

SPINACH

Spinach is one of those ubiquitous vegetables that have seeped into the British psyche as a food that is good for you. During the Second World War, nutritious everlasting (New Zealand) spinach, *Tetragonia expansa*, was widely cultivated, even in the semi-derelict front gardens of bombed-out London terraces. Spinach proper, namely *Spinacia oleracea*, only returned to favour amongst cooks once butter rationing ended in 1954. It was stewed in butter until its juices evaporated and you were left with an intensely flavoured, buttery spinach purée.

Spinach enjoyed a further vogue in the 1970s with the popularisation of frozen blanched spinach. No dinner party was complete without your hostess having whisked out some spinach from her 'oh so desirable' deep freeze to make some creamed spinach or spinach roulade. However, it was the supermarket introduction of pillow-packets of baby leaf spinach in the late 1980s that have ensured spinach's enduring popularity. Gone was the need for arduous washing and the stripping away of tough stalks; instead the contents were quickly washed and tossed into a salad or wilted in a pan. The compromise was loss of flavour, but our taste buds are changing – bitter tastes are falling from favour.

PRACTICALITIES

■ Spinach must be washed several times in fresh changes of cold water as it can be muddy. Allow 170g/6oz fresh baby leaf spinach or 250g/9oz large leaf spinach per person.

■ To prepare large mature leaves: strip away their stems by folding together each leaf (at the top of the stem, glossy side in) and pulling the stem down towards its tip and away from the leaf so you're left with two pieces of stalkless leaf. Pile in a stack, then roll and finely slice when you need to quickly 'melt' it down to a purée.

■ Blanching reduces the natural bitterness of spinach and helps retain its colour: drop into a large pan of boiling unsalted water and, as soon as it wilts, drain, cool under cold running water and squeeze dry.

CULINARY NOTES

■ Traditionally, fresh spinach is cooked in butter until its juices have evaporated and you have a tender flavoursome purée. I prefer to blanch the spinach (see left) for my recipes.

■ Cooked spinach tastes gorgeous with cream, milk, crème fraîche, yoghurt, a wide variety of cheeses, butter and eggs. Add a touch of lemon zest, nutmeg, mace, cayenne pepper or cumin for seasoning.

■ Raw spinach is lovely with vibrant dressings flavoured with fresh herbs, shallots, garlic, bacon, sherry vinegars and mustard. It's good in 'warm' salads, such as sautéed chicken livers, wild mushrooms or duck confit.

BUCKWHEAT PANCAKES WITH SPINACH AND CHEESE

Buckwheat gives these pancakes a sweet nutty flavour. They can be made in advance and freeze well. If you want to freeze them, layer them unstuffed between small sheets of greaseproof paper, then wrap in a polythene bag and seal.

SERVES 6

Pancake Batter

115g/4oz plain flour
125g/4½ oz buckwheat flour
a pinch of salt
2 medium eggs, beaten
400ml/14fl oz milk
2 tablespoons melted unsalted butter
sunflower oil for greasing

Pancake Filling

1kg/2lb 3oz washed and cleaned spinach
6 tablespoons extra virgin olive oil + extra
    for greasing
4 medium onions, finely diced
2 cloves garlic, finely chopped
225g/8oz cream cheese
finely grated zest of 1 lemon
salt and freshly ground black pepper
225g/8oz Taleggio cheese, de-rinded and diced

1 Make the pancakes: sift the flours and salt into a bowl and make a well in the centre. Slowly mix the eggs into the flour to a smooth paste. Beat in the milk, bit by bit, followed by 170ml/6fl oz cold water. Strain the batter into a jug. Stir in the butter and rest for 30 minutes.

2 Place a small heavy frying pan over a medium heat. Soak some kitchen paper in the oil and rub the inside of the pan. Once the pan is hot, lift it off the heat and pour in some batter, rotating it to ensure that the entire pan is thinly coated. Return to the heat and cook until the batter begins to set and is lightly coloured. Loosen the edges with a greased palette knife and flip over. Cook for another minute, then slip the pancake on to a plate.

3 Grease the pan and repeat the process until you have at least 24 pancakes. If not stuffing them immediately, cover with greaseproof paper and chill until needed.

4 Make the filling: drop one-sixth of the spinach into a large pan of boiling unsalted water. As soon as it wilts, remove to a colander and cool under cold running water. Repeat with the remaining spinach. Once cool, squeeze out the excess water, chop and place in a mixing bowl.

5 Set a frying pan over a low heat. Add the oil and, once hot, stir in the onions and garlic. Fry for 10 minutes, or until golden and soft. Mix into the spinach. Beat in the cream cheese and lemon zest, and season to taste.

6 Lightly oil 2 shallow ovenproof dishes. Thickly spread the stuffing on to the first pancake. Fold into quarters and arrange in the first dish. Repeat with the remaining pancakes, overlapping them. Cover with cheese, then cover and chill until needed.

7 Preheat the oven to fan 180°C/gas 5 and bake the pancakes for 30 minutes, or until hot and bubbling.

SPINACH WITH MINT AND CRÈME FRAÎCHE

This makes a wonderful dinner party vegetable as the subtle flavour of mint always takes people by surprise and you can prepare most of it in advance. You can blanch the spinach a few hours ahead and keep it chilled until needed.

SERVES 4

700g/1lb 9oz young leaf spinach, washed
2 tablespoons extra virgin olive oil
1 clove garlic, finely chopped

6 spring onions, trimmed and finely sliced
1 tablespoon finely chopped mint
5 tablespoons crème fraîche

1 Blanch the spinach as described on page 98.

2 Squeeze the excess water out of the spinach and unravel the leaves. Roughly chop, place in a bowl and chill, covered, until needed.

3 Set a saucepan over a low heat. Once hot, add the oil, garlic and spring onions. Fry gently for a minute or two, until the spring onions start to soften, then mix in the chopped spinach. Stir regularly until the spinach starts to become warm, then mix in the mint and crème fraîche. Season to taste and set aside once hot.

SPICED CHICKPEA AND SPINACH SALAD

SERVES 4

400g/14oz baby leaf spinach, washed
6 tablespoons extra virgin olive oil
4 shallots, finely sliced
1 clove garlic, finely diced
½ Thai chilli (or to taste), finely diced

1 tablespoon smoked sweet Spanish paprika
2 x 400g/14oz cans chickpeas, drained
juice of 1 lemon
salt and freshly ground black pepper

1 Blanch the spinach as described on page 98. Using your hands, squeeze dry the spinach leaves before gently unfurling them. Place in a salad bowl.

2 Set a wide saucepan over a medium-low heat. Add the olive oil and, when hot, stir in the shallots, garlic and chilli. Gently fry for 5 minutes, or until soft and golden.

3 Once soft, mix in the paprika, cook for 1 minute then add the chickpeas and continue cooking until warm and well coated. Tip into the spinach leaves, add 2 tablespoons lemon juice and mix thoroughly. Season to taste and add more lemon juice if necessary. Serve warm or at room temperature.

CLIVEDEN SPINACH AND SUMMER HERB ROULADE

The kitchens at Cliveden will vary the herbs in this roulade according to what is available from their garden.

SERVES 6

40g/1½ oz unsalted butter
40g/1½ oz plain flour
640ml/1 pint 2fl oz whole milk
340g/12oz spinach leaves
3 medium eggs, separated
salt and freshly ground black pepper

300g/10½ oz cream cheese
1 small bunch chives, finely sliced
2 tablespoons chopped basil leaves
1 teaspoon chopped tarragon leaves
finely grated zest of 1 lemon

1 Preheat the oven to fan 180°C/gas 5. Line a 20cm/8in x 30cm/12in Swiss roll tin with baking paper.

2 In a heavy-bottomed saucepan, melt the butter over a low heat. Using a wooden spoon, stir in the flour and cook for about 3 minutes, or until it turns a pale straw gold. Gradually add the milk, stirring constantly, until it forms a smooth sauce. Simmer briskly for 15 minutes, stirring regularly until it has thickened into a velvety sauce. Tip into a food processor and leave to cool while you prepare the spinach.

3 Wash the spinach leaves thoroughly, and if well grown, rip out their tough stalks (see page 98). Drop into a large saucepan of boiling water and as soon as they've wilted – a few seconds – drain and cool under cold running water. Squeeze as much water out as you can with your hands and finely chop. Place in the food processor and blend with the white sauce.

4 Add the egg yolks to the spinach mixture, one at a time, and whizz to blend. Transfer to a larger bowl and season to taste.

5 In a clean dry bowl, whisk the egg whites until they form soft peaks. Using a flat metal spoon, gently fold the whisked whites into the spinach mixture. Quickly pour into the prepared Swiss roll tin and place in the oven. Bake for 15–20 minutes, or until the mixture has risen and springs back slightly when lightly pressed. Leave to cool in the tin.

6 Put the cream cheese in a bowl and beat in the herbs and lemon zest. Adjust the seasoning to taste.

7 Loosen the edge of the spinach roulade with a knife and invert on to a large sheet of baking paper. Gently peel away the baking paper. Spread with the herb cream cheese, leaving the edges free. Then, very gently, tightly roll it up from the shorter side, using the paper underneath to help you roll. Chill for 2–3 hours, but remove from the fridge 20 minutes before needed. When ready to serve, trim the ends and slice thinly.

SPRING ONIONS

Spring onions are immature onions. They go by many names, including scallions (in America), green and salad onions. They vary in colour and shape, depending on the type of onion from which they've sprung. Red onions, for example, produce purple-flushed spring onions.

No one knows when onions were introduced into Britain, although the Romans are the chief suspects. However, once tasted by the general population, they were here to stay, along with leeks and garlic. They added an exciting flavour to the most humble pottage, and no doubt many a country wife would have plucked young spring onions from her cottage garden to flavour her pot of simmering grain and vegetables over the fire. They would have tasted good eaten with a hunk of brown bread and cheese.

Yet there is something strangely modern about spring onions. Perhaps it is their squeaky clean appearance in the supermarkets, or maybe it is because they're associated with oriental dishes, such as miso soup and stir-fried vegetables. There was a time, not so long ago, when they were regarded as being a bit too strong to serve to anyone with a sensitive palate. Yet, look closely and you'll find them mentioned in Victorian recipes for salads and relishes.

PRACTICALITIES

■ Spring onions can be pencil thin, flushed purple or fat and bulbous at the root. They're usually sold around five to ten onions to a bunch, depending on their size.

■ Choose fresh, succulent bunches, preferably with some of their roots attached, as this helps prevent them from drying out.

■ Store in the salad drawer of the fridge. Gradually their outer leaves will dry out, but they can still be used in cooked dishes. Once cut, they should be well wrapped, otherwise their smell will scent the fridge.

■ To prepare: slice off their roots, peel off any damaged or papery outer skin and trim the leaves to suit your needs.

CULINARY NOTES

■ Raw spring onions are pungent and best used in moderation. The white part of the bulb has the sweetest flavour. The greenest part of the leaf has the strongest taste.

■ Slicing affects how you perceive their flavour. Small chunks give taste explosions whereas fine slices are subtly pervasive. They are often added at the last minute in cooking, as over-cooking can give them a slimy texture.

■ Whole spring onions taste sweeter if blanched for a minute in boiling water and then cooled under the cold tap. Dress blanched spring onions like leeks or grill for salads. They're also good steamed as a vegetable accompaniment to a dish.

GRIDDLED ASPARAGUS, SPRING ONION AND FETA SALAD

This makes a beautiful early summer salad. You can add herbs and edible flowers to the salad leaves. If the weather is good, you can, of course, grill the asparagus and spring onions on a barbecue.

SERVES 4

20 stems medium asparagus (about 500g/1lb 2oz)
16 spring onions
2 tablespoons white wine vinegar
8 tablespoons extra virgin olive oil

2 teaspoons roughly chopped tarragon, leaves
salt and freshly ground black pepper
125g/4½ oz mixed young salad leaves and herbs
115g/4oz Feta, crumbled

1 Wash the asparagus and trim off the tougher ends of their stems. Drop into a saucepan of boiling unsalted water and cook for 3–5 minutes, depending on the thickness of the asparagus. Drain when the stems are tender but still retain a little bite. Spread out to cool on plates lined with kitchen paper.

2 Trim the spring onions of their roots and the raggedy tops of their green leaves. Drop into a pan of boiling water. Cook for 30 seconds, then drain immediately and spread out to cool with the asparagus.

3 In a small bowl, whisk together the wine vinegar with 6 tablespoons olive oil and the chopped tarragon. Season to taste.

4 Set a ridged cast iron griddle pan over a medium heat. Once hot, toss the asparagus and spring onions in the remaining olive oil. Lightly season and arrange half the asparagus in a single layer on the griddle pan. Cook for about 3 minutes, turning regularly until lightly seared with griddle lines. Remove to a large salad bowl. Repeat the process with the remaining asparagus, then griddle the spring onions for 1 minute, turning them regularly. Add to the bowl.

5 When you're ready to serve, add the salad leaves and herbs to the griddled asparagus. Whisk the dressing and lightly toss before adding the crumbled Feta. Mix once again and divide between 4 plates, arranging each portion into an airy pile.

PRAWN AND SPRING ONION TEMPURA

Ignore your instincts when making the batter. It must remain lumpy to ensure a crisp, lacy coating.

SERVES 4

Dipping Sauce
4 tablespoons naturally brewed soy sauce
4 tablespoons mirin
4 tablespoons sake
1 tablespoon minced ginger

Tempura
12 spring onions, trimmed
8 asparagus tips

12 king-sized raw prawns
sunflower oil for deep frying
extra plain flour, sifted

Batter
1 egg yolk
225ml/8fl oz iced water
115g/4oz plain flour, sifted

1 To make the dipping sauce, put the soy sauce, mirin, sake and ginger in a small saucepan. Simmer gently for 5 minutes. Remove from the heat and mix in 4 tablespoons warm water. Leave to cool, then pour into 4 little dipping bowls.

2 Wash and pat dry the spring onions and asparagus tips. Twist off the prawn heads and remove the shells, apart from the tail tip. Run a knife down the back of each prawn and pull away the black digestive cord. Rinse and pat dry. The prawns, spring onions and asparagus must be completely dry before being floured and battered.

3 Line a cooling rack with kitchen paper. Heat the oil to 170°C. Drop the egg yolk into a bowl. Add the iced water and roughly mix with 1 or 2 strokes. Add the flour and barely mix, so the batter is still lumpy. When the oil is ready, coat the spring onions and asparagus tips in the flour, dip into the batter and then slip into the oil. Fry for about 2 minutes, working in batches. The batter should barely colour. Leave to drain on the cooling rack.

4 Increase the oil temperature to 180°C. Flour and batter the prawns and fry for 3 minutes, turning once. Drain on the rack, then arrange the prawns on 4 plates with the spring onions and asparagus. Add the sauce in little bowls and serve immediately.

SEE ALSO

■ English sorrel salad on page 46.
■ Aubergine noodles on page 137.
■ Crispy duck with cucumber on page 110.
■ Spinach with mint and crème fraîche on page 101.
■ Sorrel sauce on page 44.
■ Tabbouleh on page 125.

CUCUMBER

We fell in love with cucumbers in the Age of Enlightenment; up until then, they had a dark reputation. As Robert Burton wrote in *The Anatomy of Melancholy* (1621): 'Among herbs to be eaten, I find gourds, cowcumbers, coleworts, melons, disallowed, but especially cabbage. It causeth troublesome dreams, and sends black vapours to the brain ... Some are of opinion that all raw herbs and sallets breed melancholy blood, except bugloss and lettuce.' Worse still, eating cucumbers was sometimes cited as the cause of death. Samuel Pepys reports of two such cases in his diary of 22 August 1663.

The development of greenhouses in the eighteenth century transformed the cucumber's reputation. Market gardeners vied to produce out of season cucumbers. Modern thought dismissed the medieval concept that you could jeopardise your health by over-indulging and thereby affect your four humours.

British cooks were soon stewing, puréeing, stuffing, baking and pickling their cucumbers. Gardeners, meanwhile, sought out many varieties to grow in their new glasshouses. Even today, you can find cucumbers growing amongst the melons in the restored greenhouse at Attingham Park in Shropshire, including old varieties such as lemon yellow Crystal Apple cucumbers.

PRACTICALITIES

■ Cucumbers divide into two main types: smooth green indoor varieties, sometimes called English or greenhouse cucumbers, that you commonly find in supermarkets wrapped in polythene; and outdoor or ridge varieties. The latter gained their name from the practice of growing them along ridges to improve the soil drainage. They come in many different shapes and sizes, including gherkins.

■ Choose plump, juicy-looking cucumbers that feel heavy for their size. Avoid spongy, wrinkled, or soft spotted ones. Store in a cool rather than a cold place for maximum flavour.

■ Older varieties of cucumber have a tendency towards bitterness, hence the common instruction to salt sliced cucumber prior to use.

CULINARY NOTES

■ The subtle flavour of cucumber is enhanced by simplicity. Think cucumber sandwiches – butter, salt, black pepper and good bread – or chilled cucumber soup made from chicken stock, bay leaf and a creamy white sauce.

■ Peppery seasonings, such as dill, borage, chervil, chives, mint, coriander, chilli and pepper, enhance cucumber, as does sugar, vinegar or lemon and mildly acidic foods, for example, fresh goat's cheese, Feta or Greek yoghurt.

■ Cucumber skin is edible if washed, although some of the older varieties have a very chewy texture. It adds fragrance to wine cups, cocktails and Pimm's.

■ Salting cucumbers will extract some of their water. Rinse and pat dry before use.

CRISPY DUCK WITH CUCUMBER AND CHINESE PANCAKES

One of the charms of cucumber is its contrasting texture. This is a perfect example of how refreshing it can be in a very modern recipe. You will need to salt the duck breasts for 8 hours before cooking. You can buy hoisin sauce and frozen Chinese pancakes from most large supermarkets.

SERVES 4

4 duck breasts
2 teaspoons fine sea salt
2 teaspoons Chinese five-spice powder
120ml/4fl oz hoisin sauce

1 bunch of spring onions, trimmed
1 cucumber, peeled, halved and seeded
1 small bunch mint, washed
16 Chinese pancakes

1 Pull the skin off the duck breasts. Neatly score the feather-side of the fat in small diamonds – this will help it crisp up later – then slice into thick strips. Cut away any sinews or bloody bits from the duck meat. Mix the salt and spice in a small bowl and rub into both the duck flesh and the skin. Place in a single layer on a large plate and store uncovered in the fridge for 8 hours. This allows the fat to dry out slightly as it salts.

2 Preheat the oven to fan 200°C/gas 7. Set a dry frying pan over a medium heat. Using kitchen paper, pat dry the duck skin and breasts. Add the duck skin to the hot pan and cook for 5 minutes, turning regularly. It will release a lot of fat as it cooks.

3 Add the breasts to the duck skin and fry for 5 minutes, turning once. Transfer the skin and breasts to a non-stick roasting pan. Add a little duck fat and roast for 10 minutes. Remove and rest for 10 minutes.

4 Meanwhile, prepare the filling: place the hoisin sauce in a pretty bowl in the centre of a serving dish. Place a teaspoon close by. Trim and wash the spring onions. Finely slice lengthways and arrange on the same plate. Cut the prepared cucumber into four evenly sized lengths – you will have eight pieces of cucumber. Finely slice each of these lengthways. Add to the serving dish. Strip the mint leaves from their stems and arrange on the plate.

5 Heat the Chinese pancakes for 20 seconds in a microwave, or for 5–6 minutes in a steamer. Keep warm.

6 Finely slice the warm, not hot, duck breasts and crispy duck skin into matchsticks. Add to the serving dish and serve immediately. Each guest can then coat a pancake with a streak of hoisin sauce before adding some spring onions, cucumber, mint and shredded crispy duck to taste.

CHICKEN AND CUCUMBER FRICASSÉE

Cucumber tastes wonderful cooked as a vegetable in a creamy chicken or fish stew, such as this modern-day chicken fricassée. I always accompany it with rice, but you could serve little new potatoes instead.

SERVES 4

6 medium thick slices back bacon, trimmed
6 tablespoons sunflower oil
salt and freshly ground black pepper
3 tablespoons plain flour
4 chicken breasts, boned, skinned and diced
1 clove garlic, finely diced

2 shallots, finely sliced
285ml/½ pint good chicken stock
3 tablespoons brandy, such as Rémy Martin
150ml/5fl oz double cream
1 cucumber, peeled

1 Trim the bacon of fat and cut into lardons. Set a large non-stick frying pan over a medium heat. When hot, add 3 tablespoons oil and briskly fry the bacon for 3 minutes, or until lightly coloured. Remove, using a slotted spoon, to a wide saucepan.

2 Season the flour. Toss the diced chicken in the flour, shaking off the excess as you do so. Add half the floured chicken to the hot frying pan and fry briskly on all sides until seared and lightly coloured on the outside but still raw on the inside. Remove with a slotted spoon to the bacon. Add a further 2 tablespoons oil and repeat the process with the remaining diced chicken. Remove to the bacon.

3 If necessary, add a further tablespoon of oil to the non-stick frying pan, reduce the heat to low and stir in the garlic and shallots. Fry gently for 5–7 minutes, or until the shallots are soft and golden. Add the stock and boil vigorously for 3 minutes, or until reduced slightly.

4 Meanwhile, add the brandy to the chicken and bacon in the cold pan, stand well back and ignite. Stir briskly as the flames shoot into the air. Set aside.

5 Add the cream to the stock, return to the boil and bubble for a further 3 minutes. Tip into the chicken and adjust the seasoning to taste. Set over a low heat and bring up to a simmer. Cook for 5 minutes.

6 Cut the cucumber in half lengthways. Remove the seeds with a teaspoon and slice the flesh into thick sickle moons. Stir these into the fricassée and continue simmering for 3 minutes or until the cucumber is just cooked. Serve piping hot.

STEWED CUCUMBERS

This recipe is the just the type of dish that would have been served at Scotney Castle in Kent in the nineteenth century. Cooked cucumbers cool very quickly, so reheat at the last moment and transfer to a warmed dish or plate.

SERVES 4

2 large cucumbers, peeled
30g/1oz unsalted butter
salt and freshly ground black pepper

2 teaspoons plain four
170ml/6fl oz good chicken stock
a pinch of ground mace

1 Peel the cucumbers, cut in half lengthways and, using a teaspoon, scrape out their seeds. Thickly slice each half.

2 Set a large frying pan over a medium heat. Add the butter and once it starts to foam, add the cucumber, lightly season and fry briskly for 2–2½ minutes. Remove with a slotted spoon and place in a sieve over a bowl.

3 Using a wooden spoon, stir the flour into the melted butter and cook over a low heat for 3 minutes. Slowly stir in the chicken stock until it forms a smooth sauce. Season to taste with the mace, salt and pepper. Bring up to a simmer. Cook gently for 5 minutes, until it no longer tastes of raw flour and forms a sauce just thick enough to lightly coat the cucumber. Add the cucumber, gently reheat and serve piping hot.

CUCUMBER, COURGETTE AND MARIGOLD MOUSSE

This summery dish comes from the National Trust archive of recipes and is irresistible to all those lucky cooks who have access to kitchen gardens filled with fragrant herbs and pot marigolds (*Calendula officinalis)*, which are the edible variety. It will still taste good without the marigolds. The mousse contains no gelatine, so it's dependent on the cheese base chilling sufficiently to form a creamy texture Try serving it for lunch with a leafy salad and crusty home-made bread, see page 312.

SERVES 6

½ cucumber, unpeeled, halved and deseeded
salt
500g/1lb 2oz local cream cheese
100ml/3½ fl oz single cream
100ml/3½ fl oz natural Greek yoghurt
2 tablespoons white wine vinegar

1 medium courgette, finely diced
3 spring onions, trimmed and finely sliced
3 tablespoons finely chopped parsley
4–6 pot marigold flowers, petals only
freshly ground black pepper

1 Sprinkle the two halves of cucumber with salt. Leave to drain for 1 hour. Rinse, drain and pat dry on kitchen paper, then finely dice, pat dry on more kitchen paper and place in a mixing bowl.

2 In a separate bowl, beat together the cream cheese, cream, yoghurt and white wine vinegar. Add the finely diced cucumber, courgette, spring onions and parsley. Roughly chop the marigold flower petals. Add to the mixture, beat thoroughly and season to taste.

3 Spoon into six 150ml/5 fl oz ramekins. Cover and chill for a minimum of 3 hours before serving.

MRS MARSHALL'S CUCUMBER ICE CREAM

This ice cream tastes of summer. The fragrant flavour of cucumber mixed with ginger liqueur and lemon is exquisite. It comes from one of my favourite books, *The Book of Ices* (1885) by Mrs Marshall. Mrs M. uses ginger brandy, but since I didn't have any to hand, I replaced it with King's ginger liqueur, first made for King George IV in 1901 by Berry Bros.

SERVES 4

½ large cucumber, peeled and seeded
170g/6oz caster sugar
85ml/3fl oz King's ginger liqueur

juice of 1 lemon
285ml/½ pint double cream
4 medium egg yolks

1 Roughly slice the peeled and seeded cucumber. Place it in a small saucepan with 55g/2oz sugar and 150ml/5fl oz water. Set over a medium heat, bring up to a boil and simmer for 15 minutes, or until tender. Tip into a food processor and liquidise to a purée. Add the ginger liqueur and lemon juice and whizz once more.

2 Pour the cream into a medium heavy-bottomed saucepan. Bring up to the boil and remove from the heat immediately. Place the egg yolks in a mixing bowl, add the remaining sugar and whisk until thick and pale. Add the hot cream in a thin stream, whisking quickly to mix it into the egg yolks, then return to the pan.

3 Set over a low heat and, using a wooden spoon, stir continuously in a figure-of-eight motion until the cream thickens enough to coat the back of the spoon. This will take between 10 and 20 minutes, depending on your confidence. Don't let it boil or the custard will split. If it feels as though it's getting too hot, just lift the pan off the heat and keep stirring.

4 As soon as it is ready, strain the custard through a sieve into the cucumber purée. Process to mix, then transfer to a bowl. Once cool, cover and chill.

5 Churn the cold custard, according to the instructions for your ice cream machine, until it reaches a soft set. Transfer to a covered container and store in the freezer. Alternatively, pour into a shallow plastic container, cover and freeze. Beat with a fork every 40 minutes until you have a smooth, soft-set ice cream.

SEE ALSO
- Broad bean, dill and rice salad on page 79.
- Salad leaves, saffron lamb and pitta bread on page 94.
- Tabbouleh on page 125.

GLOBE ARTICHOKES

As the swallows swoop in a June sky, it is easy to imagine how exotic globe artichokes might have seemed to Lord Berwick's gardeners in the kitchen garden at Attingham Park in Shropshire in the eighteenth century. Even today, these great blowsy thistles seem strangely foreign, despite the fact that they've been grown in England since at least 1530. Henry VIII was known to be very partial to them, and references appear in gardening books throughout the sixteenth century. They were a rich man's delicacy. As John Evelyn wrote in his wonderful *Acetaria: A Discourse of Sallets* (1690): 'Tis not very long since this noble thistle came first into Italy, improv'd to this magnitude by culture; and so rare in England, that were commonly sold for crowns a piece'.

It takes a gardener cook to feel confident about picking the tiny lateral buds and slicing them raw in a salad, dressed only in lemon and oil. Urban British cooks rarely see such tiny heads. Instead, they must pluck up their courage and drop the fat, tightly packed thorny heads into a pot of boiling water, and allow themselves time to linger over their preparation.

TO EAT AN ARTICHOKE

Begin by pulling off an outside leaf, hold it by its point and dip the succulent base into the sauce. Draw the base lightly through your teeth to remove the tender part. Put the inedible part of the leaf on the side of your plate. Continue, working your way around the artichoke until you reach the thin central leaves that contain little edible pulp. Use your knife and fork to cut these and the fibrous choke away from the heart, before carefully scraping away any remaining small fibres. Eat the heart with the sauce.

PRACTICALITIES

■ Choose luscious-looking unblemished heads that feel heavy for their size and give a squeaky scrunch when lightly pressed. Never buy any wrapped in plastic or that have brown tips or patches.

■ If picking your own, rid them of any insects by sitting them upside-down in a bowl of salted water for 10 minutes. Shake well and rinse.

■ To trim small artichokes, remove the outer layers of leaves until you expose their pale, soft leaves. Trim the stalk and tip, then pare around the circumference of the base. If not cooking them immediately, drop into acidulated water.

■ Traditionally, large artichokes are trimmed in a similar way with their outermost tough leaves removed before preparing as above, but in her *Vegetable Book* (1978) Jane Grigson advocates against 'deforming such a beautiful object' other than trimming the base.

■ Raw or cooked, remove the 'choke' (unopened flower) at the heart of the artichoke, or you can literally choke. Pull away the surrounding leaves and scoop out with a teaspoon.

■ Some artichoke varieties have tender edible stems – but pare away their thick skin before cooking in risottos or soups.

CULINARY NOTES

■ Cooked globe artichokes have a lovely earthy flavour, which tastes good with other sweet earthy-flavoured foods, such as salad potatoes, beetroot, caramelised onions, rice and pasta.

■ Cooked, they are often served with a piquant dipping sauce, such as vinaigrette, flavoured mayonnaise or a butter sauce.

■ Very small (before they've formed a choke) freshly picked artichokes can be eaten raw or fried. Raw: they're finely sliced and dressed Italian-style with olive oil and lemon. Cooked: they're quartered, battered and fried and served with lemon.

■ Baby artichokes and artichoke hearts can be simmered with other vegetables, such as peas, young carrots and broad beans or added to risottos.

BABY ARTICHOKE, NEW POTATO AND PARMESAN SALAD

This is a recipe for gardener cooks. If you have access to your own tiny new potatoes, use them instead as the success of this dish depends on the freshest, finest quality ingredients.

SERVES 4

500g/1lb 2oz new potatoes, such as Charlotte
    or Ratte
3 tablespoons good extra virgin olive oil
salt and freshly ground black pepper
4 red Belgium endive (chicory) or 2 radicchio

8 small artichokes
120ml/4fl oz mild olive oil
2 tablespoons roughly sliced flat-leaf parsley
55g/2oz good-quality Parmesan
1 lemon, quartered

1 Put the potatoes in a saucepan, cover with boiling water and set over a medium-high heat. Return to the boil and cook briskly for 15–20 minutes, or until tender. Drain. Once cool enough to handle, peel and slice into thick rounds. Place in a mixing bowl, toss in the extra virgin olive oil and season.

2 Shortly before you're ready to serve, divide the endive or radicchio into individual leaves and then gently fold into the potatoes. Divide between 4 plates.

3 Place a 30cm/12in non-stick frying pan on the hob and add the mild olive oil. Remove the outer layers of artichoke leaves until you expose the pale, soft leaves.

Trim the stalk and tip, then carefully pare around the circumference of the base of each artichoke

4 When you're ready to finely slice the artichoke hearts, gently heat the oil over a medium-high flame. Slip in the finely sliced artichokes, gently coat in oil and stir-fry briskly for 2–3 minutes, or until just cooked and speckled gold. Remove, drain well on kitchen paper and scatter over each salad. Sprinkle with parsley.

5 Using a potato peeler, shave off some fine curls of Parmesan over each salad. Garnish with lemon and serve immediately.

ARTICHOKE VINAIGRETTE

Large artichokes are commonly sold in Britain during the summer months. Although we've grown them for many centuries they're still regarded as an essentially foreign and rather recherché dish. You can serve these artichokes warm with melted butter or Hollandaise sauce (see page 22) or tepid with mayonnaise or vinaigrette.

SERVES 4

4 large globe artichokes
1 teaspoon Dijon mustard
salt and freshly ground black pepper
½ teaspoon caster sugar

1 tablespoon good sherry vinegar
1 tablespoon lemon juice
6 tablespoons mild extra virgin olive oil

1 Fill a very large non-reactive saucepan with a lid with enough boiling unsalted water to comfortably hold the artichokes. It is common practice to acidulate the water to prevent discolouration, but I think it imbues the artichoke with an unpleasant flavour and isn't necessary.

2 Drop the artichokes into the briskly boiling water, stem-side down, cover and return to the boil. A medium-sized artichoke will take around 30 minutes to cook; a large specimen, nearer 45 minutes. A globe artichoke is cooked when you can easily pull a leaf from its base.

3 Drain the artichokes upside-down in a colander before serving warm or at room temperature. You can,

if wished, remove the choke at this stage by opening up the artichoke and scraping it out with a teaspoon. This is not easy, I would advocate leaving it for your guests to remove later (see page 118). To make the vinaigrette, place the mustard in a bowl. Season with salt, pepper and sugar, then gradually whisk in the vinegar, lemon juice and olive oil.

4 To serve: place each artichoke on a large plate with a small bowl of sauce. You will also need to supply a small bowl of warm water with a slice of lemon for your guests to clean their fingers and a knife and fork for them to eat the heart.

TOMATOES

Some years ago, a well-known supermarket investigated whether the tomatoes in France and Italy really did taste better than ours. Overnight, they brought in freshly picked French, Italian and English tomatoes of a similar quality and conducted a blind tasting with consumers. Surprisingly, they discovered that there was no discernible difference.

Our perception of flavour is influenced by our environment and mood – a point worth noting as a cook. Thus, a tomato eaten on a holiday picnic in the Auvergne will be remembered as being more delicious than one we ate in our packed lunch at work. Of course, you need to ensure that you choose flavoursome varieties, and preferably ones that have endured stress while growing. A programmed life of drip-feeding on rockwool (a mineral insulation material) does not make for intensely flavoured tomatoes.

Happily, there are literally thousands of interesting varieties to choose from, ranging from exquisitely sweet-sour crunchy green-skinned tomatoes to huge fine-flavoured Brandywine beefsteak ones. Wander through Clumber Park's splendid 1910 greenhouse in Nottinghamshire, for example, and you will find furry peach tomatoes and flavoursome, elongated Jersey Devils in amongst the peppers, chillies and aubergines. It's easy to become a tomato connoisseur.

PRACTICALITIES

■ For maximum flavour, tomatoes should be stored uncovered at room temperature – chilling destroys their fragrance.

■ To peel: nick the skin with a small knife and place in a bowl. Cover with just-boiled water and leave for about 2 minutes, then drain and peel. Do not leave in hot water or it will start to cook the tomato flesh, giving it a woolly texture.

■ To seed: cut the tomato into quarters and cut out the seeds, or squeeze them out from a halved tomato. For whole tomatoes, cut off the top and scoop them out with a teaspoon. Strain the debris and use in vinaigrettes and sauces.

CULINARY NOTES

■ Whether using raw or cooked tomatoes, always consider their texture in relation to what you're making. Does their skin detract from a dish when used raw, such as in a salsa? Should they be seeded or not for a tomato-based stew?

■ Sautéed onion, garlic, fennel and carrots, stock and cream add sweetness to tomato soups and sauces, while lemon zest and herbs add fragrance.

■ Slow-cooking tomatoes intensifies their taste, for example, roasting or gently stewing them in olive oil with whole cloves of garlic.

ROAST TOMATO SOUP

This is a good way to use up excess tomatoes. Roasting intensifies their flavour and makes them sweeter. The soup freezes well. You can also adapt this recipe to make a gorgeous roast tomato sauce by omitting the stock and créme fraîche. Simmer with basil or tarragon instead.

SERVES 6

4 tablespoons extra virgin olive oil
2 onions, very thickly sliced
4 carrots, peeled and thickly sliced
½ fennel, thickly sliced
4 cloves garlic, peeled
1.5kg/3½ lb tomatoes, destalked

6 lemon thyme sprigs
3 parsley stems
450ml/16fl oz chicken stock
salt and freshly ground black pepper
100ml/3½ fl oz crème fraîche (optional)

1 Preheat the oven to fan 180°C/gas 5. Pour the oil into a large non-stick roasting tray and mix in the onions, carrots, fennel, garlic and whole tomatoes. Slip the thyme and parsley under the tomatoes to prevent them burning as the vegetables cook. Roast in the centre of the oven for 1½ hours, or until soft and golden.

2 Discard the thyme sprigs, then add the chicken stock to the tomatoes and deglaze the roasting pan. Scrape everything into a saucepan, add 400ml/14fl oz water and briskly boil for 15 minutes. Purée in a blender and strain into a clean container. Adjust the seasoning.

3 To serve, reheat the soup, pour into bowls and swirl a blob of crème fraîche into each serving bowl.

MARINATED SLOW ROAST TOMATOES

You can adapt this recipe to any type of tomato – just vary the cooking time according to the size.
It makes a rich accompaniment to grilled fish or meat.

SERVES 6

3 cloves garlic, sliced

2 shallots, finely sliced

½ teaspoon ground coriander

¼ teaspoon ground cinnamon

a pinch of ground cloves

a pinch of caster sugar

salt and freshly ground black pepper

12 plum tomatoes, halved

1 tablespoon finely chopped parsley

4 tablespoons extra virgin olive oil + extra
    for serving

1 Preheat the oven to fan 140°C/gas 2. Put the garlic and shallots in a bowl with the spices, sugar, salt and pepper. Add the tomatoes and oil and mix.

2 Arrange the tomatoes, cut-side up, on a roasting tray and scatter the spicy shallot mixture over them. Roast in the preheated oven for 1½ hours on a low shelf, or until meltingly tender. Transfer to a serving dish, sprinkle with parsley and drizzle with a little extra oil. Serve warm or at room temperature.

TABBOULEH

This makes a lovely packed work lunch, especially with the home-made pitta bread on page 311.

SERVES 4

115g/4oz bulgur wheat

200g/7oz ripe tomatoes, peeled

115g/4oz parsley, leaves and stems finely chopped

6 spring onions, finely sliced

½ ridge cucumber, finely diced

juice of 1 lemon

150ml/5fl oz extra virgin olive oil

salt and freshly ground black pepper

1 Pour some boiling water over the bulgur wheat and leave to soak for 15 minutes. Drain in a sieve, rinse under the cold tap and squeeze dry. Set aside.

2 Cut out the seeds from the tomatoes (saving them and their juice). Strain the juice from the seeds into a mixing bowl. Dice the tomatoes and mix into the juice with the prepared bulgur wheat. Mix in the remaining ingredients and season to taste.

FRESH TOMATO TAGLIATELLE

This is another favourite recipe. You can add grilled and peeled peppers or change the herb to basil or chives. I usually serve it for supper, but it is also good served as an accompaniment to grilled meat at a barbecue.

SERVES 4

1½ tablespoons white wine vinegar

4 tablespoons extra virgin olive oil

2 cloves garlic, finely chopped

1 teaspoon lemon thyme leaves

salt and freshly ground black pepper

500g/1lb 2oz ripe flavoursome tomatoes

12 large green olives, stoned

250g/9oz tagliatelle

250g/9oz soft fresh goat's cheese

1 Place the vinegar, olive oil, garlic and thyme in a large mixing bowl. Season to taste.

2 Cut a small nick in the skin of each tomato. Place in a separate bowl. Cover with boiling water and drain after a couple of minutes. Peel and dice the tomatoes. Mix into the vinaigrette. Stone and slice the green olives and mix into the tomatoes.

3 When you are ready to serve, cook the pasta in boiling salted water according to the packet's instructions – usually for about 10 minutes. Drain thoroughly and immediately mix into the tomato vinaigrette. Crumble the cheese into small chunks and mix into the warm pasta. Serve warm or at room temperature.

COURGETTE, TOMATO AND BASIL CHARLOTTE

This unusual recipe comes from the National Trust's archive of recipes. It could be served as a light lunch with a pretty salad. You can add any type of sweet-flavoured tomato.

SERVES 6

150ml/5fl oz extra virgin olive oil
1 large white loaf, medium sliced
a handful of fresh basil leaves
finely grated zest of 1 lemon + juice of ½ lemon
salt and freshly ground black pepper

200g/7oz sweet cherry tomatoes, quartered
15g/½ oz unsalted butter
1 clove garlic, finely chopped
250g/9oz courgettes, trimmed and diced

1 Preheat the oven to fan 190°C/gas 6. Liberally brush six 150ml/5fl oz pudding basins with olive oil. Cut off the crusts from the sliced bread. Cut out 12 small discs of bread and use 6 to line the bottom of each basin; save the remaining discs for the lids. Carefully line the sides with wide strips of bread, making sure there are no gaps, and brush with oil.

2 Place the basil leaves, lemon zest and juice in a food processor – and enough of the remaining oil to make a thick sauce when you process the mixture. Season to taste. Tip into a bowl and mix in the tomatoes.

3 Set a frying pan over a medium heat. Add the butter and, once melted, add the garlic and then the courgettes. Fry briskly for 2 minutes. Drain and mix into the tomatoes with the basil sauce. Season well and divide between the basins. Top each one with a bread lid and press down firmly. Brush with oil and bake for 15–20 minutes, or until golden. Turn each mould out on to a plate and serve warm.

TOMATO AND HERB CHEESE SANDWICHES

These are irresistible! If you love dainty sandwiches for tea, combine these with pretty watercress and prawn ones or elegant cucumber sandwiches, all carefully crusted. Perfect for an *al fresco* tea.

MAKES 6 ROUNDS OF SANDWICHES

450g/1lb large ripe tomatoes, thinly sliced
salt and freshly ground black pepper
caster sugar, to taste
150g/5½ oz cream cheese
1 small bunch chives, finely sliced

1 tablespoon finely chopped parsley
1 teaspoon finely chopped tarragon
½ teaspoon finely chopped thyme
12 slices good brown bread

1 Place the thinly sliced tomatoes on a cooling rack set over a baking tray (to catch the drips). Lightly but evenly season with salt, pepper and sugar. Leave them for 20 minutes, then turn over and very lightly season. Leave for 25 minutes.

2 Beat together the cream cheese and herbs, then season to taste. Spread on one side of each slice of bread. Lay the tomato slices on top of the cream cheese of 6 slices of bread. Gently, but firmly, press the remaining slices of bread, cream cheese-side down, and cut off the crusts. Cut into squares, fingers or triangles and serve immediately.

SEE ALSO
- Borlotti bean, tomato and spinach soup on page 219.
- Chunky vegetable soup on page 292.
- Pizza with sweet green peppers on page 142.
- Roast pepper salsa on page 141.
- Stewed borlotti beans on page 216.
- Spicy aubergine stew on page 136.
- Sweet and sour aubergine on page 133.
- Green beans with tomato and cumin on page 84.

AUBERGINES

The aubergine, just like the tomato, only became popular in Britain in the twentieth century. Both were introduced in the sixteenth century, but whereas the tomato began to be widely eaten after 1919, the aubergine had to wait for the publication of Elizabeth David's influential book *Mediterranean Food* in 1950 and the rise in package holidays to familiarise us with its delights. At first, aubergines were so exotic that you could buy them only in a specialist greengrocer. Gradually, they began to be sold in supermarkets, so that by the late 1970s, aubergine moussaka had become a favourite student dinner party standby.

Today, aubergines are regarded as commonplace. The commercial British glasshouse season for violet and deep purple varieties of aubergine starts in April and continues until late in the year. However, as a result of its foreign reputation, British cooks still look for aubergine recipes from around the world to find the best ways to cook it. Alongside the now-familiar Greek, Italian and French recipes are Middle Eastern, Indian and Thai dishes. Each region has developed its own way of cooking this beautiful vegetable, ranging from the soft grilled slices encasing mozzarella to spiced aubergine crisps. No doubt, in time, we will start to develop our own dishes, such as the aubergine noodles on page 137.

PRACTICALITIES

■ Aubergines can range widely in shape, size and colour. The smallest are pea-sized while the largest are as fat as small melons. They can be thick- or thin-skinned and range from white or green to dark purple.

■ Modern aubergines are not very bitter, so do not need to be salted to rid them of bitter juice.

■ Choose plump shiny specimens and use soon after purchase to ensure the best flavour. Store at room temperature.

CULINARY NOTES

■ Aubergine acts like a sponge. It tastes wonderful with spices, tomato, coconut, cheese and yoghurt, as well as meat, vegetables and herbs, and it can be stuffed, mashed, sliced, baked, fried or grilled.

■ Aubergines take on a lovely smoky flavour if you cook them over a flame – either on a gas hob or barbecue – and then skin them before use, as in a tahini-based dip.

■ To fry: coat aubergine in breadcrumbs, Parmesan or a tempura batter – all are good.

SPICED AUBERGINE WITH YOGHURT DIP

Try serving these as an addictive nibble as a prelude to a relaxed summer lunch – but they're only for people who don't mind messy hands. If you like crisp-fried aubergine, slice them more finely and add a little more oil. I use a potato peeler to peel my aubergine, but you can use a sharp knife.

SERVES 4

2 aubergines, peeled (optional) and trimmed
1 tablespoon ground cumin
¼ teaspoon cayenne pepper, or to taste
1 teaspoon salt

freshly ground black pepper to taste
200g/7oz natural Greek yoghurt
2 tablespoons roughly sliced coriander leaves
12 tablespoons sunflower oil

1 Slice the aubergines into 1cm/½ in thick rounds. Mix together the ground cumin, cayenne pepper, salt and freshly ground black pepper. Lay out the aubergine slices in a single layer on 2 plates. Sprinkle with half the spice mixture. Turn over and sprinkle once again.

2 Put the yoghurt in a mixing bowl. Using a fork, beat in 5 tablespoons cold water. Season to taste and stir in the chopped coriander. Transfer to a pretty bowl and place on a larger serving plate.

3 Place a large non-stick frying pan over a medium-high heat. Add 3 tablespoons oil. Once hot, add a single layer of the sliced, spiced aubergine. Fry until just golden, then flip the aubergines over and cook lightly on the other side before returning to the first side and cooking a little longer – about 5 minutes in total. As you turn them, they will release much of the oil they initially absorbed. This helps minimise the amount of oil you need.

4 Place plenty of kitchen paper on a plate. Transfer the fried aubergine slices to the paper. Wipe the hot pan clean and add another 3 tablespoons oil. Repeat the process until all the aubergine slices are cooked. Then arrange the warm cooked aubergine around the bowl, and serve with plenty of paper napkins.

SWEET AND SOUR AUBERGINE

Temperature affects our perception of certain tastes: for example, the colder food is, the less we can detect sweet and sour tastes, so this dish tastes at its best if served at room temperature. It's lovely eaten with crusty bread as a summery starter or as an accompanying salad.

SERVES 4

2 tablespoons salted capers

2 large aubergines

extra virgin olive oil

3 inner stems of celery, finely sliced

2 onions, finely sliced

450g/1lb ripe tomatoes, peeled and chopped

1 tablespoon caster sugar, or to taste

5 large green olives, stoned and quartered

3 tablespoons red wine vinegar

4 sprigs basil + a handful of leaves

salt and freshly ground black pepper

1 If the capers are preserved in salt, soak them in cold water for 15 minutes, then drain, pat dry and set aside. If they're preserved in brine, rinse in cold water, then drain and set aside.

2 Cut the aubergines into 2cm/¾ in cubes. Set a large non-stick frying pan over a medium heat. When hot, add 4–5 tablespoons olive oil and, once hot, add a single layer of the diced aubergine. Stir-fry briskly for 3 minutes, or until coloured golden brown on all sides. Remove with a slotted spoon and drain on kitchen paper.

3 Add some more olive oil and repeat the process until all the aubergine is cooked. Add 3 tablespoons olive oil and fry the sliced celery for 4 minutes, or until golden. Drain on kitchen paper.

4 Meanwhile, set a saucepan over a medium-low heat. Add 4 tablespoons olive oil and gently fry the onions for 10 minutes, or until soft and golden. Mix in the tomatoes and sugar, and boil briskly for 3 minutes, then stir in the aubergine, celery, capers, olives, vinegar and basil sprigs. Lightly season and simmer gently for 30 minutes. If you're making this the day before it's needed, cover and chill once tepid. Serve at room temperature garnished with sliced basil leaves.

GRILLED AUBERGINE WITH GREEN BEANS AND LEEKS

Aubergine is delicious cooked on the barbecue, but if you don't have one, use an oven-top griddle pan instead. If you're using slightly larger leeks, blanch them for about 4 minutes.

SERVES 6

2 tablespoons balsamic vinegar
6 tablespoons extra virgin olive oil + extra
   for brushing
salt and freshly ground black pepper
310g/11oz fine green beans, trimmed

12 baby leeks, trimmed
2 large aubergines, trimmed
3 handfuls rocket
3 mozzarellas, drained

1 Measure the balsamic vinegar into a bowl and slowly whisk in the olive oil, so that it forms a thick emulsion. Season to taste.

2 Drop the beans into a saucepan of boiling unsalted water. Cook for 6 minutes, or until tender. Drain and immediately spread them out on a plate. Allow to cool slightly, then dry with kitchen paper and place in a mixing bowl. Toss in half the vinaigrette.

3 Cut a cross in the leafy green part of each trimmed leek. Wash the leeks thoroughly in plenty of water, then drop them into a saucepan of boiling unsalted water and cook for 2 minutes, or until they are just tender. Drain and cool under cold running water. Gently squeeze dry with some kitchen paper and set aside.

4 Once the coals on the barbecue are glowing white, or your griddle is hot, cut the aubergine into 1cm/½in thick slices lengthways. Lightly brush with some olive oil, season and place over a medium-hot grill. Cook for 3 minutes on each side, or until seared a deep golden brown by the grill and cooked through. If possible, sear a diamond pattern on to each slice. Transfer to a plate and lightly coat both sides of the aubergine with some of the balsamic vinaigrette.

5 Lightly oil the leeks and grill for 2 minutes, turning regularly until they are flecked with gold. Remove and gently mix into the beans.

6 To serve, gently mix the rocket into the beans and divide between 6 plates, spreading out the tentacle-like tops of the leeks. Weave in the marinated aubergine. Cut the mozzarella into thick slices, season lightly with pepper and slip into each salad. Serve immediately.

SPICY AUBERGINE STEW

Baking aubergine rather than frying it allows you to use less oil. This dish is gorgeous eaten with the home-made pitta bread on page 311.

SERVES 2

1 aubergines, about 250g/9oz in weight

3 tablespoons extra virgin olive oil

1 small onion, finely chopped

1 clove garlic, finely chopped

1 small bunch coriander

1 teaspoon cumin seeds

1 teaspoon sweet smoked paprika

225g/8oz ripe tomatoes, peeled and chopped

400g/14oz can chickpeas, drained

salt and freshly ground black pepper

4 tablespoons natural Greek yoghurt

1 Preheat the oven to fan 200°C/ gas 7. Stab the aubergine all over with a fork and bake for 35 minutes or until soft. Remove and leave to cool.

2 Set a saucepan over a medium-low heat. Add the oil and once hot, stir in the onion and garlic. Gently fry for 8 minutes or until golden and soft. Meanwhile, strip the leaves from the coriander and finely slice the stems. Mix the stems into the onion, fry for a further 2 minutes then mix in the cumin seeds and smoked paprika.

3 Peel the tomatoes by covering them with boiling water, stabbing each tomato, then drain after a couple of minutes and peel. Roughly chop the tomatoes and stir them into the spiced onion. Bring up to the boil and cook briskly for 5 minutes or until they form a thick sauce. Add the drained chickpeas with about 200ml/ 7fl oz water. Season to taste and simmer gently while you prepare the aubergine.

4 Slice the baked aubergine in half. Cut off its cap and peel away its skin. Cut its soft flesh into chunks. Mix into the chickpeas. Adjust the seasoning to taste and simmer for 5 minutes or until you're ready. If necessary, add a little more water as the aubergine absorbs the tomato sauce.

5 Season the yoghurt to taste. When you ready to serve, add the remaining coriander leaves, spoon into two bowls and top with the yoghurt.

AUBERGINE NOODLES

Chilli oil is very easy to make and keeps well in the fridge. Measure 5 tablespoons sunflower oil into a small saucepan. Once it is hot, but not smoking, stir in 4 teaspoons chilli powder, wait 30 seconds and then remove from the heat and leave until cold. Strain through kitchen paper into a clean bowl and use as required, but take care – it's very hot. Once cold, store in a sterilised sealed container.

SERVES 4

3 aubergines

4 tablespoons naturally brewed soy sauce

2½ tablespoons honey

1 teaspoon finely chopped ginger root

1 tablespoon chilli oil (see above)

4 tablespoons toasted sesame oil

2 tablespoons lemon juice

2 tablespoons sesame seeds

200g/7oz Chinese fine egg noodles

2 red Romano peppers, halved, seeded and finely sliced

1 bunch spring onions, trimmed and finely sliced

2 large handfuls coriander leaves

1 Preheat the oven to fan 200°C/gas 7. Stab each aubergine all over with a fork and bake for 35 minutes, or until soft. Once cooked, remove and leave to cool.

2 Place the soy sauce, honey and ginger in a small saucepan. Set over a low heat and simmer for 5 minutes, or until fragrant. Remove from the heat, cool slightly, then add the chilli oil, toasted sesame oil and lemon juice.

3 Place the sesame seeds in a dry pan, set over a medium heat and stir for 30 seconds, or until they're golden. Mix into the dressing.

4 Cook the noodles according to the instructions on the packet – usually drop into a large saucepan of boiling water, remove from the heat and leave for 4 minutes, or until *al dente*. Drain thoroughly. Place in a large bowl and toss in half the sesame dressing.

5 Cut the aubergines in half lengthways and peel. Cut or tear the flesh into long strips and mix into the remaining dressing. Add the sliced red peppers, spring onions and coriander leaves. Mix into the marinated noodles and serve.

PEPPERS AND CHILLIES

One of the surprises when researching this book was the discovery that we were tentatively growing chilli peppers in the seventeenth century and cultivating them commercially by the mid-nineteenth century. According to Toby Musgrave in his fascinating book *Heritage Fruit and Vegetables* (2012), 'Mawe (1779) lists seven types of "Capsicum", including the "bell shaped". By the mid-nineteenth century the chilli was both garden grown and extensively cultivated by market gardeners around London, with the fruits "maked into pickles and seasonings" and sent to supply the Italian warehouses'. The latter were a primary source of condiments and delicatessen items for domestic British cooks. Spiced vinegars, chutneys and sauces had become very popular, as had curries, due to the British Raj.

Chillies and peppers are all part of the same capsicum family, *C. annuum*. They range in heat from very mild bell peppers to ultra-hot habaneros. As our taste for spicy food has developed, so has our interest in growing both chillies and peppers. You only have to wander around a farmers' market to discover someone selling locally grown Hungarian hot wax peppers or ultra-hot habaneros. Chillies are very addictive and the more you consume, the less sensitive you will become to their heat.

PRACTICALITIES

■ The heat in capsicums comes from capsaicin, an odourless, tasteless irritant alkaloid. This is measured by the Scoville system. Bell peppers range from 0–600, while habaneros average from 80,000 to 150,000 Scoville Heat Units.

■ Chillies from the same plant can vary in heat, but choose a variety suitable to your tolerance. If you remove the white ribs and seeds, which contain up to 80 per cent of the capsaicin, you will lessen the heat of the chilli.

■ Never rub any part of your body when you're handling fresh or dried chillies as you can get a chilli burn. Scrub your hands and equipment clean immediately after handling chillies. If you're nervous of a reaction, wear rubber gloves.

CULINARY NOTES

■ Grilling peppers or chillies imbues them with a smoky, sweet flavour. Raw green pepper has a slightly metallic taste, so match carefully to negate this or grill before use.

■ Both chillies and peppers have an affinity with New World foods, such as tomatoes, sweetcorn, dried beans and potatoes.

■ Soften the heat of chilli with yoghurt, crème fraîche or cheese.

■ Sweetness ameliorates chilli heat, but chillies are delicious in fruit salads, sorbets and chocolate cakes.

RED PEPPER PANCAKES WITH SMOKED SALMON

Roasted red peppers make surprisingly good drop pancakes, as you'll discover in this rich starter.

SERVES 4

2 red peppers
finely grated zest and juice of 1 lime
salt and freshly ground black pepper
3 medium eggs, separated
scant 55g/2oz melted unsalted butter
55g/2oz plain flour
1 teaspoon baking powder

2 sweetcorn cobs, cleaned (see page 146)
120ml/4fl oz double cream
120ml/4fl oz crème fraîche
115g/4oz finely sliced smoked salmon
85g/3oz clarified butter (see page 175)
½ bunch chives, roughly snipped

1 Quarter and seed the peppers. Place under the grill, turn to high and cook until the skin has blackened and blistered. Remove to a bowl, cover with a plate and leave until cool enough to handle. Peel both peppers. Neatly dice one whole pepper and set aside.

2 Place the remaining 4 pepper quarters in a food processor, add 1 tablespoon lime juice and whizz until it forms a purée. Add seasoning to taste, the egg yolks and 20g/¾ oz melted butter. Whizz to mix.

3 Sift the flour and baking powder together. Add to the red pepper mixture, briefly process and tip into a bowl. Whisk the egg whites in a separate bowl until they form soft peaks. Using a metal spoon, fold a spoonful into the red pepper purée to slacken the mixture, then slowly fold in the remaining whipped egg whites. Cover and chill the red pepper batter while you prepare the sauce.

4 Cut the corn kernels away from the cleaned cobs by carefully holding each cob upright and cutting down the length of each side. Melt 30g/1oz butter in a small saucepan. Add the corn kernels and gently fry for 3

minutes, or until they begin to soften, then stir in the cream and diced red pepper. Season to taste and simmer gently for 3 minutes. Reheat this corn sauce when the pancakes are ready and mix in a tablespoon of lime juice.

5 Mix the finely grated lime zest into the crème fraîche. Rip the slices of smoked salmon into attractive pieces.

6 When you're ready to serve, set a heavy-bottomed, non-stick frying pan over a medium heat. Add a tablespoon of clarified butter and thoroughly coat the bottom of the pan. Once the pan is hot, spoon 4 blobs of red pepper batter on to the pan. After about 2–3 minutes, when they've puffed up and show tiny bubbles, flip them over and cook for a further minute on the other side until flecked golden and cooked through. Keep warm on a plate (under a tea towel) and continue to cook the remaining pancakes.

7 Arrange 2 pancakes on each serving plate. Top with the lime-zest crème fraîche and some delicate slices of smoked salmon. Spoon the warm corn sauce around the pancakes and garnish with chives. Serve immediately.

ROAST PEPPER SALSA

You can serve this as either a sauce or a dip. It's particularly good as an accompaniment to grilled chicken (marinated in lemon and yoghurt) and guacamole.

SERVES 4

2 peppers, red, yellow or orange
400g/14oz ripe tomatoes, peeled
1 Thai chilli (or to taste), finely chopped
1 clove garlic, finely chopped

1 tablespoon white wine vinegar
3 tablespoons extra virgin olive oil
3 tablespoons finely chopped coriander leaves
salt and freshly ground black pepper

1 Preheat the grill or barbecue to high. Quarter and seed the peppers. Place, skin-side up, under the grill or, skin-side down, on a barbecue. Cook until the skin blisters and blackens. Remove to a bowl, cover and leave to cool.

2 Cover the tomatoes with boiling water. Quickly stab each one, wait a couple of minutes, then drain, peel and dice. Place in a mixing bowl with the finely chopped chilli, garlic, vinegar, olive oil and coriander leaves.

3 Dice the peppers to a similar size to the tomatoes. Mix into the tomatoes and season to taste. This will get hotter and more juicy the longer it sits.

PIZZA WITH SWEET GREEN PEPPERS

Sweet green 'Italian' peppers, which are sometimes called *peperoncino dolce*, are long, thin green peppers that look as though they ought to be hot but actually taste deliciously sweet. If you can't find any, replace with ordinary green bell peppers.

SERVES 2

125g/4½ oz buffalo mozzarella
250g/9oz baby plum tomatoes, halved lengthways
150g/5oz sweet or green peppers
½ quantity pizza dough (see page 310)
1 fat clove garlic, finely chopped

10 large green olives, stoned and roughly diced
salt and freshly ground black pepper
½ tablespoon extra virgin olive oil
30g/1oz finely grated Parmesan

1 Drain the mozzarella and pat dry. Slice and place in a sieve over a bowl to release some of the excess moisture. This stops the pizza from becoming soggy.

2 Lightly squeeze the halved tomatoes to release some of their juice. Place them, cut-side down, in a colander on a plate and gently press again. Save the juice – it's delicious in vinaigrettes.

3 Preheat the grill to high. If using Italian sweet peppers, place them whole under the grill and turn regularly until their skin has blistered and blackened. Remove, peel and cut away their seeds. If using green bell peppers, quarter, seed and grill, skin-side up. Remove, peel and slice into thick strips.

4 Place 2 baking sheets in the cold oven. Preheat the oven to fan 230°C/gas 9.

5 When you're ready, roll out each ball of pizza dough (as described on page 310) on to a non-stick 20cm/8in cake tin base. Season the tomatoes and divide evenly between the 2 pizzas, leaving the edges free. Sprinkle with the garlic, followed by the olives and green pepper strips. Season, drizzle with olive oil, then top with the mozzarella and Parmesan. Place each pizza on its base on a hot baking sheet.

6 Bake both pizzas for 12–20 minutes (depending on your oven), or until the dough is crisp and the mozzarella melted and flecked gold-brown. Remove and serve.

TAMARIND CHILLI SEARED BEEF

This Thai dish is lovely served with steamed rice. The clean fresh taste of the chilli is counter-balanced beautifully by the sweet-sour nature of the tamarind sauce, while its heat enhances the crunchy texture of the green beans.

SERVES 4

200g/7oz trimmed green beans

15g/½ oz tamarind pulp

2 tablespoons lime juice

2 tablespoons Thai fish sauce

1 tablespoon palm or pale muscovado sugar

500g/1lb 2oz trimmed rump steak

3 tablespoons sunflower oil

4 lime leaves, finely shredded, or finely grated zest
  of 1 lime

2 garlic cloves, finely sliced

1 red Thai chilli (or to taste), finely sliced

1 Drop the beans into a saucepan of boiling water. Return to the boil and then cook for 1 minute, or until bright green and crunchy. Drain and cool under cold running water. Set aside.

2 Place the tamarind pulp in a small bowl, then add 3 tablespoons hot water and leave for 5 minutes. Rub the pulp with your fingers, then strain into a clean bowl. Add the lime juice, fish sauce and sugar.

3 Remove any fat or tough sinews from the rump steak. Finely slice and place in a bowl. Mix in 1 tablespoon sunflower oil and, if using lime zest, mix this in with the oil. Set aside.

4 Place a large frying pan or wok over a high heat. Add the remaining oil and, once it is sizzling hot, add the lime leaves (if using) along with the garlic and chilli. Stir, then add the beans and stir-fry for a few minutes before adding the beef. Stir-fry briskly until it is brown, then immediately add the tamarind liquid. Simmer for 1–2 minutes, then serve immediately.

SEE ALSO

- Chicory, crab and avocado salad on page 256.
- Corn and pepper relish on page 152.
- Spicy green cabbage coleslaw on page 289.
- Creamy spiced chard on page 204.
- Crunchy cauliflower salad on page 166.
- Killerton Estate piccalilli on page 165.
- Oriental purple sprouting broccoli on page 24.
- Two ways with slow-cooked garlic broccoli on page 168.

SWEETCORN

Over the years, our national palate has changed. Our fondness for bitter vegetables, such as Brussels sprouts and greens, has lessened while our desire for ever-sweeter tasting foods has increased. One obvious example is sweetcorn. The older varieties of slightly floury, flavoursome corn cobs have been replaced in the shops by 'supersweet' corn. This sweetcorn has intensely sweet, juicy kernels and a long shelf life but a bland flavour.

Sweetcorn is a form of soft-kernelled maize, as opposed to hard-kernelled varieties that produce polenta, popcorn and cattle feed. In England, we began to cook with what we called Indian corn in the nineteenth century. It was stripped of its green leaves and boiled until tender, then dressed in butter. As Eliza Acton writes in her 1855 edition of *Modern Cookery for Private Families*: 'the grains may be freed from the corn-stalks with a knife, and tossed up with a slice of fresh butter and some pepper and salt, or served simply like green peas. Other modes of dressing the young maize will readily suggest themselves to an intelligent cook'. By 1937, Edward Bunyard was describing how the Americans ate their corn on the cob, turning it like a lathe. Some things never change.

PRACTICALITIES

■ Sweetcorn should be eaten as soon as possible after picking as the sugar in its kernels starts to convert to starch once it has been cut. Choose heavy heads with lush leaves and tightly packed, juicy-looking kernels. Irregular-spaced kernels indicate dry growing conditions.

■ To prepare: peel the leaves back like the skin of a banana and pull away the long hairs. Wash and either pull the leaves back over the cob or strip them away.

■ To strip the kernels: trim the stem, so that you can hold the cob upright, and use a small, serrated knife to cut the sides of the cob. The kernels will ping off but scoop them all up and place in a bowl with their starchy juice. One cob yields about 115g/4oz sweetcorn kernels.

CULINARY NOTES

■ Avoid adding sweetcorn to quiches, salads and sandwiches, especially with tuna – it tastes horrible. Sweetcorn freezes well and has a better flavour than canned corn.

■ To add a smoky flavour to sweetcorn dishes, such as relishes, dry-roast your freshly shucked raw kernels by placing them in a single layer in a dry, heavy-based frying pan and stirring over a medium heat until golden brown. Add to your dish as required.

■ Sweetcorn has an affinity with chilli, lime or lemon juice and spices. It also tastes wonderful with dairy products, such as cream, milk, butter and cheese.

INDIAN GRILLED CORN-ON-THE-COB

This is sold as a street snack in North India and is very addictive. Amchoor powder is made from dried sour mangos and is sold mainly in Asian grocery shops. Don't worry if you can't find any – it will still taste good.

SERVES 4

4 plump heads sweetcorn
2 juicy limes, halved
salt

amchoor (sour mango) powder, to taste (optional)
freshly ground black pepper (optional)

1 Strip the sweetcorn of its leaves and hairs. Wash clean and set aside. Once the coals on your barbecue are glowing hot, set your corn cobs on the grill rack, turning regularly for 7–8 minutes, or until the kernels are deep yellow and flecked brown.

2 Serve each cob on a plate with half a lime and let everyone season their own by rubbing their cob all over with the lime juice, then sprinkling with salt and a little amchoor powder – just as they would salt or pepper. As they eat, they can rub their cob into the salty lime juice and amchoor mixture left on their plate – just as they would butter.

ABOVE Sweetcorn growing in the kitchen garden at Chartwell, Kent, in August.

SCALLOP CHOWDER

I first wrote this recipe for *Modern British Food* and I still love it today. It freezes very well.

SERVES 4

5 slices medium thick slices smoked back bacon, finely diced

55g/2oz unsalted butter

1 large onion, finely diced

4 inner celery stalks, finely diced

1 large potato, peeled and finely diced

4 heads sweetcorn

3 tablespoons plain flour

285ml/½ pint dry white wine

285ml/½ pint double cream, or to taste

565ml/1 pint whole milk

1 small bay leaf

small bunch of parsley

salt and freshly ground black pepper

6–8 large scallops, without their roes

juice of ½ lemon, or to taste

1 Trim and discard the fat from the bacon. Cut the lean meat into small dice. Melt the butter in a large, heavy-bottomed saucepan over a medium heat. Add the bacon and fry briskly for 5 minutes. Reduce the heat to low and add the onion, followed by the celery and potato as you dice them.

2 Strip the corn cobs of their leaves and fine hairs. Slice off the kernels by cutting down each cob. Mix into the potatoes and cook for about 2 minutes.

3 Stir in the flour and cook for 3 minutes. Increase the heat a little and stir in the wine. Boil vigorously until it has reduced by half and then mix in the cream, milk and bay leaf. Add a couple of parsley stalks, season to taste and simmer gently for 20 minutes, or until the potatoes are soft.

4 While the soup is cooking, prepare the scallops. Check their girths to see if they have a thin black intestinal thread and a small tough white muscle. Remove these by pulling them away with your fingers. Then rinse the scallops and pat dry. Cut into large dice.

5 Remove the bay leaf from the soup and add the scallops. Simmer very gently for about 5 minutes, or until the scallops are tender. If you boil them, they'll become tough. Remove from the heat.

6 Strip the parsley leaves from their stems and finely chop. At the last minute, mix into the soup and season to taste with the lemon juice, salt and pepper.

TWICE-BAKED SWEETCORN SOUFFLÉS

Twice-baked soufflés were very fashionable in the 1980s. They're perfect for dinner parties insofar as you can make them the day before they're needed and then reheat at the last moment, when they rise again.

SERVES 6

40g/1½ oz unsalted butter + extra for greasing

4 heads sweetcorn (about 450g/1lb sweetcorn kernels)

450ml/16fl oz whipping cream

1 Thai chilli, or to taste, finely diced

40g/1½ oz plain flour

4 large eggs, separated

115g/4oz finely grated mature Cheddar

salt and freshly ground black pepper

½ teaspoon cayenne pepper, or to taste

120ml/4fl oz double cream

1 Preheat the oven to fan 190°C/gas 6. Lightly butter 6 200ml/7fl oz soufflé dishes. Place in a roasting tin. Also butter a large ovenproof china dish that can fit the soufflés, once cooked.

2 Clean the corn cobs and remove their kernels (see page 146). Place the kernels in a saucepan with the whipping cream. Set over a low heat and simmer gently for 10 minutes, or until the kernels are very soft. Purée the mixture in a food processor, then push through a medium-fine sieve. Discard the debris.

3 Melt the butter in a heavy-bottomed saucepan over a low heat. Add the diced chilli and cook for 1 minute before stirring in the flour. Cook for 2–3 minutes, or until the flour turns paler. Slowly add the puréed corn, stirring all the time, so that it forms a lump-free sauce. Simmer gently, stirring regularly, for 5 minutes, or until smooth and thick.

4 Remove from the heat and cool until tepid. Then, using a wooden spoon, beat in the egg yolks, one at a time, followed by 85g/3oz grated cheese. Season to taste with the salt, black pepper and cayenne pepper.

5 In a clean dry bowl, whisk the egg whites until they form soft peaks. Add a spoonful to the sweetcorn mixture to slacken it. Gently fold the remaining egg whites into the mixture with a flat metal spoon. Divide the mixture evenly between the buttered soufflé dishes. Pour enough boiling water into the roasting tray to come halfway up the sides of the ramekins. Bake in the preheated oven for 30 minutes, then using a cake slice, gently transfer the ramekins to a cooling rack, so that they don't continue to cook. Don't worry if the filling sinks slightly.

6 Once tepid, run a knife around their rims and gently turn each one out into the palm of your hand. Place them, right-side up, in the buttered dish. You can chill them at this stage, lightly covered in clingfilm, for 24 hours.

7 To serve, preheat the oven to fan 180°C/gas 5. Let the soufflés come up to room temperature. Spoon the cream over their tops and sprinkle them with the remaining grated cheese. Bake for 20 minutes and serve immediately.

CORN AND PEPPER RELISH

This fresh-tasting relish is perfect served with barbecued meat or fish. It keeps well for several days if covered in the fridge, but serve at room temperature. If you love spicy food, add a little fresh chilli.

SERVES 4

½ red pepper, seeded
¼ red onion, finely diced
1 small inner stem celery, finely diced
1½ tablespoons white wine vinegar

2 heads sweetcorn
1 tablespoon extra virgin olive oil
1 tablespoon finely chopped fresh coriander leaves
salt and freshly ground black pepper

1 Cut away the white ribs of the red pepper. Finely dice the pepper flesh. Place in a mixing bowl with the finely diced onion and celery. Mix in the vinegar and leave for 30 minutes.

2 Strip the corn cobs of their leaves and fine hairs. Slice off the kernels by cutting down each cob. Set a small non-stick frying pan over a medium-high heat. When hot, add the olive oil and fry the corn kernels briskly for 2 minutes, or until just tender. Mix into the diced vinegared vegetables. Add the coriander and season to taste with salt and pepper.

ANOTHER WAY TO GRILL CORN-ON-THE-COB

You can also barbecue corn cobs wrapped in their leaves. This steams the kernels as they cook.
The eater then strips back the leaves and rubs the cob in their chosen seasoning – usually butter-based.

SERVES 4

55g/2oz softened unsalted butter
finely grated zest of 1 lime + 1 tablespoon juice
½ red or green Thai chilli, or to taste, finely chopped

1 tablespoon finely chopped coriander
salt and freshly ground black pepper
4 plump heads sweetcorn

1 In a small bowl, beat the butter with the lime zest, lime juice, chilli, coriander, salt and pepper until smooth. Adjust the seasoning to taste – but remember that the chilli will get hotter as the butter sits.

2 Once the barbecue coals are medium-hot, prepare the corn: peel back the leaves of each cob like the skin of a banana and pull away the long hairs, then pull the leaves back over the cob. Wash each cob, wetting the leaves to help prevent them from burning. Grill for 7–8 minutes, turning regularly so that each cob is evenly cooked.

3 To serve, remove the cooked cobs and allow each person to peel back their leaves and spoon the butter on to the hot cob, so that it melts and flavours the corn.

SEE ALSO

- Red pepper pancakes with smoked salmon on page 140.

AUTUMN

AUTUMN

The dew hangs heavy in early September. Carrot leaves tremble with its drops and in the soft morning light, every vegetable in the garden takes on a blowsy appearance. Red-flushed beet leaves, tumbling climbing beans and bedraggled marrow plants are all showing the effects of that last burst of energy to produce plump roots and fat fruit.

Autumn has arrived and with it comes one of the richest times for British cooks. Were you to slip into the kitchen garden at Greys Court in Oxfordshire you might find amidst the riotous growth of trailing borlotti beans and pumpkin vines, great clumps of rainbow chard, lovage and fennel. There are pungent new shallots and the first parsnips to cook, along with cauliflower and broccoli. There are wonderful preserves to make and favourite recipes to be rediscovered.

Presented with such a cornucopia of colourful autumn vegetables, every British cook has the luxury of being able to indulge in a wide variety of dishes that address the needs of the changing season. Light dishes that hint at the passing of summer, such as sour cream and onion tart, fennel, chicory and fig salad, and courgette chips are perfect for the last warm days of September. Intensely flavoured, hearty dishes, such as slow-cooked garlic broccoli, beef and carrot pie and sticky blackcurrant shallots, are ideal for the frosty nights of November.

PRESERVING AUTUMN VEGETABLES

In the past, British cooks spent a considerable amount of time preserving their vegetables for the winter months. In a world where most relied on local produce, it was essential to save as much as possible of the autumn crop. Cauliflower, cucumber and onion would be turned into piccalilli; onions, gherkins, garlic and beetroot into pickles; and marrow into chutney. Beans and mushrooms would have been dried, although the latter were also often turned into ketchup or potted.

With the year-round availability of many vegetables, and our increasingly pressurised lives, the need and time to make preserves has declined. Nevertheless, our taste for such relishes has remained and, as a result, many cooks focus on making just one or two preserves each year, supplemented by 'quick' relishes, such as a horseradish sauce or sticky onion 'jam'.

ABOVE Crisp autumn leaves fall in the gardens of Avebury Manor, Wiltshire.

Meanwhile, gluts of certain vegetables, such as garden marrows, still weigh heavily on the cook's conscience, since no one likes to waste good produce. In the 1970s, when it was fashionable to experiment with self-sufficiency, a great many recipes were written about what to do with marrows. The best I've come across was a recipe for marrow and ginger jam, variants of which both Jane Grigson and Mary Norwak published in 1978 – it's delicious.

Today, with the benefit of freezers, there is also much to be said in favour of freezing your autumnal vegetables as ready-made dishes. Soups, stews and tarts all freeze well, and time and money can be saved if you cook in bulk when vegetables are at their prime. Slow-cooked dishes, such as stewed borlotti beans and roasted beetroot soup are perfect candidates.

A NEW APPROACH TO GLUTS

Another approach to autumnal gluts of vegetables is to create a wider range of vegetable-based dishes for everyday consumption – this is most obviously seen with the creation of sweet dishes. In the past, country cooks used pumpkin in sweet tarts and carrots in jam, but today's cooks can turn parsnips, carrots or beetroot into cakes and puddings, and a wide variety of squash into soufflés, custards and ice creams.

Careful spicing is needed with such produce. Parsnips, for example, can take on a slightly sappy, woody flavour in sweet dishes, and beetroot can make a cake taste mildly bitter. It is worth dipping into a wide variety of recipe books for inspiration. The delicate bitterness of the eighteenth-century inspired beetroot pancakes on page 175 is perfectly balanced if you serve them with an orange-infused crème fraîche. The slightly cloying taste of a carrot cake can be removed if you add the fresh Persian inspired flavouring of cardamom and drizzle it in a rosewater lemon icing.

FASHIONABLE VEGETABLES

As anyone who has wandered around the glasshouses and kitchen gardens of National Trust properties will know, vegetables come into and go out of fashion. Beetroot is very à la mode at the moment, yet few people are familiar with the equally delicious and once fashionable scorzonera and salsify.

During the autumn months, you will find in the grounds of Clumber Park in Nottinghamshire rare Clayworth Prize Pink celery and fat golden-skinned Reliance onions. These local vegetables enjoyed widespread popularity in the nineteenth century but have since slipped out of cultivation. This is partly because gardeners rely less on home-grown seeds but also because seed companies have become increasingly commercial in their choice of stock.

Many of the National Trust properties plant rare seeds that visitors have donated, such as the once common hardy Cottager's kale, which is now grown at Knightshayes Court in Devon. Many also act as seed guardians for the Heritage Seed Library of Garden Organic at Ryton Gardens near Coventry. This was set up to save local, family and regional vegetables that have fallen from commercial seed production. Each guardian harvests the seeds of certain designated plants and returns them to the HSL whose members can then grow six rare varieties for pleasure during the following year. Thus, this autumn Clumber Park might harvest the seeds from downy, sweet Garden Peach tomatoes or Major Cook's pretty purple-flecked beans, which an HSL seed adoptee can enjoy growing next year.

DISCOVER NEW VEGETABLES

Autumn is the perfect time to seek out these unusual vegetables. Many National Trust properties sell some of their unusual garden produce or offer cookery demonstrations, but you can also quiz the growers at your local farmers' markets. After all, this is the time of year when gardeners and farmers alike receive their seed catalogues and start to plan for next year. Once you've eaten scorzonera tossed in cream and mustard, or lovage mixed into a beetroot and goat's cheese salad, you're going to want to get your hands on more.

CAULIFLOWER
AND BROCCOLI

Were you to wander around the walled kitchen garden of Clumber Park in Nottinghamshire in the early autumn, you might be surprised to see beds of purple- and orange-curded cauliflowers growing under the nets. These are Graffiti and Cauliflower 'Cheddar', both modern F-1 hybrid cauliflowers that taste as gorgeous as they look. They are the latest in a long line of beautiful cauliflower and broccoli plants that have been cultivated to capture the imagination of gardeners and cooks alike.

The cauliflower, like broccoli, is a form of wild cabbage (*Brassica oleracea*), which has been selectively bred for its flower head. It was introduced into England in the seventeenth century; broccoli followed during the next century. The early varieties needed warmth, and, as a result, cauliflower was widely regarded as an exotic, and therefore highly desirable, vegetable.

How fickle we British cooks are! By the nineteenth century, both had been bred to withstand our cold weather and, as a result, had become cheap and therefore commonplace. Cauliflower, in particular, was demoted from elegant side-dish to a homely boiled staple. Our consumption has fallen dramatically – sales have dropped by around one-third in the last decade.

Broccoli, meanwhile, has managed to retain some of its glamour, due in part to clever marketing as a dinner party staple. Even today, you are more likely to find broccoli, in some shape or form, on a restaurant menu than cauliflower. Seared scallops, for example, might be served with a jade-green broccoli purée and garnished by wafer-thin slices of broccoli carpaccio.

Naturally, cauliflower growers are fighting back with new coloured varieties, such as Graffiti and Cheddar, as well as introducing older strains, including the exotic-looking lime-green Italian cultivar 'Romanesco Minaret', which tastes half of cauliflower, half of broccoli. From the cook's perspective, old-fashioned white cauliflowers are to be treasured as much as broccoli. Treated correctly, both are wonderful vegetables that add character and variety to our cooking.

PRACTICALITIES

■ Broccoli is divided into two types: headed and sprouting (see the latter on page 20). You can adapt either to broccoli recipes, so turn to pages 22–5 for more ideas.

■ All parts of cauliflower and broccoli are edible, including the leaves. Whatever the colour, always choose tight, compact heads to ensure even cooking. Avoid those with discoloured or slimy curds. Store unwashed and lightly wrapped in the fridge.

■ If cooking a whole cauliflower – not something I would recommend as it cooks unevenly – drop it into a sink filled with cold salted water first and then swirl the head around to dislodge any lurking caterpillars.

■ For florets, remove the outer leaves, then cut out the central stem as a cone, so that the florets are severed.

CULINARY NOTES

■ Cauliflower and broccoli are mildly bitter vegetables. Slow cooking intensifies their flavour and tastes wonderful in North Indian-style dry curries and Italian dishes (see page 168).

■ Raw cauliflower is delicious cut into florets or finely sliced on a mandoline to make cauliflower carpaccio. In either case, robust seasonings bring out its sweetness, either in dressings flavoured with mustard, vinegar or lemon juice; garlic, capers, olives or parsley; or dips, such as walnut, herb and cream cheese, hummus, or a creamy curried mayonnaise.

■ Broccoli and cauliflower both taste sweeter if lightly cooked, especially in British dishes flavoured with butter, milk, cream, and mace, cayenne, nutmeg or cheese – for example, a cauliflower gratin or broccoli soup.

■ Stir-fried they develop a nutty flavour, which is delicious seasoned with salt and dried chilli, or ginger, spring onions, soy sauce, sesame oil, dried mustard seeds, sesame seeds, fish sauce or lime leaves.

■ Cauliflowers make an excellent pickle, the most famous of which is piccalilli (see page 165).

SPICY CAULIFLOWER FRITTERS

The soft, succulent texture of cauliflower makes it ideal for fritters, or pakoras as they're known in India. The key is to twice-fry the fritters as this ensures a crisp coating and soft interior. You can cook sliced small (raw) potatoes and onion rings in the same way. Serve these fritters as party nibbles.

SERVES 6

Fritters
corn oil for deep-frying
1 cauliflower
½ teaspoon each of salt, garam masala and
    chilli powder

Batter
170g/6oz gram flour
1 teaspoon each of garam masala and salt
½ teaspoon each of ground turmeric and
    chilli powder

Chilli Dip
2 tablespoons granulated sugar
1 teaspoon chilli flakes, or to taste
2½ tablespoons white wine vinegar

1 Heat the oil in a deep-fat fryer to 190°C. Cut the cauliflower into medium-thick florets. Pat dry on kitchen paper and mix with the salt and spices.

2 Sift all the batter ingredients into a bowl and slowly beat in 200ml/7fl oz water until you have a smooth, thick batter. Dip the cauliflower into the batter and fry in batches for 5–6 minutes. Shake off the excess oil and leave to cool on crumpled kitchen paper.

3 For the dip, place the granulated sugar and chilli flakes in a small bowl. Mix in 5 tablespoons boiling water and stir until the sugar has dissolved. Mix in the vinegar and pour into a small dipping bowl.

4 Reheat the oil to 190°C and refry the cauliflower fritters for 2–3 minutes, or until golden and crisp. Drain on kitchen paper and serve hot, warm or cold, arranged on a plate around the spicy chilli dip.

KILLERTON ESTATE PICCALILLI

This recipe comes from the Killerton Estate in Devon. They use all their own produce and recommend leaving it for four weeks before eating, but it is even better if you can wait for a further couple of months!

MAKES JUST OVER 3.5kg/7lb 14oz

450g/1lb fine sea salt
625g/1lb 6oz small cauliflower florets
625g/1lb 6oz diced onions
1 cucumber
225g/8oz courgettes
350g/12½ oz granulated sugar
2 cloves garlic, finely sliced
1.5 litres/2½ pints malt vinegar

1 teaspoon ground mixed spice
1 teaspoon finely grated nutmeg
2 fresh red chillies
55g/2oz plain flour
35g/1¼ oz English mustard powder
20g/¾ oz ground turmeric
15g/½ oz ground ginger

1 Mix the salt with 4.5 litres/7½ pints boiling water. Leave until cold, then divide the brine between 2 large china bowls.

2 Add the cauliflower florets and diced onions to one bowl of brine. Cut the cucumber and courgettes in half lengthways. Seed the cucumber and cut both into quarter moons. Place in the second bowl of brine. Cover each bowl with a plate, making sure that the plate pushes the vegetables under the water. Leave for 12 hours in the fridge.

3 Drain each bowl of vegetables into a separate colander – they need to be kept separate. Rinse well under cold running water and drain thoroughly.

4 Put the sugar, garlic and 1.1 litres/2 pints of malt vinegar into a large non-corrosive pan. Bring to the boil, then add the cauliflower, onions, mixed spice and nutmeg. Cook for just 3 minutes. Immediately add the courgette, cucumber and chillies. Cook for a further 4–5 minutes, so that the vegetables are just cooked and still retain a little crunch. Using a large sieve, lift the vegetables out of the vinegar, shake well and tip into a large clean bowl. Set aside while you finish the sauce.

5 Mix the flour, mustard, turmeric and ginger in a bowl. Gradually stir in the remaining 375ml/13 fl oz cold malt vinegar, so that it forms a smooth paste. Dilute further with some of the hot, spiced vinegar, then mix the thin mustard paste into the remaining hot vinegar in the pan. Bring to the boil, stirring, then simmer for 15–20 minutes, or until you can no longer taste the flour.

6 Stir the sauce into the vegetables, spoon into warm sterilised jars (see page 83) and seal with vinegar-proof lids. Label and leave for at least four weeks for the flavours to develop.

CRUNCHY CAULIFLOWER SALAD

This hearty salad can be eaten on its own or served as a delicious accompaniment to grilled steak.

SERVES 4

2 teaspoons wholegrain Dijon mustard

1 clove garlic, finely chopped

2 tablespoons white wine vinegar

6 tablespoons extra virgin olive oil

3 tablespoons capers (in brine), rinsed

salt and freshly ground black pepper

1 small cauliflower

1 x 400g/14oz can butter beans, drained

1 red pepper, quartered and seeded

4 leeks, trimmed and finely sliced

a small bunch of parsley, finely chopped

1 In a large mixing bowl, whisk together the mustard, garlic, vinegar and olive oil. Pat dry the rinsed capers and add to the dressing. Season to taste.

2 Wash the cauliflower, cut into small florets and pat dry on kitchen paper. Rinse the drained butter beans and pat dry. Mix into the vinaigrette with the cauliflower florets. The salad can be set aside to soak up the vinaigrette at this stage. If chilled, return it to room temperature before continuing.

3 Shortly before serving, cut the red pepper into similar-sized chunks to the beans. Drop the sliced leeks into a saucepan of boiling water, return to the boil, drain thoroughly and mix, while warm, into the salad with the diced peppers and parsley. Adjust the seasoning to taste, adding more oil or vinegar as necessary.

CAULIFLOWER CHEESE

Always choose a good mature artisan-made Cheddar for this recipe. You can, of course, omit the bacon if you're vegetarian – try adding some sautéed mushrooms instead.

SERVES 2

300ml/10½ fl oz milk

2 bay leaves

4 black peppercorns

1 cauliflower, cut into large florets

2 tablespoons extra virgin olive oil

115g/4oz back bacon, trimmed and diced

1 onion, finely diced

8 cherry tomatoes, halved

30g/1oz unsalted butter

30g/1oz plain flour

3 tablespoons single cream

85g/3oz mature Cheddar

½ teaspoon English mustard powder

salt and freshly ground black pepper

1 Put the milk in a saucepan with one bay leaf and the black peppercorns. Slowly bring up to the boil, then cover the pan and remove from the heat. Set aside to infuse for 20 minutes.

2 Drop the cauliflower florets and remaining bay leaf into a saucepan of boiling unsalted water. Return to the boil, then simmer for 4 minutes, or until *al dente*. Drain thoroughly and place in a gratin dish.

3 Set a frying pan over a high heat. Add the olive oil, followed by the bacon. Fry briskly for 4 minutes, or until lightly coloured, then reduce the heat and stir in the onion and fry gently for 5–10 minutes, or until softened and golden. Mix into the cauliflower with the halved cherry tomatoes.

4 Preheat the grill to medium-high. Melt the butter in a saucepan over a low heat. Stir in the flour to make a roux and cook gently for 2 minutes. Strain the milk and slowly add to the roux, stirring all the time with a wooden spoon to ensure it forms a thick smooth paste. Continue stirring until all the milk has been added. Mix in the cream and simmer for 8 minutes, stirring regularly. Remove the pan from the heat. Mix in 55g/2oz grated cheese and the mustard powder, and season to taste. Pour evenly over the cauliflower and sprinkle with the remaining cheese.

5 Place under the hot grill, and grill until bubbling hot and golden. Serve immediately.

TWO WAYS WITH SLOW-COOKED GARLIC BROCCOLI

The British are famous for over-cooking their vegetables, but in this case, it feels wrong to cook the broccoli until it is meltingly soft. Ignore your instincts and take a risk – it's not pretty but it tastes wonderful. The picture opposite shows the broccoli just after it has gone into the pan. The first two steps of this recipe make a robust-flavoured vegetable dish; the last step transforms the broccoli into a pecorino-rich sauce for penne.

SERVES 2

250g/9oz broccoli (one head)
4 tablespoons extra virgin olive oil
2 cloves garlic
1 fresh or dried red chilli
salt and freshly ground black pepper

For Pasta
115g/4oz penne
55g/2oz pecorino cheese, finely grated

1 Separate the broccoli stalks from the florets, trying to create even-sized pieces. Using a potato peeler, pare away the tough outer skin of the thick stalk and cut into even-sized lengths, similar in size to the florets. Drop them into a saucepan of boiling unsalted water. Cook for 3 minutes, then drain.

2 Meanwhile, set a heavy-bottomed saucepan over a low heat. Add the oil, whole garlic cloves and chilli. Once hot, mix in the broccoli and season to taste. Cover the pan and reduce the heat to low. Cook gently, stirring regularly, for about 30 minutes, or until the broccoli is meltingly soft. Discard the chilli and garlic cloves. Serve immediately as a vegetable or mix in the pasta at this stage.

3 If you are making the slow-cooked broccoli with penne, drop the penne into a large saucepan of boiling salted water about 10 minutes before the broccoli is ready. Cook the pasta briskly until *al dente*, drain and quickly tip into the cooked broccoli while the water is still clinging to the penne. Add the grated pecorino and mix thoroughly. Serve immediately.

SEE ALSO

- Oriental purple sprouting broccoli on page 24.
- Purple sprouting broccoli with Hollandaise sauce on page 22.
- Stuffed parathas on page 302.
- Tahini dressed purple sprouting broccoli on page 23.

BEETROOT

Beetroot is currently enjoying a renaissance. You will find the red-flushed leaves of Bull's Blood in many a formal flower bed, while no National Trust vegetable garden is complete without its compliment of old beetroot varieties. Clumber Park in Nottinghamshire, for example, grows the long-rooted, fine-flavoured Crapaudine, pink-and-white striped Chioggia and the pretty yellow-rooted Burpee's golden.

Leafy sea beet is indigenous to Britain, but the root appears to have come into cultivation during the sixteenth century, when it was introduced into Britain. Its intense red colour and sweet taste proved popular, and it appears in various recipes through the centuries, from eighteenth-century sweet pancakes to nineteenth-century chilli-spiced pickles. The Victorians even ate cold sliced boiled beetroot with their cheese course. It fell from popularity after the Second World War – too much spam and pickled beetroot.

In recent years the beetroot's fortunes have revived, perhaps helped by the fashionable belief in the health-giving virtues of brightly coloured vegetables. The desire to incorporate beetroot into all sorts of dishes has led domestic cooks to add it to sweet dishes, such as spiced cakes and chocolate puddings. Chefs, meanwhile, have taken to scattering beetroot across their menus, including exquisite-tasting tiny yellow or white beetroot. These are often added as a last-minute garnish to some elegant fish or meat dish; just as their seventeenth-century predecessors garnished their savoury dishes with Roman red beetroot cut into 'divers forms and fashions'.

PRACTICALITIES

■ The younger the beetroot, the sweeter it is. Choose well-shaped, firm roots with fresh green tops. Misshapen roots may have a poor flavour.

■ Twist off the leaves 2.5cm/1in from the root and store unwashed in the bottom of the fridge.

■ To bake beetroot the size of a large egg, wrap in a baggy parcel of oiled foil and roast at fan 170°C/gas 4 for about 45 minutes. To boil the same-sized beetroot will take about 30 minutes from when the water starts boiling. Cooking times vary according to the age of the root; to test, rub the skin with your thumb – if it peels easily, the beetroot is cooked.

CULINARY NOTES

■ Beetroot can be served raw, peeled and either finely sliced or grated and then marinated in an acidic dressing. Test your beetroot before preparing, as some are surprisingly bitter when eaten raw.

■ Sour ingredients, such as vinegar, citrus juice, pickled gherkins, rye bread, sour cream, yoghurt and soft cheeses, bring out the natural sweetness in beetroot.

■ Intense flavourings, such as cumin, dill, chives, citrus zest and horseradish, enhance the taste of beetroot, as do smoky and toasty flavours, such as cured fish and game, and toasted nuts.

UPTON HOUSE BUTTERED AND SPICED BEETS

This curious recipe is from Upton House in Warwickshire and is believed to date back to 1920s. I've included it out of interest, but it is only for those who possess that peculiar English taste for tart, spiced dishes.

SERVES 4

4 medium-sized beetroot
2 tablespoons white wine vinegar
2 tablespoons hot water
a pinch of salt

1 teaspoon paprika
$\frac{1}{8}$ teaspoon English mustard powder
a very small pinch of ground cloves (optional)
1 tablespoon melted unsalted butter

1 Cook the beetroot by baking or boiling until tender (see page 170). Drain and as soon as they're cool enough to handle, peel and cut into pretty slices.

2 Put the vinegar, hot water, salt, paprika, mustard and ground cloves in a small saucepan. Set over a medium heat and then whisk in the butter until it amalgamates with the vinegar and spice. As soon as it is piping hot, add the warm beetroot slices. Mix thoroughly, and serve immediately.

HAM HOUSE ROASTED BEETROOT SOUP WITH HORSERADISH CREAM

If there is one home-grown vegetable that every National Trust restaurant serves, it is beetroot, in all its different shapes, sizes and colours. Every property has its own favourite recipe. This simple, intensely-flavoured soup comes from Sue Lown, a volunteer cookery demonstrator for the kitchen garden at Ham House. She recommends serving it with walnut bread or home-made vegetable crisps (see page 269).

SERVES 6

800g/1¾ lb fresh beetroot
8 sprigs thyme
1 clove garlic, skin on
3 tablespoons extra virgin olive oil
8 shallots, peeled and chopped
2 teaspoons fennel seeds

750ml/1 pint 6fl oz good chicken or vegetable stock
salt and freshly ground black pepper
2½ teaspoons freshly grated horseradish
  (see page 65)
5 tablespoons soured cream
1 tablespoon finely sliced chives

1 Preheat the oven to fan 180°C/gas 5. Scrub the beetroot well to remove any dirt. Top and tail but do not peel. If the beetroot are large, halve or quarter. Place them on a large sheet of aluminium foil with 4 sprigs of thyme and the garlic clove. Toss in 1 tablespoon olive oil and wrap into a baggy parcel. Place on a baking sheet.

2 Bake in the preheated oven for 1–1½ hours, or until the beetroot is tender when pierced with a knife. Allow to cool slightly. Discard the thyme. Squeeze the garlic out of its husk and keep with any roasting juices. Peel the cooked beetroot with a small knife and roughly dice.

3 Set a large saucepan over a medium low heat. Once hot, add the remaining olive oil and gently fry the shallots and fennel seeds for 10 minutes, or until soft and golden. Add the leaves from the remaining thyme and cook for 1 minute, then mix in the diced beetroot, roasted garlic and any roasting juices. Add the stock, bring up to the boil and simmer for 20 minutes, or until all the vegetables are very soft. Liquidise and season to taste. You may need to thin the soup with a little water.

4 To serve, mix the grated horseradish into the soured cream. Heat the soup, divide between 6 bowls and swirl in the horseradish cream. Sprinkle with the sliced chives and serve immediately.

SWEET BEETROOT PANCAKES

This wonderful eighteenth-century sweet pancake is often demonstrated at Wordsworth House, the childhood home of William and Dorothy Wordsworth in Cockermouth, Cumbria. It is based on a recipe 'To make a pink coloured pancake' from the 1787 edition of Elizabeth Raffald's *The Experienced English Housekeeper* (1769). The author recommends garnishing these with 'green sweetmeats, preserved apricots or green sprigs of myrtle – it is a pretty corner-dish for either dinner or supper.' Alternatively, try serving it as a pudding with this lovely orange cream.

SERVES 4

Clarified Butter
85g/3oz unsalted butter

Orange Cream
finely grated zest of 1 orange
2 tablespoons icing sugar
200ml/7fl oz crème fraîche
2 tablespoons Grand Marnier

Pancakes
170g/6oz peeled cooked beetroot
2 tablespoons plain flour
2 teaspoons caster sugar
1 teaspoon grated nutmeg
4 medium egg yolks
3 tablespoons double cream
3 tablespoons brandy

1 Begin by making the clarified butter: slowly melt 85g/3oz butter in a heavy-bottomed saucepan over a very low heat. Once it has melted, gently simmer for 15 minutes, then strain through a muslin-lined sieve to remove any froth or sediment, taking care to leave any milky liquid at the bottom of the pan. This will be more than enough but it keeps well in the fridge.

2 Whisk the orange zest and icing sugar into the crème fraîche before adding the Grand Marnier. Whisk until thick, then chill, covered, until needed.

3 Place the beetroot in a blender and process until it forms a paste. Add the flour, sugar and nutmeg. Whizz to blend, then gradually add the egg yolks, followed by the double cream and brandy. Whizz or beat thoroughly.

4 Set a non-stick frying pan over a medium-low heat. Add 3 spoonfuls of clarified butter. As soon as it is hot, drop 4 small spoonfuls of the beetroot batter into the hot pan so that they look like burgundy blinis. Cook for about 2 minutes, taking care that they don't catch as they burn easily. As soon as they begin to form bubbles, flip them over and cook for another minute or two, then transfer to a warm plate.

5 If necessary, wipe out the pan. Add a little more butter, then repeat the process until you have 16 small pancakes. Serve warm, sprinkled with caster sugar and accompanied by the orange cream.

SEE ALSO
■ Beetroot, lovage and goat's cheese salad on page 212.

CARROTS AND PARSNIPS

As the first frost nips the hedgerows, cooks start to think of warming dishes. Few can resist the pleasure of eating honey roast parsnips or an aromatic beef and carrot pie on a cold frosty night. The sweet flavour and unctuous texture of carrots and parsnips are an integral part of British cooking.

Both are indigenous to Britain, although the wild ancestors of the orange carrots we eat today originated from Afghanistan. Flemish refugees introduced them into England in the fifteenth century. The early varieties were purple, yellow, white and red and only became orange in the sixteenth century. No one knows when our wild parsnip was first cultivated, but it's an ancient traditional food.

By the sixteenth century, carrots and parsnips, along with turnips and cabbages, were grown in market gardens around large towns, such as Norwich and Worcester, to feed the lower classes. According to Thomas Cogan in his *Haven of Health* (1584), they were 'common meate among the common people, all the time of autumne, and chiefly upon fish daies'.

Today, we are spoilt for choice with flavoursome varieties of parsnips and carrots. As our interest grows in cooking with locally grown produce, it is likely that we will create ever more recipes around these two roots, as both store well throughout the winter and early spring months.

Perhaps we should echo our Elizabethan ancestors' approach by turning them into 'common meate'. Carrots, in particular, are a good vegetable to bulk out all manner of dishes, from salads and soups to stews, curries and tarts. They absorb flavourings in a delicious way, from meaty broths to creamy spice-infused sweet tarts. In savoury dishes, carrots are perfectly balanced by caramelised onion, a hint of garlic and, on occasion, a little celery. In sweet dishes, they need spices and lemon or orange zest to bring out their aroma.

Intensely sweet parsnips require a lighter touch. They, too, complement meat and game and work well with creamy foods, but often need a little acidity and/or spice to stop them from becoming cloying.

PRACTICALITIES

■ Choose fresh-looking perky roots, regardless of size. They keep better if unwashed, with some of their green shoots still attached.

■ Young carrots can be scrubbed clean, rather than peeled, but older specimens should be peeled. Carrots taste the same, regardless of whether they're white, yellow, orange or red.

■ Parsnips require peeling, but for maximum flavour and a fluffy texture, peel them after being par-boiled or peel and steam, otherwise they become waterlogged.

■ Large or old parsnips have a tough core, which should always be cut out before steaming or post par-boiling.

■ For the fluffiest parsnip mash, pass through the finest disc of a mouli-legume, otherwise opt for a more silky texture with a food processor.

CULINARY NOTES

■ Carrots are delicious both raw and cooked, while parsnips require cooking.

■ Both have an affinity cooked with meat, especially beef, game and fowl, and both benefit from being cooked with lots of butter and cream. Both taste good cooked with mustard; or 'curry' spices; or herbs, such as parsley, thyme or rosemary. And both work well with tart apples, caramelised shallots and garlic.

■ No plate of crudités is complete without its raw carrots, but they are also wonderful grated into citrus-dressed salads or finely sliced and marinated with a fragrant herbal dressing.

■ Parsnips are delicious roasted, especially when seasoned with cinnamon or black pepper, and honey, maple syrup or even sugar. They make lovely crisps and can be blanched and deep-fried coated in breadcrumbs seasoned with Parmesan.

■ The sweetness of carrots makes them perfect for sweet dishes, ranging from orange-flavoured conserve to cardamom-flavoured halwa. They can also be used in cakes and sweet custard.

HERITAGE CARROT SALAD

Older varieties of purple, white and yellow carrots are currently enjoying a renaissance and this recipe is a good way to show off their pretty colour while enjoying their pure carrot flavour. If using purple carrots with other colours, marinate separately and mix at the last minute. This recipe can be made a day ahead, if wished.

SERVES 4

juice of 1 lemon
2 tablespoons extra virgin olive oil
salt and freshly ground black pepper
1/8 teaspoon ground cumin (optional)

1/8 teaspoon cayenne pepper (or to taste)
1/2 teaspoon caster sugar
450g/1lb carrots
a large handful of mint leaves, roughly chopped

1 Measure the lemon juice, olive oil, salt, black pepper, cumin, cayenne pepper and sugar into a large mixing bowl. Peel the carrots and finely slice into rounds or sticks – they need to be very thin. Toss in the lemon marinade, making sure that they are thoroughly coated.

Cover and chill in the fridge for a minimum of 1–2 hours.

2 When you're ready to serve the salad, mix in the mint leaves and adjust the seasoning to taste.

A DISHFUL OF CARROTS

Mature carrots taste wonderful when cooked in this simple way. You can alter the herbs to taste, for example, by adding tarragon and chervil instead of rosemary, and you can also enrich the dish by adding a little cream and bubbling briskly until the sauce has thickened slightly and achieved the right consistency.

SERVES 4

30g/1oz unsalted butter
2 shallots, finely diced
1 small clove garlic, finely diced
450g/1lb carrots, peeled and cut into batons

½ teaspoon finely chopped fresh rosemary
salt and freshly ground black pepper
55ml/2fl oz good chicken stock
1 tablespoon finely chopped parsley

1 Melt the butter in a wide saucepan over a medium-low heat. Add the shallots and garlic and then gently fry for 8 minutes, or until soft and golden. Mix in the carrots and rosemary and season to taste.

2 Add the stock, bring up to the boil, then cover and simmer for 10 minutes. Mix in the parsley and serve.

ABOVE Freshly picked carrots from the kitchen garden at Knightshayes Court, Devon.

BEEF AND CARROT PIE

The sweet nature of carrots counterbalances the slightly bitter taste of beer. I've suggested using small Chantenay carrots, a sweet French nineteenth-century variety, which is still available, but you can use any type or shape of carrot. If your carrots are large, peel them and cut into rounds.

SERVES 4

Filling
900g/2lb trimmed stewing steak
3 tablespoons plain flour
salt and freshly ground black pepper
7 tablespoons sunflower oil
2 onions, finely diced
1 clove garlic, finely diced
2 sticks celery, finely diced
370g/13oz Chantenay carrots, trimmed

2 teaspoons pale Muscovado sugar
2 tablespoons cider vinegar
250ml/9fl oz British pale ale
1 bay leaf + some parsley and thyme sprigs

Pie Crust
225g/8oz puff pastry (flour weight), see page 309
½ egg, roughly beaten

1 Both the beef filling and pastry can be prepared in advance. Remove any tough fibres running through the beef before cutting into 5cm/2in chunks. Place the flour in a large mixing bowl and season liberally. Set a large pan over a medium heat. Once hot, add 3 tablespoons oil. Take a large handful of meat and toss in the seasoned flour, shaking the excess flour back into the bowl. Add the floured meat to the pan in a single layer.

2 Fry briskly, turning regularly, for about 3 minutes, or until browned on all sides. Using a slotted spoon, transfer the meat to a bowl. Repeat the process with the remaining diced steak, adding a little more oil as you need it. Save the remaining seasoned flour.

3 Once the meat is browned, lower the heat and, if necessary, add a further 2 tablespoons of oil to the pan. Stir in the onions, garlic, celery and carrots, and gently fry for about 8 minutes, or until soft. Increase the heat slightly and mix in the brown sugar and seasoned

flour. Cook for a minute, then add the vinegar, pale ale, 300ml/10½ fl oz water, the herbs and the meat with its juices. Bring up to the boil, then turn down the heat to very low. Season to taste, cover and simmer very gently for a good hour. Set aside to cool.

4 Preheat the oven to fan 180°C/gas 5. On a lightly floured surface, roll out the pastry to a piece large enough to fit comfortably over the top of your pie dish. Line the rim of the pie dish with a strip of pastry and lightly brush with some beaten egg. Fill the dish with the cold or tepid stew. Add a pie vent. Using the rolling pin, gently cover the dish with the pastry lid. Seal the edges with a fork. Brush the lid with some beaten egg and prick with a small knife.

5 Bake in the preheated oven for 40 minutes, or until the pastry is crisp and golden. If you have time, leave the pie to sit for 10 minutes before serving, so that the juices are reabsorbed into the meat.

CARROT AND CARDAMOM CAKE

This is a gorgeous, aromatic cake, perfect for an autumnal tea. Carrots, cardamoms and sugar are a flavour match made in heaven, as every eastern cook knows, from Iranian carrot jam to Indian carrot halwa. Here is a very British interpretation, which creates a gorgeous cake, perfect for an autumn tea.

SERVES 8

2 lemons
250g/9oz carrots, peeled
55g/2oz plain flour, sifted
1 teaspoon baking powder
a pinch of salt
15 green cardamoms

250g/9oz ground almonds
5 medium eggs, separated
200g/7oz unrefined caster sugar
200g/7oz icing sugar
2 teaspoons distilled orange flower water
8 whole blanched almonds, lightly roasted

1 Preheat the oven to fan 180°C/gas 5. Line the sides and removable base of a 23cm/9in round cake tin with Bakewell paper.

2 Finely grate the lemons and place the zest in a mixing bowl with 2 tablespoons lemon juice. Set aside 2 tablespoons lemon juice for the icing. Finely grate the carrots. Mix into the lemon zest and juice and set aside.

3 Sift the flour, baking powder and salt into a bowl. Roughly crush the cardamoms with a pestle and mortar or under a rolling pin. Remove the little black seeds and grind them into a powder. Mix into the flour with the ground almonds.

4 Place the egg whites in a large dry bowl. Whisk until they form soft peaks. Add 2 tablespoons caster sugar and continue to whisk, gradually adding the remaining sugar until it is all used and the egg white forms a glossy, floppy meringue.

5 Roughly beat the egg yolks. Fold them into the egg whites with a metal spoon, followed by one-third of the almond flour mixture, then one-third of the carrots – you'll need to separate out the grated carrots and sprinkle them over the mixture. Repeat until all the ingredients are mixed into the meringue. Pour into the prepared cake tin and bake in the middle of the preheated oven for about 30 minutes, or until the cake springs back when pressed and an inserted skewer comes out clean.

6 Remove from the oven. Once cold, remove the cake from the baking tin and peel off the paper.

7 To make the lemon icing, sift the icing sugar into a bowl. Using a wooden spoon, stir in the lemon juice, followed by the orange flower water, until you have a thick, smooth icing. Spread the icing all over the cake, using a wet knife, if necessary. Once the icing begins to set, press in eight roasted almonds around the edge.

SPICED PARSNIP SOUP

The coconut cream adds a luscious richness to this simple soup. You can garnish it with fresh coriander leaves, finely sliced chilli or even a swirl of crème fraîche, depending on your mood.

SERVES 4

4 tablespoons sunflower oil
1 onion, roughly diced
1 large clove garlic, roughly chopped
1 tablespoon mild korma curry powder

680g/1½ lb parsnips, peeled and roughly chopped
320ml/11fl oz organic coconut cream
salt and freshly ground black pepper
½ lemon, juiced or to taste

1 Set a large saucepan over a medium-low heat. Add the oil and, once hot, stir in the onion and garlic. Fry gently for 8 minutes, or until soft and golden. Mix in the curry powder, cook for a couple of minutes, then add the chopped parsnips. Cover and continue to cook gently for 10 minutes, stirring occasionally.

2 Add the coconut cream and 400ml/14 fl oz water, then bring up to the boil, season to taste and simmer gently for 30 minutes, or until the ingredients are meltingly soft. Purée and return to the pan, then thin to taste with about 565ml/1 pint water. Reheat the soup when ready to serve. Add the lemon juice, salt and freshly ground black pepper to taste.

CRISPY PARSNIP CAKES

I sometimes serve these as an alternative to potatoes. They can be made a few hours ahead, cooled, lightly covered and stored in the fridge, then reheated in a hot oven (fan 190°C/gas 6).

SERVES 4

500g/1lb 2oz parsnips
1 onion, roughly grated
1 teaspoon fresh lemon thyme leaves
1 tablespoon plain flour

2 small eggs, roughly beaten
salt and freshly ground black pepper
extra virgin olive oil

1 If cooking the parsnip cakes shortly before serving, preheat the oven to fan 140°C/gas 2. Top, tail and peel the parsnips. Roughly grate them and place in a mixing bowl with the onion, thyme and flour. Mix thoroughly, then mix in the beaten eggs and season to taste.

2 Set one or two non-stick frying pans over a medium heat. Once hot, add 3 tablespoons olive oil to each pan and drop 3 separate blobs of parsnip mix into each pan.

Neatly flatten with a palette knife until each blob forms a compact, thin, round cake. Fry for about 4 minutes, or until golden and set, then turn over and cook for a further 4 minutes. Once cooked, transfer the cakes to a non-stick baking sheet and keep warm in the oven while you continue to fry the remaining parsnip mixture. The mixture should make 12 cakes in all. If you only have one pan, repeat the process, adding more oil, if necessary.

CINNAMON HONEY PARSNIPS

If you like really fluffy sweet parsnips, then this is the perfect dish for you. You can also adapt this recipe to salsify and scorzonera (see page 194).

SERVES 6

750g/1lb 10oz medium parsnips
40g/1½ oz melted unsalted butter
¾ tablespoon honey

¾ tablespoon cinnamon
salt and freshly ground black pepper

1 Preheat the oven to fan 180°C/gas 5. Scrub the parsnips clean and drop them whole into a large saucepan filled with boiling unsalted water. Boil for 10 minutes, or until they are half cooked, then drain and allow to cool. Once they're warm but not hot, top and tail each parsnip.

2 Cut each parsnip in half, so that you have a thick upper end and thin lower end. Using a small knife, peel off the skin – this winds off easily if you work around the parsnip, but don't pull it lengthways. Once the parsnips are peeled, cut each half lengthways into wedges

3 Put the butter, honey and cinnamon in a small saucepan and melt over a low heat. Place the parsnips in a non-stick roasting tray and thoroughly coat in the spicy sweet butter. Season with salt and freshly ground black pepper. Bake in the oven for 40 minutes, turning regularly, until soft and flecked golden.

SEE ALSO
- Celeriac crips on page 269.
- Wild mushroom and barley risotto on page 244.

TURNIPS AND SWEDES

It's a strange fact, but in Britain vegetables are often cited as a term of abuse, for example, 'turnip-head' or 'stop sitting like a sack of potatoes'. The lower the social status of the vegetable, the more likely it is to be denigrated. Turnips and swedes, in particular, have suffered from their association with poverty and their widespread use as an animal feed, despite the fact that both make excellent culinary vegetables.

Turnips (*Brassica rapa*) have been cultivated in Britain since Roman times. Some writers have extolled their virtues, particularly when young and sweet, but their fate was sealed when Charles Townshend, 2nd Viscount Townshend, demonstrated their use as a winter animal feed in the early eighteenth century. They formed an important part of his new agricultural system in which animals no longer needed to be slaughtered in the autumn and crops were rotated. The Agricultural Revolution quickly followed and we became a nation of beef eaters.

Large orange- or yellow-fleshed swedes (*Brassica napus*) were introduced into Britain from Sweden in 1781, although Jane Grigson suggests in her *Vegetable Book* (1978) that they were originally developed in Bohemia. The plant evolved as a hybrid between a turnip and cabbage or kale and was originally grown for both human and animal consumption. Swedes became so popular in Scotland as a culinary vegetable, that the Scots changed their name to turnips or 'neeps', hence widespread confusion in England. The Americans, meanwhile, call a swede a rutabaga.

PRACTICALITIES

■ Turnips come in many forms, from round, white-fleshed ones to yellow-fleshed spheres and long-rooted Japanese varieties.

■ Young turnips can be harvested from June onwards. They have a delicate peppery taste, quite unlike the mature turnips that appear in the autumn. Don't buy large turnips – they have an unpleasantly strong flavour. Turnip tops can be eaten in the spring.

■ Trim and peel swedes before cooking. They soak up liquid, so cook carefully by steaming or by simmering in a small amount of flavoursome liquor, such as chicken stock, bay leaf and butter.

CULINARY NOTES

■ Swede is a traditional ingredient in a Cornish pasty and an integral part of a Robbie Burns' dinner, where haggis is accompanied by bashed neeps and washed down with whisky. The neep must be mashed with liberal amounts of butter.

■ Try simmering swede in a hearty beef stew with lots of root vegetables and caramelised onions. It also tastes good with butter, cream, milk and spices, such as nutmeg and mace.

■ Young turnips are superb cooked with butter, sherry or stock, especially with sugar or honey, or tossed in mustardy herbal vinaigrettes. They go well with duck, lamb, beef and gammon.

HONEY AND MUSTARD BABY TURNIPS

Turnips are an acquired taste but baby ones are irresistible when seductively dressed in honey and mustard. This dish is lovely eaten with seared duck breast or steak. I usually serve it warm, but it's good cold on a warm summer's day.

SERVES 4

450g/1lb baby turnips with some leaf stems
1 tablespoon wholegrain Dijon mustard
½ tablespoon honey
1 tablespoon white wine vinegar

3 tablespoons extra virgin olive oil
salt and freshly ground black pepper
½ bunch chives, roughly snipped

1 Trim the turnips of their leaves, leaving about 2.5cm/1in of green stems attached to the root (if you wish, you can cook the young leaves like spinach). Take a small, serrated knife and cut off the little tail root, then, under cold running water, use your knife to pare away any dirt from the join between the stem and the bulb. Finally, scrub the roots clean.

2 Drop the roots into a saucepan of boiling water and cook for about 8 minutes, or until they're just tender. Drain and lightly dry with kitchen paper.

3 While the turnips are cooking, mix together the mustard and honey in a bowl large enough to hold the turnips. Whisk in the vinegar, followed by the olive oil, and season to taste. Toss the drained hot turnips in the dressing, then add the snipped chives, and serve warm or at room temperature.

SALT-BAKED BUTTERED 'NEEPS'

Swedes have a tendency towards wateriness, especially if they are boiled, but this unusual cooking method makes them taste amazingly sweet. This dish is perfect for Burns' Night.

SERVES 2

1 medium trimmed swede, about 370g/13oz
2 medium egg whites
500g/1lb 2oz rock or sea salt

55g/2oz unsalted butter
salt and freshly ground black pepper
freshly grated nutmeg

1 Preheat the oven to 180°C/gas 5. Wash and dry the swede. In a large bowl, mix together the egg whites and rock or sea salt until you have a thick paste.

2 Place a sheet of baking paper on a roasting tray. Shape a flat disc of salt paste on the paper and sit the base of the swede on top. Pile up the salt mixture around the swede until it is completely encased in the salt paste. This will be about 1cm/½ in thick on the top but thicker nearer the base, where you need to pile it up.

3 Bake the swede in the preheated oven for 1 hour 20 minutes. Remove and cool slightly, then, using a rolling pin, crack open the salt crust. Extract the swede and peel away its skin.

4 Cut the flesh into chunks and place them in a saucepan. Set over a low heat and add the butter, and season to taste with salt, pepper and nutmeg. Mash thoroughly, until the swede forms a fragrant, buttery mash. Serve immediately.

HANBURY HOUSE ROAST ROOT VEGETABLES

The cooks at Hanbury House in Worcestershire vary this popular dish according to the season, and they flavour it with a variety of different herbs, such as lovage, rosemary and thyme – all freshly picked from their own kitchen garden. It's delicious served with roast meat.

SERVES 8

1 swede
½ celeriac
2 parsnips
2 beetroot
½ butternut squash

2 sprigs rosemary
2 cloves garlic, finely diced
salt and freshly ground black pepper
4 tablespoons extra virgin olive oil

1 Preheat the oven to fan 180°C/gas 5. Prepare your chosen vegetables by trimming, peeling and cutting them into similar-sized pieces. If using squash or pumpkin, remove the seeds. Mix together and divide between 2 roasting trays.

2 Strip the rosemary leaves from their stems. Finely chop and scatter over the vegetables with the chopped garlic. Season to taste and, using your hands, thoroughly mix in the olive oil.

3 Bake in the preheated oven for about 1¼ hours, tossing the vegetables occasionally in the oil, or until soft and golden.

SCORZONERA AND SALSIFY

There are some vegetables that deserve to be reinstated. At Ham House in Surrey, for example, in the seventeenth-century inspired vegetable bed in the kitchen garden, you will find pretty yellow flowers bedecking great bushy clumps of raggedy leaves. These belong to scorzonera (*Scorzonera hispanica*, see opposite), a delectable, pearly-fleshed long root now unfamiliar to British cooks, as is its equally delicious cousin salsify (*Tragopogon porrifolius*). Both are still widely grown on the Continent.

Salsify has a long thin white-skinned root and mauve flowers. Its white flesh has a subtle earthy sweetness. It belongs to the same family, *Compositae* (*Asteraceae*), as scorzonera. The two are often confused as scorzonera looks and tastes very similar to salsify, once cooked. However, the latter has a thick black skin – hence its other name, black salsify. Both require careful work to dig them out of the soil, which may account for the fact that, although they were grown in refined kitchen gardens from the sixteenth century onwards, they never caught the popular imagination. They continued to be grown right up to the nineteenth century, but the familiar taste and plump flesh of easy-to-grow parsnips won out.

PRACTICALITIES

■ Allow about 170g/6oz uncleaned root of either salsify or scorzonera per person.

■ Once cut, they discolour very quickly. Set aside a bowl of acidulated water before cleaning the roots. Add 1 tablespoon lemon juice or vinegar to 1 litre/1¾ pints cold water. Using a potato peeler, quickly pare off its skin under cold running water. Drop the roots into the acidulated water as you go – they release a sticky sap as you peel, but it disappears with cooking. Cut into the required lengths but keep in the bowl until ready to cook.

■ Both are normally boiled before further cooking. Cover with cold water, bring to the boil and cook for 10–15 minutes. Salsify can be boiled in large unpeeled pieces – drain, cool and peel before cutting to the required length.

CULINARY NOTES

■ Scorzonera and salsify have a wonderful sweet flavour that is unique. Cooked, it hints at both celeriac and root artichoke, while its texture is a cross between a carrot and a potato. Scorzonera is slightly more intensely flavoured.

■ Traditionally, both are normally boiled before being turned into fritters, gratins or simply fried in butter and finished with lemon.

■ Once boiled, dress with a light hand, even when strewing with parsley. You can toss them in a creamy sauce, flavoured with nutmeg or a tiny amount of cheese; or season them with a hint of sharpness, such as lemon or a mustard vinaigrette, to bring out their sweetness.

HAM HOUSE SALSIFY GRATIN

The kitchen gardeners at Ham House in Surrey always grow scorzonera or salsify. The roots are then offered up in the Orangery Restaurant for diners to sample. This is one of their favourite recipes for either root – it's very rich.

SERVES 4

15g/½ oz unsalted butter
1 tablespoon lemon juice or vinegar
680g/1½ lb salsify or scorzonera
salt and freshly ground black pepper

100ml/3½ fl oz double cream
4 tablespoons white breadcrumbs
3 tablespoons finely grated Parmesan

1 Preheat the oven to 190°C/gas 6. Liberally butter a shallow gratin dish.

2 Measure 1 tablespoon lemon juice or vinegar and 1 litre/1¾ pints cold water into a large bowl. Thoroughly wash the salsify or scorzonera. Trim off both ends of the first root and peel under cold running water. Immerse in acidulated water (see page 194) and continue with the remaining roots – this helps prevent discolouring. Once all are peeled, cut into even-sized lengths, about 3.5cm/1½ in long, returning them to the water as you cut.

3 Drain and place in a saucepan. Cover with cold water, bring up to the boil and cook briskly for 10–15 minutes, or until tender. Drain thoroughly, shaking dry, and then tip into your buttered dish. Season lightly and toss in the cream. Mix together the breadcrumbs and cheese and sprinkle over the top. Bake in the oven for 20 minutes, or until bubbling hot and flecked golden brown.

SAUTÉED SCORZONERA

Scorzonera or salsify can be served instead of potato. It develops a wonderful nutty flavour when fried, but it will not be as crisp as a sautéed potato as it contains too much sugar. Try serving with grilled fish or steak.

SERVES 4

680g/1½ lb salsify or scorzonera
1 tablespoon lemon juice or vinegar
3 tablespoons extra virgin olive oil

15g/½ oz unsalted butter
salt and freshly ground black pepper
3 tablespoons finely chopped parsley

1 Prepare the scorzonera or salsify, as described on page 196, dropping it into acidulated water. Drain and place in a saucepan. Cover with unsalted cold water, bring up to the boil and cook briskly for 10–15 minutes, or until tender. Drain thoroughly and leave to dry slightly, so that it does not spit when it is added to the hot fat.

2 Set a large non-stick frying pan over a medium heat. Once hot, add the oil and butter. As soon as the butter is sizzling, add the scorzonera or salsify, season to taste and fry briskly, turning regularly, until well coloured. Remove with a slotted spoon, tip on to kitchen paper, then toss in a bowl with the parsley and, if needed, extra salt. Serve immediately.

SCORZONERA WITH CREAM AND MUSTARD

In Victorian times, scorzonera would have been simmered in a thin béchamel sauce, but this is a modern, lighter interpretation. I've added wholegrain mustard as it tastes wonderful, especially if served with roast beef.

SERVES 4

680g/1½ lb scorzonera or salsify
1 tablespoon lemon juice or vinegar
100ml/3½ fl oz double cream

2 teaspoons wholegrain mustard
salt and freshly ground black pepper

1 Prepare the scorzonera or salsify, as described on page 196. Drain and place in a saucepan. Cover with cold water, then bring up to the boil and cook briskly for 10–15 minutes, or until tender. Drain thoroughly.

2 Pour the cream into a clean saucepan. Bring up to the boil, then add the hot drained scorzonera or salsify. Mix in the mustard and season to taste. Serve immediately.

CHARD

It is hard to resist the idea of buying a bunch of rainbow or Swiss chard, *Beta vulgaris*, when you slip into the organic kitchen garden at Greys Court in Oxfordshire. It looks so pretty, growing in amongst the pink and white flowering tobacco plants and the bright yellow flowers of the edible chrysanthemum greens. On a warm autumn day, pert chard leaves beg to be wilted and tossed in pasta with chilli, lemon and oil or turned into a creamy gratin.

However, chard often fills the urban cook with a sense of guilt. Week after week, gorgeous bunches of red-, yellow- and pink-stemmed chard gets tucked into their organic boxes. Few growers can resist such a beautiful, hardy and prolific plant, but what do you make after the first few gratins and tarts? All too often, the chard ends up in the bin.

Once you've wearied of your normal culinary repertoire, an analytical approach is needed. First, remember that mature chard needs to be separated – leaf from stalk – and that each has a different flavour and texture. Sliced chard stems can be added to stir-fried vegetables or sautéed onions as part of a vegetable base for soups, stews, tarts and pies. The leaves can then be blanched or cooked at the last moment, a little like tough spinach. Think cheesy soufflés, stuffed cannelloni and fish parcels.

PRACTICALITIES

■ Always wash chard thoroughly. Young leaves can be left whole and mixed raw into salads. The coloured stems fade with cooking.

■ To prepare: cut the stalk 1cm/½ in below the leaf or, if mature, fold the two shiny long sides of the leaf together and pull the stem up and away from the leaf towards the leaf tip – like a zip. Pull away or pare any stringy fibres from the stem. Keep leaves and stem separate.

■ Cook the leaves in the same way as spinach, either blanched for a minute in a saucepan of boiling water and refreshed under the cold tap before drying and dressing, or wilted in a pan with a little butter or olive oil.

CULINARY NOTES

■ Chard leaves taste like a stronger version of spinach and work well with fish or meat. They are good seasoned with butter, olive oil, chilli, lemon juice or garlic as well as soy sauce, sesame oil and sesame seeds.

■ Blanched chard stems can be baked in gratins, with or without the blanched leaves. Dress in a white sauce or cream seasoned with a strong-flavoured cheese or mustard.

■ The stems can be added to sautéed onions and cooked with other vegetables, from meat stews to spiced tomato dishes. Add the blanched leaves at the end of cooking.

SWISS CHARD GRATIN

In this dish, you only use the Swiss chard stems. Save the leaves for another dish. This is lovely eaten with a green salad or some baked cherry tomatoes.

SERVES 2

15g/½ oz unsalted butter + extra for greasing
1 bay leaf
3 black peppercorns
1 blade of mace
285ml/½ pint whole milk

250g/9oz cleaned Swiss chard stems
2 teaspoons plain flour
55g/2oz Emmental, roughly grated
salt and freshly ground black pepper
15g/½ oz finely grated Parmesan

1 Preheat the oven to fan 190°C/gas 6. Liberally butter a shallow gratin dish.

2 Put the bay leaf, peppercorns, mace and milk in a saucepan. Bring slowly up to boiling point, then remove from the heat and leave to infuse for 20 minutes.

3 Lightly pare the chard stems with a potato peeler. Cut into short lengths. Drop into a saucepan of boiling water for 5–7 minutes, or until tender. Drain, cool under the running cold tap and pat dry on kitchen paper. Place in the buttered gratin dish.

4 Melt the butter in a saucepan over a low heat. Stir in the flour and cook gently for 2 minutes, or until it starts to look paler. Strain the warm milk and, using a wooden spoon, gradually add to the buttery flour, stirring all the time, until all the milk has been added. Simmer very gently for 25 minutes, stirring regularly, or until it loses its floury taste. It will reduce and thicken as you simmer. Stir in the Emmental cheese and season to taste.

5 Pour the sauce over the chard stems. Sprinkle with the Parmesan cheese. It can be covered and chilled at this stage, until you're ready to eat. Bake in the preheated oven for 20 minutes, or until bubbling hot and flecked golden brown.

CHARD WITH MUSTARD AND CREAM

This intensely flavoured dish is lovely eaten with roast chicken. Chard is one of those vegetables that soaks up flavour, so it's often served with a strong tasting sauce. The mustard and cheese add a delicious bite.

SERVES 4

450g/1lb chard
100ml/3½ fl oz double cream
30g/1oz finely grated Gruyère

2 teaspoons smooth Dijon mustard
salt and freshly ground black pepper

1 Separate the stems from the chard leaves (see page 200). Cut the stems into short lengths and drop into a saucepan of boiling unsalted water. Cook for 3 minutes, or until just tender, then remove to a colander. Add the leaves to the boiling water and cook for 2 minutes, then drain thoroughly.

2 Meanwhile, pour the cream into a clean saucepan. Bring up to the boil, stir in the cheese and, once it has melted, mix in the mustard, followed by the hot drained chard. Season to taste. Serve immediately.

ABOVE Ruby chard growing in the kitchen garden at Tyntesfield, Somerset.

CREAMY SPICED CHARD

This is one of those early autumn dishes you can eat with some bread, a pilaff or serve as an accompaniment to spiced meat. If you wish to make it with rainbow chard, reduce the cooking time for the sliced stems and cook until tender.

SERVES 4

340g/12oz Swiss chard
3 tablespoons sunflower oil
1 onion, finely diced
1 clove garlic, finely diced
1 small Thai red chilli (or to taste), finely diced
½ teaspoon ground turmeric

½ teaspoon ground cumin
1 small stick cinnamon, halved
340g/12oz ripe tomatoes, peeled and diced
55ml/2fl oz crème fraîche
salt

1 Prepare the chard, as described on page 200. Thickly slice the stems, set aside, and then thickly slice the leaves. Set aside.

2 Set a wide pan on a medium-low heat. Once hot, add the oil, followed by the onion, garlic and chilli. Fry gently for 10 minutes, or until soft and golden, then mix in the spices. Cook for 5 minutes, then stir in the white chard stems. Continue to fry for 3 minutes.

3 Peel the tomatoes by placing them in a bowl. Make a small nick in each tomato, cover with boiling water and leave for 2 minutes. Drain, peel and roughly chop. Mix the tomatoes into the chard. Increase the heat slightly, and boil briskly until the tomatoes form a thick purée.

4 Stir in the crème fraîche and 250ml/9fl oz boiling water to form a sauce. Season to taste with salt, bring up to the boil, then simmer for 25–30 minutes, or until the chard stems are almost tender. Add the chard leaves and cook for a further 7 minutes, or until tender.

CELERY, FENNEL AND LOVAGE

You'll find the delicate fronds of wild celery (*Apium graveolens*) growing along the damp banks of rivers and marshland fens. It's strange to think that this indigenous plant was picked by cooks for centuries before the arrival of domesticated celery in the late seventeenth century. And even then, it was another hundred years before the plump-stemmed cultivated varieties became popular.

According to Christopher Stocks, in his book *Forgotten Fruits* (2009), there was a time when Victorian cooks eschewed cooking white-stemmed celery in favour of pink varieties, which have a richer flavour. Clayworth Prize Pink from Lincolnshire was renowned for its fine taste in the late nineteenth century but has since vanished from our seed catalogues. Anxious to preserve its seeds, Clumber Park, in nearby Nottinghamshire, grows and harvests its seeds, along with Reliance, a local onion that dates back to the 1880s.

Sweet-tasting Florence fennel (*Foeniculum vulgare*) meanwhile, was introduced into England from Italy in the early eighteenth century. It, too, took a good hundred years to become popular in Britain. Florence fennel is unrelated to celery, but since both are used in place of one another in dishes, I've put them together in this section. I've also added lovage (*Levisticum officinale*) for good measure, due to its strong celery flavour. It has become a fashionable ingredient among Michelin-starred chefs who use it in both sweet and savoury dishes, including lovage ice cream.

Celery and fennel both taste fabulous raw, especially when nibbled with sea salt or an intensely flavoured British cheese. They're also delicious dipped into an anise- (Pernod) or dill-flavoured mayonnaise, accompanied by quail's eggs and other crunchy raw vegetables. However, many people love their mellow sweet flavour when slowly baked in stock or cooked in a cheese-encrusted gratin.

Lovage, on the other hand, is best used with a light hand. It makes a lovely peppery addition to salads and tastes particularly good with sweet vegetables, such as beetroot, carrot and potato. It is also wonderful simmered in soups or used to infuse a sweet custard or syrup for tarts, ice cream, jellies and sorbets.

PRACTICALITIES

■ To preapre celery or fennel: trim the base of their stems and wash thoroughly. The outer stems of old varieties of celery sometimes need to be pared to remove tough threads. Trim their tips and, if wished, strip away the leaves. These can also be used for garnish.

■ Trim and save the outermost layers of celery or fennel for stock, but make sure you cut away and discard any bruised or damaged bits.

■ Always choose lively-looking specimens. Store celery and lovage loosely wrapped in the salad drawer of the fridge. Once you separate celery stems, they will start to wilt.

■ Lovage leaves, rather than their stems, are mainly used in cooking. Always use with a light hand: you only need 4 tablespoons chopped leaves for a soup made with 500g/ 1lb 2oz potatoes.

CULINARY NOTES

■ The raw flesh and leaves of all celery, fennel and lovage add a fresh note to salads and dressings. They have an affinity with citrus fruit, apples, pears and figs, chicory, beetroot, carrot and cabbage, as well as different cheeses and nuts.

■ Peppery fresh herbs, such as dill, chervil, wild fennel, parsley, watercress and coriander, enhance their taste.

■ Their flavour mellows and sweetens with cooking, especially when slow-cooked in gratins, braises, soups and stews. They add a depth of flavour to stews, risottos, soups and sauces, which is heightened with lemon or orange zest, pepper and fennel seeds.

■ Fennel develops a sweet smoky flavour when finely sliced, tossed in oil and chargrilled.

CELERY SOUP WITH TRUFFLE OIL

Truffle oil adds a lovely aroma to this celery soup. However, you need to buy a good-quality oil as cheap brands use synthetic flavourings, which leave a nasty after-taste.

SERVES 6

1 head celery
4 tablespoons extra virgin olive oil
2 onions, roughly diced
450g/1lb potatoes, peeled and diced

500ml/18fl oz good chicken stock
salt and freshly ground black pepper
120ml/4fl oz crème fraîche
a few drops of white truffle oil (optional)

1 Trim and wash the celery. If wished, you can save the celery leaves and use them to garnish the soup when you serve it. Roughly dice the remaining celery.

2 Set a large saucepan over a medium heat. Add the oil and, once hot, stir in the onions and celery. Fry gently while you prepare the potatoes. Add the potatoes and fry for 5 minutes, or until beginning to soften. Add the stock and 500ml/18fl oz water. Bring up to the boil, then reduce the heat and simmer briskly for 20 minutes, or until the vegetables are very soft.

3 Purée the soup and, if the celery is fibrous, push through a sieve. Season to taste and reheat when needed. Swirl in the crème fraîche and add a drop or two of the truffle oil. Be careful – it's very strong. Garnish with the celery leaves, if wished.

FENNEL, CHICORY AND FIG SALAD

You can use any form of chicory, ranging from curly endive or batavia to radicchio or Belgian endive, in this salad. Allow a handful of leaves per person.

SERVES 4

2 tablespoons lemon juice
6 tablespoons walnut oil
salt and freshly ground black pepper

8 ripe figs, de-stalked
2 Florence fennel
4 Belgian endive, separated

1 In a medium bowl, whisk together the lemon juice and walnut oil. Season to taste. Finely dice 4 figs and mix into the lemon dressing. Leave to macerate for 30 minutes.

2 Top and tail the fennel. Cut each in half lengthways, so that you're left with 2 thin halves. Finely slice each half into fine fans and place in a large mixing bowl. Slice the chicory leaves lengthways, and add to the fennel. Cut each of the remaining figs into eighths and mix them into the salad.

3 Add the fig vinaigrette, gently mix everything together and then divide between 4 plates. Serve immediately.

GRILLED FENNEL GRATIN

This makes a delicious light lunch dish if it is accompanied by a salad. It tastes particularly good with a peppery watercress and pear salad.

SERVES 4

4 Florence fennel
1 red onion, finely sliced
2 tablespoons extra virgin olive oil

salt and freshly ground black pepper
6 tablespoons finely grated Parmesan
170g/6oz cold Taleggio

1 Preheat the oven to fan 200°C/gas 7. Preheat an oven-top griddle pan over a high heat on the hob. Trim the fennel bulbs by topping and tailing, halve lengthways and remove any tough or damaged outer leaves. Finely slice the fennel into fans and place in a large mixing bowl. Mix in the sliced red onion, olive oil and seasoning to taste.

2 Spread a layer – about one-third – of the oiled fennel and red onion on to the griddle pan. Lightly cook for 3–4 minutes, until just flecked gold on both sides but still crunchy. Place in a gratin dish and sprinkle with 2 tablespoons Parmesan. Repeat the process with the remaining fennel mixture until all is griddled and layered in the gratin dish with the Parmesan.

3 Cut off the Taleggio rind and thinly slice the cheese. Arrange evenly over the top of the griddled fennel. When you're ready, bake in the preheated oven for 15 minutes, or until bubbling hot and golden.

BEETROOT, LOVAGE AND GOAT'S CHEESE SALAD

Lovage has an intense celery-like flavour that goes particularly well with freshly cooked beetroot. I love eating this for lunch – it tastes of the end of summer. Follow with fresh plums.

SERVES 4

2 tablespoons cider or perry vinegar
6 tablespoons extra virgin olive oil
salt and freshly ground black pepper
600g/1lb 5oz cooked and peeled beetroot
    (see page 170)

30g/1oz lovage leaves
1 bunch chives, roughly snipped
3 x 60g/2¼ oz Innes button goat's cheeses or other
    soft, fresh goat's cheese

1 In a large mixing bowl, whisk together the vinegar, olive oil, salt and black pepper. Cut the beetroot into chunks, place in a bowl and mix thoroughly.

2 Shortly before serving strip the lovage leaves from their stems and roughly rip. Add to the beetroot with the roughly snipped chives. Toss and divide between 4 plates. Cut the goat's cheese into chunks, roughly the

same size as the beetroot, and delicately slip into each salad, so that the cheese doesn't turn a shocking pink. Serve immediately.

3 Or you can be inspired like Karen Thomas, the photographer, and serve each element separately as shown opposite, because it's so beautiful.

SEE ALSO
- Beef and carrot pie on page 181.
- Broad bean, dill and rice salad on page 79.
- Corn and pepper relish on page 152.
- Scallop chowder on page 149.
- Spicy green cabbage coleslaw on page 289.
- Sweet and sour aubergine on page 133.

BORLOTTI BEANS

In recent years, fresh borlotti beans have become fashionable in British cooking. They belong to the *Phaseolus* family, which includes haricot, kidney, cannellini, flageolet, black and pinto beans. English cooks and gardeners alike have been seduced by their wonderful magenta-and-white marbled pods, which hide equally beautiful pink-flecked, cream-coloured beans. As the beans dry, they turn a deep pink mottled with brown (as shown in the picture). As they cook, borlotti beans develop a luscious, creamy texture. They soak up the flavour of their dressing or sauce, which makes them ideal for hearty soups, stews and salads.

By the autumn, borlotti beans are hanging semi-dried from their vines, perfect for podding and simmering in a tomato-based soup, although you can also use them when they're young and tender in August. Curiously, acidic broths will help retain the skin structure of semi-dried and dried beans, so borlotti beans won't dissolve into a mush if you're cooking them with tomatoes or a rich wine sauce. Similarly, hard water can slow or even prevent dried or semi-dried beans from softening as they cook. If you have problems with their texture, try cooking them in soft mineral water.

PRACTICALITIES

■ Around 500g/1lb 2oz fresh borlotti beans (in their pods) will yield 200g/7oz shelled beans. As the pods dry, the proportion of shelled beans to pod will increase slightly. The drier the freshly-picked bean, the longer the cooking time; allow 45–60 minutes cooking time.

■ As with all pulses, don't add salt until the end of the cooking process, as it toughens the skin of the bean. This slows the rate of water absorption and lengthens the cooking time.

■ Semi-dried beans in their pods don't need to be soaked, but soak dried podded beans for 12 hours before cooking. To cook dried, soaked beans: drain, rinse and cover with cold water. Bring up to the boil and boil vigorously for 10 minutes, then simmer gently until tender.

CULINARY NOTES

■ Borlotti beans have a mild, sweet taste that absorbs other flavours. They work well with strong flavours, such as cumin, chilli, rosemary, parsley, bacon, prawns and lamb, as well as lemon, tomato and chicken stock. They also taste very good with bitter foods, such as cabbage or chicory.

■ Their soft, creamy texture has to be carefully balanced with other soft-textured foods, such as spinach or green beans, when composing a dish.

STEWED BORLOTTI BEANS

This dish is gorgeous with seared or roast lamb. You can add a little chopped parsley before serving or flavour the beans with lemon thyme or cumin seeds.

SERVES 4

3 tablespoons extra virgin olive oil
4 shallots, finely sliced
2 cloves garlic, finely diced
400g/14oz ripe tomatoes

400g/14oz shelled borlotti beans
400ml/14fl oz good chicken stock (or water)
salt and freshly ground black pepper

1 Set a saucepan over a medium-low heat. Add the oil and then mix in the shallots and garlic and fry them for 10 minutes, or until soft and golden.

2 Peel the tomatoes by placing them in a bowl. Make a small nick in each tomato, cover with boiling water and leave for 2 minutes. Drain, peel and roughly chop. Add to the shallots and fry briskly for 10 minutes, or until they form a thick paste and release their oil.

3 Add the shelled beans and stock. Bring up to the boil, then reduce the heat and simmer for 45–60 minutes, or until tender. If necessary, top up the stock with some hot water. Once the beans are very soft, reduce the liquid so that it forms a thick sauce. Season to taste and serve.

ANOTHER BEAN SALAD

This makes a simple late summer lunch and tastes delicious with seared salmon. If possible, choose a fruity olive oil as the borlotti beans soak up its flavour. You can, of course, use canned or dried borlotti beans for this recipe.

SERVES 4

400g/14oz shelled borlotti beans
2 tablespoons lemon juice
6 tablespoons extra virgin olive oil + extra
salt and freshly ground black pepper

1 medium red onion, halved and finely sliced
500g/1lb 2oz green beans, trimmed
1 escarole (broad-leaved endive or Batavia) heart,
    ripped

1 Cook your fresh or dried borlotti beans, as instructed on page 214. Meanwhile, whisk together the lemon juice and olive oil in a large mixing bowl. Season to taste. As soon as your beans are cooked, drain thoroughly and mix into the lemon dressing with the red onion.

2 Top and tail the green beans. If long, cut in half. Drop them into a saucepan of boiling unsalted water and cook briskly for 5–8 minutes, or until tender. Drain and spread out on kitchen paper. Pat dry and toss into the dressed borlotti beans. Season to taste.

3 When you're ready to serve, roughly rip the escarole heart into easy-to-eat pieces. Arrange on a serving plate and top with the bean salad. Drizzle with a little extra olive oil and serve.

BORLOTTI BEAN, TOMATO AND SPINACH SOUP

This can be made throughout September when fresh borlotti beans are available and home-grown tomatoes are bursting with flavour. You can, of course, use other beans, such as cannellini or flageolet. This soup freezes well.

SERVES 8

5 tablespoons extra virgin olive oil
3 large onions, finely diced
4 cloves garlic, finely diced
1 teaspoon dried chilli flakes
¼ teaspoon cumin seeds
1.5kg/3½ lb ripe tomatoes

1.25kg/2lb 12oz fresh borlotti beans
    (650g/1lb 7oz shelled weight)
1 small bay leaf
200g/7oz baby leaf spinach, washed
salt and freshly ground black pepper

1 Set a large saucepan over a low heat. Add the oil and, once hot, stir in the diced onions and garlic. Fry gently for 15 minutes, then stir in the spices and continue cooking for a further 5 minutes, or until the onions are soft and golden.

2 Peel the tomatoes (see stage 2 on page 216). Roughly chop them and mix into the softened onions. Increase the heat slightly and bring up to the boil, then cook briskly for 10–15 minutes, stirring regularly, until the tomatoes form a thick sauce.

3 Add the shelled beans, bay leaf and 1.5 litres/2½ pints water. Turn the heat to high and bring up to the boil (this will take about 15 minutes), then reduce the temperature to low and simmer gently for just under 2½ hours. Once the beans are tender and the soup tastes flavoursome, stir in the baby spinach. Season to taste and remove the bay leaf before serving.

ONIONS, SHALLOTS AND GARLIC

Every autumn, the long rows of onions, shallots and garlic were forked up and spread out to dry before being suspended from the eaves of our woodshed. Their smell mingled with the scent of wood chips and dust. Shallots were for fine French sauces, garlic for vinaigrettes and onions for everyday use. As William Ellis wrote in *The Country Housewife's Family Companion* (1750) regarding the preservation of onions, garlic and shallots: 'These roots are so necessary for family uses, that none should be without them'.

The genus *Allium* contains around 500 species, including leeks, chives and spring onions as well as onions and garlic. Shallots are considered to be a variety of onion. No one knows when their seeds were first introduced to Britain; some speculate that they may have been grown before the Romans. They appear to have always formed an important part of our diet. As Thomas Tusser wrote in the November section of his 1571 guide to farmers, *A Hundrethe Good Points of Husbandrie*:

'Set garlike and beans at St. Edmond the king,
The moon in the wane, thereon hangeth a thing:
Th' increase of a pottle [2 quarts], (well proved of some,)
Shall pleasure thy household, ere peascod time come.'

Over the millennia, both rich and poor alike have enjoyed their aromatic flavour, from a seventeenth-century countryman dining on roast onion, bread and parsley to a nineteenth-century cook flavouring her roast leg of mutton with a hint of garlic. Their pungent flavour has led, at times, to members of the *Allium* family falling out of favour with the refined, but they're always reinstated – they're too good to be ignored.

PRACTICALITIES

■ Choose firm, dry onions, shallots and garlic. Avoid any that are sprouting, soft or show signs of mould. Green shoots are edible but coarsen the flavour of the onion or garlic.

■ Ideally, onions and shallots should be stored in a cool, dry and dark place, but not the fridge. Light encourages them to sprout and to lose their pungency.

■ British-grown green garlic comes into season in June. Gradually, as it matures, its skin becomes papery. Mature garlic should be stored somewhere cool, dry and airy.

■ Small flat button onions and white-skinned pearl (cocktail) onions are perfect for pickles, stews and sauces.

■ Always prepare onions, shallots and garlic at the last moment, otherwise they oxidise and take on an unpleasant flavour. Never use a food processor to chop them – it gives them a nasty taste. Hand-chopped garlic has a sweeter, milder flavour than crushed garlic.

CULINARY NOTES

■ Finely diced shallots or red onion are excellent in vinaigrettes, especially when combined with sherry vinegar and fresh herbs.

■ Alternatively, finely chop some shallots, cover with a good white wine vinegar and serve with oysters, lemon wedges and crusty bread.

■ Slowly caramelised onions, shallots and garlic, whether roasted or fried, develop an ultra-sweet taste that can add depth of flavour to dishes.

■ Grilling onions or shallots adds a smoky aroma, which is delicious on pizzas or in salads (see salad leaves, saffron lamb and pitta bread on page 94).

■ To make crisp deep-fried shallots: finely slice a good cupful of shallots, add to medium-hot oil in a wok and, once the oil has bubbled up and then recovered, reduce the heat slightly and cook until nutty and golden. Cool on kitchen paper and then leave until crisp.

■ Always consider the balance of flavours when you are using onions, shallots or garlic – less can often be more.

■ Celery, ginger, wine, lemongrass or lemon zest (not together) add freshness; carrot, celeriac and fennel provide sweetness; chilli adds excitement; and mushrooms, tomatoes, soy sauce, stock and cream contribute to a greater intensity (umami) of flavour.

DEEP-FRIED ONION RINGS

Onions become intensely sweet when they are fried, so these are soaked in buttermilk before cooking to lessen this, and then dipped in semolina to make an extra crisp coating.

SERVES 4

3 medium onions
285ml/½ pint buttermilk
285ml/½ pint full fat milk

corn oil for deep frying
115g/4oz semolina
salt and freshly ground black pepper

1 Cut the onions into slices about 1cm/½ in-thick slices. Separate the rings and place in a bowl. Add the buttermilk and milk and mix thoroughly, then cover and chill for 1 hour.

2 Heat the oil in a deep-fat fryer to 180°C. Put the semolina in a shallow bowl and lightly season. Drain the onion rings and toss one-quarter of them in the seasoned semolina. Shake well and then deep-fry for 1–2 minutes, or until crisp and golden. Shake dry of oil and tip on to a plate lined with lots of crumpled kitchen paper. Continue to cook the onion rings in batches. When all are cooked, serve immediately.

ONION TART

Soured cream is used in this tart to counterbalance the intense rich sweetness of the fried onions. This is one of those tarts that should be packed for a picnic as its flavour improves the following day. It also freezes well.

SERVES 4–6

225g/8oz shortcrust pastry (see page 308)
4 tablespoons extra virgin olive oil
2 large or 3 medium onions, finely diced
salt and freshly ground black pepper

1 medium egg
1 medium egg yolk
200ml/7fl oz soured cream
30g/1oz Emmental cheese, roughly grated

1 Roll out the pastry on a lightly floured surface and line a 23cm/9in shallow quiche dish. Prick the base of the pastry, line with greaseproof paper or foil and fill with baking beans. Chill for 30 minutes. Preheat the oven to fan 180°C/gas 5.

2 Bake the pastry case in the preheated oven for 15 minutes, then remove the paper or foil and beans and return to the oven for a further 5 minutes.

3 Meanwhile, place a non-stick frying pan over a medium heat. Add the oil and, once hot, gently fry the onions for 20 minutes, or until soft and golden. Season to taste and spoon into the pastry case.

4 Beat together the egg, egg yolk and soured cream. Season to taste and pour into the pastry case, mixing it with a fork into the onion. Sprinkle with the cheese and bake for 25 minutes, or until golden and set. Serve the tart warm or cold.

THYME, BUTTON ONION AND CREAM SAUCE

Button onions only appear in the shops for a few brief weeks in the autumn. Enthusiasts turn them into pickles, but I love them in this simple sauce, which is wonderful with chicken, veal and meaty-textured white fish. It freezes well.

SERVES 6

450g/1lb button or cocktail onions
3 tablespoons extra virgin olive oil
6 thick slices smoked bacon, cut into lardons
450ml/16fl oz dry white wine

450ml/16fl oz good chicken stock
450ml/16fl oz double cream
1 teaspoon finely chopped lemon thyme leaves
freshly ground black pepper

1 Peel the onions. This can take longer than expected, as both button and cocktail onions tend to be tightly wrapped. Set aside.

2 Set a medium-sized non-corrosive saucepan over a low heat. Add the oil and, once hot, mix in the onions. Fry gently for 10 minutes, stirring regularly, until the onions start to colour and soften. Mix in the bacon and fry gently for 5 minutes, stirring occasionally, until the bacon has coloured.

3 Add the wine, then increase the heat and boil for 15 minutes, or until it has reduced to 3 tablespoons of liquid. Add the stock, return to the boil and simmer briskly for 15 minutes, or until the liquid has reduced by two-thirds.

4 Add the cream and thyme, return to the boil, then simmer briskly for about 10 minutes, or until it thickens into a luscious sauce. Season with a little black pepper. Reheat when needed.

ROAST GARLIC DRESSING

This simple dressing is for garlic lovers. It relies on the sweetness of roast garlic and has an intense flavour. You can serve it with roast chicken or barbecued meat or even toss it into the crisp leaves of a cos lettuce salad.

SERVES 6

2 whole heads garlic
2 tablespoons sherry vinegar
a handful of curly parsley leaves

1½ tablespoons lemon juice, or to taste
120ml/4fl oz extra virgin olive oil
salt and freshly ground black pepper

1 Preheat the oven to fan 140°C/gas 2. Place the whole heads of garlic on a small baking tray and roast in the oven for 1 hour, or until very soft. Remove and set aside to cool.

2 Once cold, cut each head in half and squeeze out the soft garlic cloves into a food processor. Discard the papery skin. Add the vinegar, parsley leaves and lemon juice. Process until it forms a purée, then slowly add the olive oil, so that it forms a thick emulsion. Season to taste, adding extra lemon juice if wished.

3 Transfer to a clean container and cover. Store in the fridge. Bring up to room temperature before serving.

STICKY BLACKCURRANT SHALLOTS

This ultra-sticky shallot confit will keep for several weeks covered in the fridge. It tastes amazing in blue cheese sandwiches or as an accompaniment to roast venison or steak.

SERVES 6–8

3 tablespoons extra virgin olive oil
450g/1lb smallish shallots, peeled
salt and freshly ground black pepper

150ml/5fl oz full-bodied red wine
150ml/5fl oz crème de cassis
1½ tablespoons red wine vinegar

1 Set a wide sauté pan over a low heat. Add the oil and, once warm, mix in the peeled shallots. Season lightly and fry gently, stirring regularly, for 10 minutes, until they start to colour, then cover the pan with some dampened crumpled greaseproof paper and a lid. Cook gently over a low heat for 20 minutes, or until very soft, remembering to give the pan the odd shake.

2 Remove the lid and paper. Add the wine, crème de cassis and vinegar. Return to the boil, then simmer gently for 30–35 minutes, or until the liquid has evaporated into a sticky juice and the shallots are dark and soft. Season to taste and transfer to a clean container. Once cool, cover and chill until needed. Gently reheat to serve.

SEE ALSO

- Another bean salad on page 217.
- Chicken with chanterelles on page 246.
- Roast beef salad with radicchio and red onions on page 257.
- Salad leaves, saffron lamb and pitta bread on page 94.
- New potatoes in paper parcels on page 66.

COURGETTES, SQUASH AND PUMPKINS

Early in the thirteenth century, no English monastic garden was complete without its pumpkins. These coarse-textured gourds were far removed from the fine-flavoured *pompion* (pumpkin) introduced from France and the New World in the sixteenth century. Pumpkins became fashionable and the rich indulged in luxuriously spiced and layered sweet egg custard pies of pumpkin, currants and apples.

However, as the novelty wore off, so did the appeal of pumpkins and various thick-skinned squash. They gradually slipped from upper-class tables to rural working-class kitchens, where they were appreciated for their ability to keep through the long winter months.

Soft-skinned marrows were introduced from the New World at the same time as their hard-skinned siblings. They, too, have long been regarded in Britain as a worthy stomach filler rather than something delicious to eat, although the marrow and ginger conserve on page 236 may change such opinions.

Courgettes and their myriad small cousins, however, are another matter. They belong to the early twentieth century when Italian plant breeders created wonderful tender baby marrows by hybridisation. These quickly became popular in America when Italian migrants arrived there in the 1920s, but they took another 30 years to enter the consciousness of domestic cooks in Britain. Jane Grigson credits Elizabeth David as the first person to write about them as something natural to eat in 1950, in her revolutionary *A Book of Mediterranean Food*.

How the world has changed. Today, British cooks think nothing of roasting great chunks of exotic-looking turban squash or cooking pretty yellow and green patty pan squash in garlic-infused tomato sauce. The sweet taste of butternut squash has so captured the national imagination that you will find it in pasta sauces, tarts and gratins.

PRACTICALITIES

■ Courgettes, squash and pumpkins all belong to the genus *Cucurbita*. Immature or soft-skinned fruit, such as courgettes, patty pans, custard-marrows and marrows, are sometimes called summer squash. Winter squash refers to hard-skinned mature fruits, ranging from pumpkins to turban squash.

■ In the summer, courgette flowers are sold with a small courgette attached to one end. The flowers are edible and have a delicate courgette flavour.

■ Hard-skinned squash and marrows need to be seeded before cooking. Their flesh can be cooked in sweet and savoury dishes.

■ Acorn and Little Gem squash have a delicate taste and soft, pulpy flesh, which makes them useful for stuffing and baking as an individual portion.

■ In Britain, pumpkins are bred for carving at Hallowe'en rather than for cooking. One small pumpkin yields about 400g/14oz watery flesh, which can be cooked down for soups, pies or pumpkin bread. The seeds can be lightly roasted and eaten. Large West Indian pumpkins are sold by the wedge and have lush, flavoursome flesh.

CULINARY NOTES

■ Courgettes taste best lightly cooked, especially if partnered with olive oil and garlic. Add sweet herbs, tomatoes or piquant fresh cheeses and you will create wonderful dishes, whether they are summer soups, char-grilled slices or courgette fritters.

■ Squash responds to slower cooking. Its predominantly sweet taste needs to be counterbalanced by sourness in savoury dishes, for example, with sour cream, crème fraîche, cooking apple or a tart tomato sauce. Spices, such as chilli, cumin, turmeric, garam masala and coriander, enliven its flavour.

■ Butternut squash is widely used in squash and pumpkin dishes, although the blue-skinned, orange-fleshed Crown Prince has a finer flavour and firmer texture. Kabocha squash has a more fibrous texture and stronger flavour.

COURGETTE FLOWER RISOTTO

Although I have included courgettes in the autumn section, this recipe really belongs in summer, when you have an abundance of courgette flowers and tiny courgettes. You can, of course, adapt this recipe purely to courgettes.

SERVES 4 AS A MAIN COURSE

1 litre/1¾ pints good chicken stock (see page 307)
salt
a pinch of saffron threads
4 tablespoons extra virgin olive oil
30g/1oz unsalted butter, diced
1 small onion, finely diced

300g/10½ oz Arborio or Carnaroli rice
100ml/3½ fl oz dry white wine
freshly ground black pepper
15g/½ oz Parmesan, finely grated
6 courgette flowers (with courgettes attached)
a handful of parsley, finely chopped

1 Bring the stock up to simmering point in a saucepan. Add a tiny pinch of salt to the saffron threads and roughly crush under a teaspoon. Mix into the hot stock.

2 Heat 2 tablespoons olive oil with half the butter in a wide, heavy-bottomed saucepan and gently fry the diced onion for 5 minutes, or until very soft. Add the rice and stir until it looks translucent, then mix in the wine. As soon as this has almost evaporated, stir in a ladleful of hot stock. This should simmer briskly. Stir regularly, adding another ladleful of stock as each becomes absorbed. After about 18–20 minutes, the rice should be tender and cooked but with a sauce.

3 Remove the pan from the heat, season to taste and then mix in the remaining butter and Parmesan.

4 Shortly before the risotto is ready, halve the courgettes lengthways and slice into rounds or half moons. Roughly slice the courgette flowers. Set a non-stick frying pan over a high heat, add the remaining olive oil and stir-fry the courgettes for 1 minute. Add the flowers, season to taste and fry for a further minute, then mix into the rice with the chopped parsley. Serve the risotto immediately.

COURGETTE CHIPS

These make a delicious alternative to potatoes and are very easy to make. Alternatively, you can serve them as an appetiser in the Greek style, piping hot after frying in a shallow pan of olive oil, with a cucumber yoghurt dip.

SERVES 2

300g/10½ oz young courgettes
salt
corn oil for deep-frying

plain flour
freshly ground black pepper

1 Wash, pat dry and trim the courgettes. Cut into medium thick chips, place in a bowl, sprinkle with salt and mix thoroughly. Leave for 30 minutes, so they have time to release any bitter juices.

2 If you have a deep-fat fryer, heat the oil to 180°C. If not, choose a sturdy deep saucepan and clip a jam thermometer on to the sides. If you don't have a thermometer – cut a few cubes of white bread. Add enough oil to come about one-third of the way up the side of the pan – you don't want too much oil or it could erupt over the top.

3 Set over a medium-low heat. If you don't have a thermometer, test the temperature by adding a cube of bread. The bread will take 40 seconds to brown when the oil has reached 180°C.

4 Tip the courgettes into a sieve and then on to kitchen paper. Pat dry carefully. Put a few tablespoons of plain flour in a large mixing bowl. Season with black pepper.

5 Once ready to cook, quickly mix the courgettes into the flour until they're lightly coated. Place them in a deep-fry basket and lower into the hot oil. If you have a small fryer, you might have to do this in batches, so that the temperature remains at 180°C. Fry for 2–3 minutes, or until golden and crisp, then tip on to crumpled kitchen paper to remove any excess oil. Serve immediately.

MARROW AND GINGER CONSERVE

This makes a beautiful and unusual conserve. It turns a translucent gold and tastes of late summer – all lemon and ginger. You will need a marrow that is slightly over 1.8kg/4lb in weight for this recipe.

MAKES ABOUT 625g/1lb 6oz OR 3 ASSORTED JARS

1kg/2lb 3oz peeled, seeded and diced marrow
625g/1lb 6oz preserving sugar
3 lemons

15g/½ oz peeled root ginger
½ small white grapefruit, juiced

1 First tackle your marrow: cut off its ends, then cut through the middle and set each half upright on one end before slicing off its thick skin. Quarter the peeled marrow lengthways and cut away and discard the seeds. Finally, cut the flesh into 2cm/1in cubes and weigh.

2 Place the cubed marrow in a large mixing bowl with the sugar. Mix thoroughly. Use a julienne zester and finely zest and juice one lemon. Add to the sugared marrow. Cover and leave overnight – by morning, it will be swimming in liquid.

3 The next day, scrape everything into a preserving pan. Roughly bash the root ginger with a rolling pin. Wrap the ginger into a square of muslin and tie into a bag. Place in the sugary liquid. Squeeze the juice from the remaining lemons and the grapefruit half and add to the pan.

4 Sterilise your jam jars by washing them in hot soapy water, rinsing in very hot water, and then placing them in a cool oven, fan 130°C/gas 1 to dry. Alternatively, wash in the dishwasher, then leave to dry with the dishwasher door partially open.

5 Clip a jam thermometer to the preserving pan. Set over a medium heat and stir regularly until all the sugar has dissolved. Bring slowly up to the boil and boil steadily until the marrow looks transparent and the syrup has really reduced and thickened – it should reach a little over 106°C/220°F on the thermometer. Discard the ginger. Pour into the hot sterilised jars. If using screw-top lids, wait until cold, then cover. Otherwise, cover with waxed paper discs and transparent covers.

BUTTERNUT SQUASH AND SAGE SOUP

You can use pumpkin or other types of hard-skinned squash for this recipe. The Parmesan adds a savoury umami note, which enhances the natural sweetness of the squash.

SERVES 6

2–3 sprigs sage leaves
4 tablespoons extra virgin olive oil
2 onions, roughly chopped
2 cloves garlic, roughly chopped
1 butternut squash

1 litre/1¾ pints chicken stock
70g/2½ oz Parmesan rind
250ml/9fl oz crème fraîche
salt and freshly ground black pepper

1 Strip the leaves from the sage sprigs. Set a small frying pan over a medium-high heat. Add 4 tablespoons oil and, as soon as it is hot, fry about 6 sage leaves (for the garnish) in a single layer until crisp. Carefully remove from the oil and drain on kitchen paper.

2 Tip the 'sage' oil into a large saucepan. Set the pan over a medium-low heat, and stir in the onions and garlic. Fry gently for 10 minutes, or until melting soft and golden.

3 Top and tail the squash. Cut through its waist and then cut away its skin before slicing in half lengthways and discarding the seeds. Roughly dice the flesh.

4 Stir the squash flesh into the caramelised onions. Cover and continue to cook for about 10 minutes, stirring occasionally, until it begins to soften. Add the stock, 3 sage leaves and Parmesan rind. Simmer for 45 minutes, or until the vegetables are meltingly soft. Discard the cheese and sage leaves, then liquidise the soup. Add half the crème fraîche and season to taste.

5 Reheat the soup until it is piping hot, and divide between 6 bowls. Spoon a swirl of crème fraîche into each bowl, then add a deep-fried sage leaf and serve.

SWEET PUMPKIN CUSTARDS

You can adapt this recipe to use any type of hard-skinned squash. Like other sweet-fleshed vegetables, they work well in sweet dishes, ranging from custard pies to ice cream.

SERVES 4

400g/14oz pumpkin (or squash) flesh
80g/2¾ oz caster sugar
finely grated zest of 2 lemons
3 tablespoons dry sherry
½ teaspoon ground cinnamon

150ml/5fl oz double cream
4 medium egg yolks
unsalted butter for greasing
icing sugar, for dusting

1 Preheat the oven to fan 180°C/gas 5. Dice the pumpkin or squash flesh into small cubes. Place in a saucepan with 200ml/7fl oz water. Bring up to the boil, then cover and simmer for 30 minutes, or until very soft. Continue to cook if the pumpkin or squash is watery. Once dry, purée with the sugar, lemon zest, sherry, cinnamon, cream and egg yolks.

2 Lightly butter 4 x 150ml/5fl oz soufflé dishes. Place them in a small roasting tray. Fill the dishes with the custard and pour enough boiling water into the tray around them to come halfway up their sides. Bake in the preheated oven for 30 minutes, or until the custards have a slight wobble. Serve warm or cold, liberally dusted in icing sugar.

SEE ALSO

- Cucumber, courgette and marigold mousse on page 113.
- Courgette, tomato and basil charlotte on page 128.
- Killerton Estate piccalilli on page 165.

MUSHROOMS

Tucked behind the Orangery at Hanbury Hall in Worcestershire is a small windowless outhouse. Slip through its door, down two steps, and you'll find yourself in a dark room. The air smells damp and musty. As your eyes adjust to the gloom, you will see three slate beds speckled with white mushrooms. Built in the 1860s, this building supplied the kitchens all year round with button, cup and flat field mushrooms. An inner wall acts as a double skin to keep a regular ambient temperature – perfect for growing mushrooms and forcing two other Victorian favourites: rhubarb and sea kale.

These days, a wide variety of exotic mushrooms are cultivated in Britain, including shiitake, pleurotte and enoki mushrooms, but in the past, British cooks sought out what was to hand. We dried, pickled, potted and powdered our field mushrooms. For centuries, we made an intensely-flavoured spiced field mushroom ketchup, which was used as a seasoning. Other types of wild mushrooms are rarely mentioned in British cook books, but I suspect that country cooks collected what was to hand and dried penny buns (ceps), fairy mushrooms and chanterelles for winter soups, stews and pies.

PRACTICALITIES

■ As mushrooms absorb water like a sponge, wipe them clean with a damp cloth or lightly brush. Tough stalks should be removed or pared (as with ceps), and thick skin peeled.

■ Store mushrooms in the fridge, but don't let them get damp. They keep best when loosely covered in paper bags where they can breathe rather than sweat.

■ Novices desirous of foraging for wild mushrooms must ensure that their finds are checked by an expert as mistakenly eating a poisonous mushroom can be fatal.

CULINARY NOTES

■ Mushrooms are best appreciated in moderation as they can add an intensity of flavour to a dish that benefits from being cut by other ingredients, such as lemon, ham or sherry.

■ Mushrooms add complexity of flavour to recipes and combine well with starchy foods, such as rice, pasta, pizza and pastry. They also taste good with dairy products, including butter, cream, cheese and eggs.

■ Fresh-flavoured ingredients enhance their taste; for example, lemon zest, mace, nutmeg, ginger, garlic, chilli, chives, tarragon, parsley and soured cream.

GRILLED SPICED MUSHROOMS

Country cooks would serve freshly picked field mushrooms fried or potted in butter that was flavoured with mace, cayenne pepper and lemon juice. It works equally well with grilled mushrooms – perfect for breakfast or dinner.

SERVES 2

6 large flat mushrooms

55g/2oz unsalted butter, softened

¼ teaspoon ground mace

a pinch of cayenne pepper, or to taste

1 tablespoon lemon juice

salt and freshly ground black pepper

1 Preheat the grill to high. Peel and stalk the mushrooms and place in a grill-proof dish. In a small bowl, beat the softened butter with the spices, lemon juice and seasoning. Divide equally between the mushrooms.

2 Set the mushroom dish 7.5cm/3in under the grill and cook for 8–10 minutes, or until the mushrooms are soft and succulent. Serve immediately.

ABOVE The Mushroom House at Hanbury Hall, Worcestershire.

HANBURY HALL MUSHROOM FLAN

During the summer months, the tea room at Hanbury Hall in Worcestershire can be inundated with mushrooms from the Estate's mushroom house. One of the dishes they prepare with them is this very light, cheesy mushroom tart. They don't add shallots, as many of their customers prefer a plain tart, so omit, if wished.

SERVES 4–6

225g/8oz shortcrust pastry (see page 308)
30g/1oz unsalted butter
1 shallot, finely diced (optional)
285g/10oz button, cup or flat mushrooms, sliced
salt and freshly ground black pepper

115g/4oz finely grated Cheddar cheese
2 tablespoons finely chopped parsley
3 medium eggs
120ml/4fl oz whole milk
55ml/2fl oz double cream

1 Preheat the oven to fan 180°C/gas 5. Roll out the pastry on a lightly floured surface and use to line a 23cm/9in quiche dish. Prick the base of the pastry with a fork, line with greaseproof paper or foil and fill with baking beans. Chill for 30 minutes.

2 Bake the pastry case for 15 minutes, then remove the paper or foil and beans and return to the oven for a further 5–10 minutes, or until the pastry no longer looks raw. Reduce the oven temperature to fan 160°C/gas 3.

3 While the pastry is cooking, place a non-stick frying pan over a medium-low heat. Add the butter and, once melted, add the shallots. Fry for 5 minutes, or until soft, then add the mushrooms, increase the heat and fry briskly for 3 minutes, or until they've collapsed and their juice has evaporated. Season to taste. Spoon into the pastry case and sprinkle with the cheese.

4 Beat together the chopped parsley, eggs, milk and cream. Season to taste and carefully pour into the pastry case. Bake in the preheated oven for 30 minutes, or until golden and set. Serve warm or cold.

WILD MUSHROOM AND BARLEY RISOTTO

Barley risotto has a lovely earthy flavour, which tastes good with mushrooms. Use wild or cultivated ones for this recipe. If using wild, look out for chanterelles, sometimes sold under their French name of girolles (July to October) or ceps (August to October). If using cultivated, use a mixture of button, oyster and shiitake mushrooms.

SERVES 2

6 medium thick slices smoked back bacon
3 tablespoons extra virgin olive oil
1 fat clove garlic, finely chopped
2 inner stalks celery, finely diced
1 carrot, finely diced
140g/5oz wild mushrooms

115g/4oz pearl barley
4 tablespoons dry white wine
285ml/½ pint good chicken stock
salt and freshly ground black pepper
1 tablespoon finely chopped parsley (optional)

1 Trim the bacon of fat and cut into dice. Set a heavy-bottomed saucepan over a medium heat. Add the oil and, once hot, fry the bacon for 2 minutes, or until lightly coloured. Add the garlic, celery and carrot and reduce the heat. Fry gently, stirring occasionally, for about 5 minutes, or until the vegetables are soft and golden.

2 Prepare your mushrooms: wipe clean with a damp cloth and trim their stems. If large, rip into slightly smaller pieces. Increase the heat slightly and mix the mushrooms into the softened vegetables. Fry briskly for 2 minutes, stirring regularly, until they're lightly cooked.

3 Mix in the barley, cook for 1 minute and then add the wine. Boil briskly until it has almost evaporated, then stir in the stock. Bring to the boil, cover and simmer for 30 minutes, or until the barley is plump, tender and has absorbed most of the stock. If it is too liquid, boil uncovered to reduce the stock. Season to taste and stir in the parsley just before serving.

CHICKEN WITH CHANTERELLES

This is a luxurious fricassée, which is ideal for supper on a warm September evening. It tastes equally good eaten with rice or fluffy mashed potato. I love it with peas, but then I love most things with peas.

SERVES 2

2 skinless boned chicken breasts
1 tablespoon plain flour
salt and freshly ground black pepper
3 tablespoons extra virgin olive oil
15g/½ oz unsalted butter
3 shallots, finely sliced

1 fat clove garlic, finely chopped
85g/3oz fresh chanterelles
100ml/3½ fl oz dry white wine
2 finely pared strips lemon zest
100ml/3½ fl oz good chicken stock (see page 307)
85ml/3fl oz double cream

1 Trim the chicken of any fat or bloody flesh. Cut into approximately 2.5cm/1in dice. Mix the flour, salt and pepper in a small bowl.

2 Set a wide heavy-bottomed saucepan over a high heat. Add the olive oil and, once hot, toss the chicken pieces in the seasoned flour, shake free of any excess flour and fry in a single layer for about 2–3 minutes. As soon as they start to turn golden, turn them and colour on the other side for a further minute or so. Remove with a slotted spoon.

3 Immediately reduce the temperature to low. Add the butter, quickly followed by the shallots and garlic. Fry gently for 4 minutes, or until soft and golden.

4 Meanwhile, wipe the chanterelles clean with a damp cloth. Trim their stalks and, if large, rip into large chunks. Increase the heat to high and add the mushrooms to the shallots. Stir-fry briskly for about 5 minutes, or until they become soft and collapse.

5 Add the wine and lemon zest and boil briskly until the liquid has reduced to a few tablespoons, then add the stock and boil vigorously until it has reduced by two-thirds – it will only take a few minutes. Mix in the cream and continue to boil until it thickens slightly into a luscious sauce. Season to taste. Finally, add the chicken. As soon as the mixture starts to simmer, reduce the heat to low and simmer gently for 5 minutes, or until the chicken is tender. Remove from the heat and allow the fricassée to rest for 10 minutes before serving, so that the juice can be reabsorbed into the chicken. Remove the lemon zest when you plate the chicken.

STIR-FRIED RICE

There is something deeply satisfying about this recipe, which I make for supper when the fridge is almost bare. You can use shiitake mushrooms instead, if wished.

SERVES 2

425g/15oz cooked rice (200g/7oz uncooked rice)
2 eggs, roughly beaten
a pinch of salt
3 tablespoons sunflower oil
4 slices lean back bacon, cut into small strips
2 fine slices fresh ginger, peeled and finely sliced

55g/2oz frozen or fresh petits pois
55g/2oz button mushrooms, cut into pea-sized dice
1 tablespoon naturally brewed soy sauce
1 tablespoon sake, or dry sherry
1 tablespoon sesame oil
3 spring onions, finely sliced

1 If you don't have any cooked rice – I never do – cook your favourite rice. I use basmati and I measure out a cup, which is around 200g/7oz, and add 2 cups of cold water. Bring it up to the boil, cover the pan and reduce the heat to low. Simmer for about 15 minutes, or until all the water is absorbed. Turn off the heat and leave for another 5 minutes. Beat the eggs with a pinch of salt and set aside.

2 Set a large non-stick frying pan over a medium heat. Add the sunflower oil and, once hot, add the bacon. Stir-fry briskly for 5 minutes, or until crispy, then add

the ginger and sizzle for 1 minute. Add the peas and mushrooms. Stir-fry for 1 minute, then add the soy sauce and sake and let it bubble up until the liquid has evaporated.

3 Tip in the rice and stir-fry until well coated in the mixture. Part the rice to reveal a large patch of frying pan. Add the sesame oil, quickly followed by the beaten eggs. Allow them to cook for 1–2 minutes, then mix into the rice. Immediately mix in the spring onions and season to taste. Stir-fry until piping hot and eat straight away.

SEE ALSO
- Warm artichoke mousse with dried ceps on page 278.
- Creamy fish pie on page 301.

WINTER

WINTER

Winter defines British cooks. As the sun gleams low over the horizon, catching the dark tracery of the bare trees in its fading light, cooks across the country take pleasure in the bright warmth of their kitchens. From December until the end of February, they transform winter vegetables into delicious dishes that will keep out the invasive cold of winter. Fat leeks, brilliant-coloured chicories and muddy potatoes are all converted into tempting delicacies, from jewel-like salads to fragrant pies and dainty puffs.

Whereas the cooking of spring, summer and autumn in Britain can subtly merge into one another, winter is a clearly defined culinary season. It has its own unique rhythm, starting with December when producers ensure that we have access to a wide variety of vegetables. These are mainly used in festive recipes, ranging from party dishes, such as chicory, crab and avocado salad, and Jerusalem artichoke mousse with dried ceps to Christmas classics, such as Brussels sprouts with bacon and chestnuts, and sweet and sour red cabbage.

In January, our cooking changes in response to our desire for simplicity. Vegetables are embraced as a cheap, healthy food that sits comfortably with our post-festive state of mind. Yet, at the same time, the choice of home-grown vegetables available to us shrinks. We're left with the hardiest of brassicas, alliums, celery and chicories, stored roots and squash, and frozen vegetables.

By February, our mood has changed again. The days start to lengthen, but the icy weather takes it toll, and cooks seek solace in creating comforting flavoursome food, such as creamy fish pie, chunky vegetable soup, and stir-fried cabbage with pork balls.

FLAVOURING WINTER VEGETABLES

Flavourings are often intensified in January and February, although whether this is to counteract the limited repertoire of vegetables or simply because we love the excitement of change I cannot say. Citrus juice, chilli, mustard, mature cheese and soy sauce are all excellent seasonings for winter vegetables, although they work in slightly different ways.

The acidity in citrus juice brings out any natural sweetness in a vegetable. Mildly bitter chicory, for example, will taste much sweeter if it is simmered in orange juice, butter and dessert wine.

ABOVE Bare Himalayan birch trees in the winter gardens at Anglesey Abbey, Cambridgeshire.

Similarly, if you dress a coleslaw in lime juice and olive oil, they will enhance the sweet notes in the cabbage and carrot.

Chilli contains an odourless, tasteless chemical called capsaicin, which heightens our sense of taste, flavour and texture by exciting our palate. This makes everything you eat taste more intriguing. It can be added in different forms, from fresh chillies to ground cayenne pepper. Chilli is an acquired taste, and the less often you eat it, the more sensitive you'll be to its heat. It works well as a flavouring for most winter vegetables.

Mustard is predominantly a bitter seasoning; it brings out any natural sweetness in a vegetable, while adding a sophisticated note. Always choose a good-quality mustard for cooking. It's important that you like its flavour licked from the spoon, otherwise, it won't enhance your dish regardless of whether it's in a vinaigrette or the cream sauce for a leek and bacon pie. You can also add dried mustard seeds to potato or cabbage dishes.

Mature cheese, such as a good Cheddar or Parmesan, adds an umami salty, savoury taste to most vegetables, making your chosen ingredient taste sweeter and more tasty. Compare the taste of the celeriac and potato fluff with that of the celeriac Parmesan soufflé and you will immediately understand its effect.

Soy sauce works in the same way as mature cheese, but take care to buy only the naturally brewed type as some brands contain monosodium glutamate, which is a flavour enhancer. Soy sauce tastes good with brassicas, greens and mushrooms but, in my view, does not work so well with root vegetables unless you're cooking them in a Japanese style.

SEEKING NEW IDEAS

During the winter months, when you're tied more closely to home, it's worth experimenting with different ways of cooking vegetables. Of course, you can seek out ideas from the other sections in this book as many of the vegetables are still in season in early winter. Don't forget to consider frozen peas, broad beans and sweetcorn when you're feeling in need of new recipes, but I'd also recommend exploring other cultures. Cooking parathas stuffed with potatoes on a snowy day will transport you to the warmth of North India. Our winter cabbages lend themselves to Italian dishes, such as slow-cooked vegetable soups infused with Parmesan rind, evoking evening wood smoke in the Tuscan hills.

NEW RESOLUTIONS

In the quiet days of January, many Britons resolve to live a different life. For some, this revolves around trying to eat a healthy diet, but for others it encompasses the idea of trying to create a sustainable way of life.

Throughout the pages of this book, I've tried to explore some of the different ways of sourcing vegetables, but there is one last area that ought to be considered and that is allotments. These are not easy to come by, but since 2009 the National Trust has created over 1,000 new allotments and growing spaces on their land, and more are still being dug. These vary in how they operate: some, such as those at Dene Place walled garden within the Hatchlands Park estate in Surrey, work as a co-operative. They have both private allotments and a community kitchen garden, which is similar to a CSA scheme (see page 72). Others, such as Minnowburn community allotments in South Belfast, and Lytes Cary Manor allotments in Somerset, offer plots for both local families and community groups. Some have beds specially designed for the disabled, and many offer support to novice gardeners. All have created a greater sense of local community. Winter is the perfect time to seek out such schemes and sign up.

CHICORY AND ENDIVE

Chicories and endives belong to two closely related botanical families, namely *Cichorium intybus* and *Cichorium endivia*. Their common names cause British cooks much confusion, as both are known as chicory and endive. Luckily, all are good with their distinctive bitter sweet taste.

The chicory family (*C. intybus*) includes all the red chicories and blanched Belgian endive, which is also known as witloof or chicory. There are many different red varieties, ranging in appearance from elegant long-leaved magenta heads to fat rose-coloured cabbage heads.

The endive family (*C. endivia*) is divided between curly- and broad-leaved varieties. If grown in sunlight, these would all be green, but to ensure greater sweetness, they are blanched (grown in the dark), so that their hearts remain white or pale yellow. The curly-leaved varieties are commonly called curly endive, chicory frisée or frisée. The broad-leaved endives are known as escarole or Batavia. Escarole can be flecked with red.

Both chicory and endive have been cultivated in Britain since the seventeenth century and were widely regarded as a welcome addition to the winter diet. Their beauty is best appreciated in salads, especially warm ones, where their succulent bitter leaves hold their shape. They become even more unctuous in slow-cooked dishes.

PRACTICALITIES

■ Choose crisp, fresh-looking heads; avoid any that have brown patches or are wilting. Do not buy any blanched or red chicory that is turning green – it will taste very bitter.

■ Trim off the outer leaves as these are often bruised or damaged. Discard the outermost dark-green leaves of curly endive as they tend to be bitter and tough.

■ Keep blanched endive and red chicories wrapped in paper, preferably in the salad drawer of the fridge. If they're exposed to light, they will turn green.

CULINARY NOTES

■ All forms of chicory and endive can be used in salads. As they're slightly bitter, sour or salty ingredients will bring out their natural sweetness, for example, citrus fruit, Feta, bacon, chorizo or confit of duck.

■ Both chicory and endive can be cooked. Radicchio, trevisse and Belgian endive gain a deep, woody flavour when lightly grilled, while escarole is excellent when stir-fried with garlic and chilli.

■ Belgian endive is particularly good slowly roasted in olive oil, garlic and thyme, or wrapped in prosciutto and turned into a gratin with a creamy sauce.

CHICORY, CRAB AND AVOCADO SALAD

You can easily turn this recipe into a party nibble just by filling the chicory leaves with a teaspoonful of the dressed crab and finely diced avocado mixture.

SERVES 4

400g/14oz white crab meat

1 Thai red chilli, or to taste, finely diced

2 limes, finely grated and juiced

salt and freshly ground black pepper

4 plump Belgian endives, trimmed

2 bunches watercress, washed and cut into sprigs

4 spring onions, trimmed and finely sliced

2 ripe avocados, halved, stoned and peeled

4 tablespoons extra virgin olive oil

1 Squeeze the excess liquid out of the crab meat. Spread it out on a plate and pick out any tiny pieces of shell, then place in a bowl. Add the chilli with the lime zest and about 2 tablespoons lime juice to taste. Season lightly and set aside.

2 Slice the endive leaves lengthways. Place in a mixing bowl with the watercress sprigs and spring onions. Slice the avocados lengthways and place in another bowl with 2 tablespoons lime juice and the olive oil. Season to taste and gently mix. Divide between 4 plates and arrange the crab into 4 piles on each side of each plate.

ROAST BEEF SALAD WITH RADICCHIO AND RED ONIONS

This salad is perfect for dinner parties as it can be prepared in advance and assembled at the last minute, accompanied by some buttered salad potatoes. If you can't find any radicchio, use another type of red chicory.

SERVES 6

1 kg/2lb 3oz trimmed fillet of beef
salt and freshly ground black pepper
a few splashes of Worcestershire sauce
3 tablespoons extra virgin olive oil
3 bay leaves, ripped

Dressing
8 anchovy fillets, finely chopped
2 teaspoons Dijon mustard
3 tablespoons white wine vinegar

9 tablespoons extra virgin olive oil
freshly ground black pepper
1 small bunch parsley, finely chopped

Salad
600g/1lb 5oz green beans, trimmed
3 red onions, thickly sliced into rounds
olive oil, for brushing
15g/½ oz fat green olives, stoned and quartered
2 heads radicchio, leaves separated

1 Preheat the oven to fan 220°C/gas 8. Lightly season the beef with salt, freshly ground black pepper and Worcestershire sauce. Heat the olive oil in a roasting tray over a medium-high heat. Add the meat and brown on all sides. Tuck the bay leaves around the beef and place in the centre of the preheated oven. Roast for 25–30 minutes for medium-rare. If you like your meat rare, roast for about 15–20 minutes. Remove and, once cold, chill, covered, until needed.

2 To make the dressing, whisk together the anchovies, mustard, vinegar and oil in a small bowl, Season with pepper to taste. Add the parsley at the last moment.

3 Prepare the salad ingredients: drop the beans into a saucepan of boiling unsalted water and cook for 6 minutes, or until tender. Drain and cool. Pat dry and place in a mixing bowl. Mix in half the dressing.

4 Set a griddle pan over a medium heat. Once hot, brush the red onion slices with olive oil. Season to taste and grill on both sides until flecked gold. Set aside on a plate.

5 Cut the beef into slices and arrange with the onions, dressed green beans, olives and radicchio leaves on a shallow serving dish. Spoon over the remaining dressing and serve immediately.

ORANGE COOKED ENDIVES

This intensely flavoured version of simmered endives is wonderful as an accompaniment to game. Choose a richly floral white dessert wine, such as Beaumes de Venise, for this recipe.

SERVES 4

juice of 2 oranges
285ml/½ pint sweet white dessert wine
5 sprigs lemon thyme

6 small heads Belgian endive (chicory)
salt and freshly ground black pepper
55g/2oz unsalted butter

1 Put the orange juice, dessert wine and lemon thyme in a shallow wide non-corrosive saucepan.

2 Trim the base of the Belgian endives and remove any battered outer leaves. Slice in half lengthways and place in one layer in the saucepan – making sure each half is thoroughly coated in the orange juice. Season to taste and fleck the top with half the butter.

3 Roughly crumple up some greaseproof paper, then gently press over the Belgian endive and liquid to prevent the endive from discolouring. Simmer for 20 minutes, or until tender.

4 Remove the endive from the pan, but keep warm. Boil the cooking liquid vigorously until it has reduced to a syrupy sauce. Remove from the heat, swirl in the remaining butter and adjust the seasoning to taste. Return the endive to the pan and serve immediately.

SEE ALSO

- Baby artichoke, new potato and Parmesan salad on page 119.
- Fennel, chicory and fig salad on page 210.
- Leek vinaigrette with hazelnuts on page 264.
- Papaya, mint and watercress salad on page 59.

LEEKS

Under the espaliered apple and pear trees in the organic kitchen garden at Greys Court in Oxfordshire, you will find lush clumps of leeks. Look more closely at this pretty hotchpotch of vegetables, flowers and herbs, and you'll see leeks growing amongst the delicate leaves of carrots and beetroot. Their pungent aroma helps deter aphids and white fly, much as it must have in medieval times, when no cottage garden was complete without its leeks, cabbages, onions and garlic. Vegetable patches were often called 'the leek garden' at that time.

It is hard for a British cook to imagine life without leeks. The Romans introduced them, and while we quickly forgot their sophisticated plumbing, we clung on to the humble leek as an ingredient that enhanced our cooking and withstood our harsh winters. They can replace onions in a wide variety of dishes, from tarts, pies and savoury puddings to soups, sauces and soufflés. They can be served in salads or as a vegetable in their own right. Better still, leeks taste wonderful with eggs and dairy products as well as potatoes, carrots, spinach, bacon, chicken, beef and fish.

PRACTICALITIES

■ Small and medium-sized leeks have the best flavour. Choose squeaky, pert specimens. They keep best with some root and outer leaves attached.

■ To prepare: top and tail, then make a light cut down the length of the stem and peel away and discard the tough outer leaves. Cut away the darkest part of the green stem and unwrap until you reach the tender light green inner core. Use the light green stem alongside the white and light green part of each leek.

■ For sliced leeks, cut in half lengthways and wash thoroughly in cold water before slicing or dicing. For whole leeks, cut a deep cross down from the green end, before washing in plenty of cold water – the mud should wash out. If not, you'll have to cut a small cross in their white base.

CULINARY NOTES

■ The whiter the leek leaf, the finer the flavour. Avoid adding dark green leek leaves to stock – they imbue it with a harsh flavour.

■ Leeks are best if they are lightly cooked. Always blanch before char-grilling or griddling or serving in a gratin. Over-cooked leeks develop a slimy texture.

■ Lemongrass, chives, wild garlic, garlic, tarragon, watercress and thyme all work well with leeks, as do mace, nutmeg, mustard and nut oils.

■ Leeks taste good combined with other vegetables, particularly spinach, carrots and beetroot.

■ Dairy products add a luscious sweetness to leeks, especially cream, eggs and butter.

CHEESE AND LEEK BREAD AND BUTTER PUDDING

I have slightly adapted this unusual recipe from the National Trust, adding an extra leek. As a general rule, many of the National Trust's chefs use a light hand with alliums. If you can't find a curd cheese, use a full-fat fromage frais.

SERVES 4

55g/2oz softened unsalted butter + extra
    for greasing
3 leeks, trimmed, washed and finely sliced
565ml/1 pint milk
6 medium slices good white bread
225g/8oz West Country curd cheese

30g/1oz toasted walnuts, roughly chopped
85g/3oz mature Cheddar, roughly grated
2 medium eggs
½ teaspoon English mustard powder
a pinch of nutmeg
salt and freshly ground black pepper

1 Lightly butter a shallow 2 litre/3½ pint ovenproof dish. Set a saucepan over a low heat. Add half the butter and, once melted, half of the sliced leeks. Gently fry them for 10 minutes, or until very soft, then add half the milk and simmer for 15 minutes.

2 Meanwhile, spread the remaining butter on one side of each slice of bread. Cut off the crusts. Beat together the curd cheese, chopped walnuts and the remaining finely sliced raw leek. Spread thickly on to the unbuttered side of the sliced bread.

3 Sprinkle with one-third of the grated Cheddar. Firmly press together the curd cheese sides of the bread to make 3 sandwiches. Cut each into triangles and place in the buttered baking dish, making sure that the triangles slightly overlap one another.

4 Liquidise the hot milk and leeks until smooth. Add the remaining cold milk, then briefly whizz and beat in the eggs and mustard powder. Strain into a jug, and season to taste with nutmeg, salt and pepper. Pour over the sandwiches. Lightly cover and leave to soak for 30 minutes in the fridge.

5 Preheat the oven to fan 160°C/gas 3. Scatter the top with the remaining grated cheese and bake for 45–60 minutes, or until lightly set with a slight wobble and a crisp golden topping. Serve hot or warm.

LEEK, BACON AND MUSTARD PIE

This is gorgeous served hot, warm or cold with mini-jacket potatoes, pickle and a salad. I use a non-stick pastry ring on a non-stick baking tray to make this recipe, but you could use a quiche dish or even a shallow cake tin.

SERVES 4–6

340g/12 oz (flour weight) shortcrust pastry (see page 308)
200g/7oz sliced smoked back bacon
500g/1lb 2oz leeks
2 tablespoons extra virgin olive oil

3 egg yolks, beaten
200ml/7fl oz double cream
2 tablespoons Dijon wholegrain mustard
salt and freshly ground black pepper

1 Preheat the oven to fan 180°C/gas 5. Roll out two-thirds of the pastry and use to line the base and sides of a buttered 20 x 3.5cm/8 x 1½ in non-stick quiche dish (see above), letting the pastry slightly overlap the rim. Prick with a fork. Roll the remaining pastry into a circle large enough to cover the pie. Place the pastry lid on a plate and chill both base and lid.

2 Trim the fat from the bacon and cut into lardons. Slice the leeks in half lengthways and wash thoroughly in a sinkful of cold water. Drain and slice.

3 Set a frying pan over a medium-high heat. Add the oil and once hot, stir in the bacon and fry briskly for 3 minutes, or until it is lightly coloured. Add the leeks and continue cooking briskly for 5 minutes, or until they have collapsed. Tip into a bowl.

4 Using a fork, roughly beat together the egg yolks and double cream in a bowl. Set aside a spoonful for sealing and glazing the pie. Stir the mustard into the main bowl of cream and season to taste. Mix into the leeks and check the seasoning.

5 Tip the mixture into the pastry case. Brush the rim with the spare egg and cream mix, then press on the pastry lid. Seal the 2 pastries together by pressing down with a fork on the pastry rim, and then trim neatly with a sharp knife. Pierce the top with a knife and brush with the egg mix. Bake in the preheated oven for 40 minutes, or until the pastry is golden.

LEEK VINAIGRETTE WITH HAZELNUTS

Hazelnut oil is not easy to find, so if you don't wish to buy it online, you can use walnut oil instead. Add some soft goat's cheese and hazelnut bread and you will have a lovely winter lunch.

SERVES 6

55g/2oz hazelnuts
450g/1lb baby leeks
2 tablespoons cider vinegar

6 tablespoons hazelnut oil (or walnut)
salt and freshly ground black pepper
4 heads red chicory, separated

1 Preheat the oven to fan 180°C/gas 5. Place the hazelnuts on a baking tray and roast in the oven for 10 minutes, or until they smell really nutty. Tip the nuts into a clean tea towel and rub off the brown skins. Once cold, very roughly chop and set aside.

2 Trim the leeks, cut away their roots and the darkest part of their leaves. Remove their tough outer leaves and cut a cross in the pale green sections – to create a mop-like effect. Wash them thoroughly in a sink filled with cold water.

3 Bring a large saucepan of unsalted water to the boil and add the leeks. Return to the boil and cook briskly for 2–3 minutes, or until the leeks are just tender. Drain and cool under cold running water, then pat dry on kitchen paper.

4 Put the vinegar and oil in a large mixing bowl. Whisk together and season to taste. Add the leeks and chopped hazelnuts. Slice the larger chicory leaves in half lengthways. Add all the chicory leaves to the leeks, gently toss and divide between 6 plates. Serve immediately.

SEE ALSO
- Crunchy cauliflower salad on page 166.
- Grilled aubergine with green bean and leeks on page 134.
- Nettle and leek soup on page 34.

CELERIAC

Dug fresh from the earth, celeriac (*Apium graviolens* var. *rapaceum*) looks like an octopus with its tangle of hairy roots sprouting from the swollen base of its stem. Its roots and bitter leaves are discarded in favour of the sweet-tasting fat round 'hypocotyl' at the base of the stem.

Celeriac is a relative newcomer to our tables. Even today, many British cooks are unfamiliar with this close relative of the celery. It is thought that it was bred some time in the seventeenth century. Stephen Switzer, the gardener and seedsman, appears to be the first person in England to write about it in 1728. It quickly gained favour on the Continent, yet its delicate nutty flavour, which subtly hints at celery, never became widely popular in Britain.

After nearly 300 years, the celeriac's fortunes appear to be finally changing. Chefs have started using it widely on their menus, cookery writers are including it in their books and, most importantly, over the last ten years, it has become widely available to domestic cooks. Celeriac is being tossed raw in the lightest of salads, deep-fried into nutty flavoured crisps and salt-baked to create succulent fragrant chunks.

PRACTICALITIES

■ Celeriac keeps well, but don't leave supermarket-bought celeriac in its plastic wrapping for too long as it has a tendency to rot if kept sealed.

■ Allow for plenty of wastage when you're preparing celeriac. Slice off the top and bottom, cut away and discard its thick skin, then slice off any dark-veined crevices, where the roots once sprouted. Wash thoroughly. Large celeriac is often slightly hollow in the centre.

■ Raw celeriac discolours once cut, so you need to submerge it in acidulated water as soon as it is cut. Allow 1 tablespoon lemon juice or vinegar to 1 litre/1¾ pints cold water.

CULINARY NOTES

■ Celeriac has a delicate, sweet celery flavour which will woo any non-celery lover. It can be served raw or cooked – the latter brings out its sweetness.

■ The sharp, clean notes of wholegrain mustard, crème fraîche, lemon juice and vinegar work well with the nutty peppery flavour of raw celeriac. Dessert apples, nuts, blue cheese and parsley taste good, too.

■ Cooked celeriac acts like a sponge to other flavours and tastes particularly delicious with butter, cream and milk. It also works well with chicken or beef 'jus' regardless of whether it is mashed, par-boiled or roasted.

CELERIAC, APPLE AND WALNUT SALAD

This salad is a simple but pretty winter appetiser. The raw celeriac is mixed into a rémoulade dressing before being mixed into the salad. You can also serve it without the accompanying salad with cold meat or fish.

SERVES 4

170g/6oz crème fraîche
1 heaped tablespoon wholegrain Dijon mustard
scant 2½ tablespoons lemon juice
salt and freshly ground black pepper
1 medium celeriac

2 tablespoons walnut oil
2 medium or 3 small apples, such as Cox or Braeburn
2 heads chicory
55g/2oz walnut halves
3 tablespoons finely chopped parsley

1 Mix together the crème fraîche, Dijon mustard and 4 teaspoons lemon juice in a bowl. Season to taste.

2 Prepare the celeriac: slice off the top and bottom, then cut away and discard the thick skin. Rinse, then pat dry and cut in half lengthways. Lay each half flat and finely slice into half moons. Build a stack and finely slice into fine matchsticks. As you slice a batch, mix it into the dressing to prevent it from discolouring.

3 To serve: whisk together ½ tablespoon lemon juice with the walnut oil in a mixing bowl and season to taste. Core the apples by cutting 4 segments, one from each side of the apple, so you're left with a square-shaped core. Discard the core. Cut each apple segment into thin half moons, tossing them into the dressing as you go.

4 Separate out the chicory leaves and slice them lengthways into strips. Mix into the apples with the walnuts. Divide the salad between 4 appetiser plates, placing a spoonful of celeriac salad in the middle. Scatter with the chopped parsley and serve.

CELERIAC CRISPS

Celeriac crisps have a gorgeous smoky sweet flavour. Their high sugar content prevents them from becoming quite as crunchy as a potato crisp but, nevertheless, they're very addictive as either a nibble or accompaniment to roast game. If you'd like to make mixed vegetable crisps, see stage 4 below. For further guidance on deep frying see page 234.

SERVES 6

1 tablespoon lemon juice or vinegar
3 small celeriac

oil for deep-frying
fine sea salt

1 Fill a large bowl with cold water. Add a tablespoon of lemon juice or vinegar to prevent the celeriac from discolouring. Slice off the top and bottom, then cut away and discard its thick skin. Cut the celeriac in half lengthways and thinly slice, using either a food processor or a mandoline. Mix into the acidulated water and leave to soak for 10 minutes.

2 Heat the oil to 190°C in a deep-fat fryer. Drain the celeriac and rinse under a cold tap to remove any excess starch as this causes crisps to burn. Spin in a salad spinner and then pat dry on kitchen paper to remove the water.

3 Add in small batches to the hot oil. Cook for 4 minutes, or until golden, remembering that they will continue to colour a little even after they are removed from the oil. The celeriac slices will crinkle up as they cook, but will not become crisp until they begin to cool. Repeat until finished. Toss on kitchen paper and set aside in a large bowl. Season to taste with salt.

4 You can adapt this method to make mixed vegetable crisps: omit the lemon juice or vinegar from the water and fry potatoes for 3 minutes; parsnips and beetroot for 4 minutes each.

SALT-BAKED CELERIAC

British vegetables are as susceptible to culinary fashions as any other food. The latest restaurant trend is to salt-bake root vegetables, which makes celeriac taste amazing. It might seem slightly wasteful of salt, but the method intensifies the flavour of the vegetable and requires little effort on the part of the cook.

SERVES 2–3

1 celeriac, about 700g/1lb 9oz weight
500g/1lb 2oz rock salt
2 medium egg whites

1 Preheat the oven to fan 180°C/gas 5. Wash the celeriac and then dry thoroughly on kitchen paper. Trim the base and cut out any muddy crevices. In a bowl, mix together the salt and egg whites until you have a thick paste.

2 Place a sheet of baking paper on a roasting tray. Shape a flat disc of salt paste on the paper and sit the base of the celeriac on top. Pile up the salt mixture around the celeriac, so that it is completely encased in salt paste. This will be about 1cm/½ in thick on the top but thicker nearer the base, where you need to pile it up.

3 Immediately, bake in the preheated oven for 1 hour for *al dente* or for 70 minutes if you want to mash the celeriac. Remove and allow to cool slightly.

4 Break open the crust and pull out the celeriac. Cut away its skin and serve as wished. You can dice it or cut into small lengths; then serve plain with a stew or tossed in a pan with melted butter and/or cream with or without chopped parsley.

CELERIAC PARMESAN SOUFFLÉ

This unusual soufflé is very easy to prepare and makes an excellent light supper, especially if you follow it with a classic green bean salad. If entertaining, prepare the soufflé base , then whisk and fold in the egg whites at the last moment.

SERVES 4

625g/1lb 6oz celeriac, untrimmed
150ml/5fl oz celeriac cooking liquor (see below)
55g/2oz unsalted butter + extra for greasing
5 tablespoons finely grated Parmesan
1 tablespoon fresh breadcrumbs

40g/1½ oz plain flour
120ml/4fl oz milk
4 medium egg yolks
salt and freshly ground black pepper
5 medium egg whites

1 Peel the celeriac as described on page 266. Cut into large chunks. Place in a saucepan, cover with water, cover and bring up to the boil. Remove the lid and cook briskly for 25 minutes, or until tender. Remove the celeriac – saving 150ml/5fl oz of the cooking water – and leave in a colander to steam dry.

2 Preheat the oven to fan 180°C/gas 5. Liberally butter a 1.5 litre/2½ pint soufflé dish. In a small bowl, mix together one tablespoon freshly grated Parmesan with the breadcrumbs. Tip them into the buttered dish and slowly rotate until its sides and bottom are fully coated. Return the debris to the small bowl.

3 Melt the butter in a large pan over a low heat. Stir in the flour and cook for a few minutes. Using a wooden spoon, slowly stir in the milk, so that it forms a smooth paste. Continue by gradually adding the measured celeriac water, followed by the remaining Parmesan. Remove from the heat.

4 Purée 200g/7oz cooked celeriac in a food processor. Add the white sauce and egg yolks. Process until blended, then season to taste. The egg whites will dilute the seasoning, so you want it quite strongly seasoned. Transfer to a large bowl.

5 Place the egg whites in a clean dry bowl. Whisk until they form stiff peaks, then, using a metal spoon, gently fold the egg whites into the purée. Spoon the mixture into the soufflé dish and bake in the preheated oven for 35–40 minutes, or until well risen but still slightly wobbly. Serve immediately.

CELERIAC AND POTATO FLUFF

This is one of my favourite ways of eating celeriac – the potato adds a fluffy lightness of texture. It is the perfect accompaniment to stews, pies and game.

SERVES 4

1 celeriac
2 medium potatoes
30g/1oz unsalted butter

1 clove garlic, finely chopped (optional)
3 tablespoons double cream
salt and freshly ground black pepper

1 Prepare the celeriac as described on page 266. Cut into large chunks and place in a saucepan, covered with water. Cover the pan and bring up to the boil. Cook briskly for 25 minutes, or until tender. Drain and leave in a colander to steam dry.

2 Peel the potatoes and cut them into quarters. Place in a saucepan, covered with water, then cover with a lid and bring up to the boil. Cook briskly for 20 minutes, or until soft. Drain and then leave to steam dry in the sieve over the pan.

3 If you have a mouli, force the cooked potatoes and celeriac through a medium-fine grater; otherwise, vigorously mash the vegetables with a potato masher.

4 Melt the butter in heavy-bottomed saucepan over a low heat. Add the garlic and fry very gently for a few minutes, or until very soft but not coloured. Stir in the cream and simmer for 3 minutes. Add the mashed celeriac and potato and beat vigorously to make it really fluffy. Season to taste and remove from the heat. Reheat over a low heat when needed.

SEE ALSO
- Chunky vegetable soup on page 292.
- Hanbury House roast root vegetables on page 193.

JERUSALEM ARTICHOKES

There is something mysterious about Jerusalem artichokes. They grow to the height of a man in great tall clumps. If the summer is long and hot, they will burst into bright yellow flowers that turn to follow the sun, just like their close relative, the sunflower. You'd never guess that underneath their lush growth lie countless sweet-tasting tubers that can be turned into soups, sauces and salads.

At first bite, they have a subtle, almost smoky, flavour, which hints at their namesake, the globe artichoke. However, they have a problem: in the words of John Goodyer, who grew them in the early sixteenth century, 'But in my judgment, which way soever they be drest and eaten they stir up and cause a filthie loathewsome stinking winde with the bodie, thereby causing the belly to bee much pained and tormented'. It is true that they cause flatulence – but they taste so good! The only solution is to eat them in moderation.

They are native to north-east America and, despite Mr Goodyer's warnings, soon became popular amongst the poorer classes in Britain as a cheap nutritious food. They've remained in cultivation ever since and are currently enjoying a renaissance amongst chefs who value their sophisticated flavour without having to worry about the consequences.

PRACTICALITIES

■ Choose firm artichokes, which are heavy for their size. Scrub clean with plenty of water to remove any dirt from their crevices. Cut away any whiskery roots and dark tips.

■ If your Jerusalem artichokes are relatively smooth, steaming or boiling in their skins and then peeling gives the best texture and flavour. However, if they're knobbly, it's easier to peel them before cooking, in which case, drop into acidulated water as you peel them to prevent discolouration, and steam to ensure they retain their shape.

■ I usually leave them unpeeled for artichoke soup. This makes a lightly flecked soup. If you want a perfect purée, peel before cooking.

CULINARY NOTES

■ Jerusalem artichokes have a wonderful earthy, nutty flavour, which is vaguely reminiscent of artichoke hearts. Sour or piquant-tasting ingredients, such as lemon juice, vinegar or mustard, work well with them as do bitter, salty and sweet foods – for example, Batavia, bacon, chicken stock and caramelised onions.

■ Like all root vegetables, Jerusalem artichokes can be turned into gratins, chips or simply sautéed in butter and oil (adapt the recipe for scorzonera on page 197).

■ They are excellent served warm in hearty salads with endive leaves and crispy bacon, or turned into a silky puréed sauce and served with seared scallops or beef.

JERUSALEM ARTICHOKE BOULANGÈRE

This recipe can be adapted to potatoes. You can also alter the flavourings slightly, such as by adding a little finely sliced celery in place of some of the onion.

SERVES 4

55g/2oz unsalted butter
2 onions, finely sliced
1 clove garlic, finely diced
1kg/2lb 3oz Jerusalem artichokes

salt and freshly ground black pepper
285ml/½ pint good chicken or vegetable stock
 (see pages 306–7)

1 Preheat the oven to fan 180°C/gas 5 and lightly butter a gratin dish. Melt 30g/1oz butter in a frying pan over a medium heat. Add the onions and garlic and gently fry until soft and golden. Remove from the heat.

2 Peel and finely slice the artichokes. Mix into the onions and season to taste. Arrange the vegetables in even layers in the buttered gratin dish. Add enough stock to reach just beneath the top layer. Dot with the remaining butter and bake in the preheated oven for 50 minutes, or until meltingly soft.

PRAWN AND JERUSALEM ARTICHOKE SALAD

This warm salad makes an excellent winter lunch. In this recipe, I used a sweet sherry vinegar, which has been aged like balsamic vinegar, but you can season with different vinegars as you see fit.

SERVES 4

6 tablespoons extra virgin olive oil
1 medium onion, finely sliced
400g/14oz Jerusalem artichokes, scrubbed clean
1 tablespoon sweet sherry vinegar
salt and freshly ground black pepper
400g/14oz cooked, peeled North Atlantic prawns

a handful of parsley leaves, chopped
4 little gem lettuce hearts, separated
55g/2oz wild rocket
1 lemon, quartered

1 Set a frying pan over a medium-low heat. Add 3 tablespoons olive oil and, when hot, stir in the sliced onion. Fry gently for 20 minutes, stirring regularly, until the onion is golden and crisp. Tip on to kitchen paper and pat dry.

2 As soon as the onion is cooking, put the Jerusalem artichokes in a saucepan. Cover with plenty of cold water, cover with a lid and bring up to the boil. Uncover and cook briskly for about 10–15 minutes, or until tender. Drain and, as soon as they are cool enough to handle, peel away their skin and any nodules before cutting into large dice.

3 In a small bowl, whisk together the sherry vinegar with 3 tablespoons olive oil. Season to taste and mix into the warm diced Jerusalem artichokes. Tip the prawns on to kitchen paper and pat dry. Mix into the warm artichokes with the warm onions and chopped parsley. Adjust the seasoning to taste.

4 In a separate bowl, mix together the little gem lettuce leaves and rocket. Divide the undressed leaves between 4 plates. Spoon the warm artichokes on to the salad leaves, garnish with lemon wedges and serve.

WARM ARTICHOKE MOUSSE WITH DRIED CEPS

This is a wonderful winter starter. If you're vegetarian, gently fry roughly crumbled 200g/7oz vacuum-packed chestnuts instead of using the smoked bacon.

SERVES 4

Mousse
unsalted butter for greasing
15g/½ oz dried ceps
450g/1lb Jerusalem artichokes
2 medium eggs
120ml/4fl oz double cream
salt and freshly ground black pepper

Salad
200g/7oz smoked bacon, trimmed of fat
  (or chestnuts, see above)
2 tablespoons extra virgin olive oil
1 clove garlic, finely diced
2 teaspoons sherry vinegar
2 tablespoons walnut oil
115g/4oz mixed baby salad leaves

1 Preheat the oven to fan 140°C/gas 2. Line a deep roasting tray with a few sheets of kitchen paper. Liberally butter four 150ml/5fl oz dariole moulds. Cut out and liberally butter 4 circles of baking paper to fit their tops and 4 to fit their bottoms. Line the bottom of each mould with a paper disc and place in the roasting tray.

2 Put the dried ceps into a small saucepan and cover with cold water. Bring up to the boil, then strain the water into another saucepan. Finely dice the ceps.

3 Peel the Jerusalem artichokes. If large, quarter and place in the pan with the cep water. Cover with cold water from the tap and bring up to the boil. Cook briskly for about 15–20 minutes, or until tender. Drain thoroughly. Purée the artichokes until smooth in a food processor. Add the eggs, cream and seasoning and blend.

4 Divide half the artichoke custard between the buttered ramekins. Sprinkle the diced ceps over each, and add the remaining custard. It won't come up to the top of the ramekin. Cover each with a baking paper disc, butter-side down. Pour enough just-boiled water into the roasting tray to come halfway up the sides of the pots. Bake in the preheated oven for 45 minutes, or until the mousses are set.

5 Meanwhile, cut the bacon into lardons (or prepare your chestnuts). Once the mousses are ready, place a non-stick frying pan over a medium-high heat. Add the olive oil and, once hot, add the bacon lardons or chestnuts. Fry the bacon briskly for 5 minutes, or until crisp; otherwise, fry the chestnuts for 3 minutes, or until hot.

6 Whisk together the garlic, sherry vinegar and walnut oil in a mixing bowl. Season to taste. Mix in the salad leaves and hot bacon or chestnuts. Remove the paper from the mousses and, using a small knife, gently loosen the custard from the sides, then invert each one onto a plate with a sharp shake. Garnish with the salad and serve immediately.

BRUSSELS SPROUTS

There is a certain pleasure in picking Brussels sprouts on a bright frosty morning. The faint heat of a pale sun and the promise of new growth in the depths of winter gladdens one's spirit, as does the knowledge that a warm kitchen awaits, followed by a fragrant roast lunch accompanied by a pretty dish of Brussels sprouts. There are few things as sublime as roast pheasant, gravy and sprouts.

Brussels sprouts belong to the cabbage family, *Brassica oleracea*. To many, they are the epitome of British taste, which you either love or hate. It is uncertain why they have taken on this peculiar role. They only entered our gardens in the nineteenth century, and Toby Musgrave suggests in his fascinating book *Heritage Fruits & Vegetables* (2012) that they do not appear to have been particularly popular. Nevertheless, by the twentieth century, Brussels sprouts had taken off and no Christmas dinner was complete without them.

There are two schools of thought on cooking Brussels sprouts – one is that they should be lightly cooked; the other that, like broccoli, they can taste wonderful overcooked with butter and garlic. I favour the former, but it is purely a matter of taste.

PRACTICALITIES

■ Choose fresh, perky-looking Brussels sprouts – always avoid any that are turning yellow or look limp. In theory, sprouts sold on their stalk should retain greater freshness. Purple Brussels sprouts taste the same as green sprouts.

■ To prepare: trim the bottom of each sprout, peel off any tough outer leaves and, if the sprout is large, cut a cross in its base.

■ Brussels tops are the loose-hearted floppy heads at the top of a Brussels sprout plant. They appear in January and should be treated like spring greens (see page 26 for further ideas).

CULINARY NOTES

■ Brussels sprouts need simplicity. Think mini-green cabbages and you can't go wrong. Steamed or lightly boiled until tender suits them perfectly, but current fashions favour stir-frying or puréeing.

■ Their bitterness brings out the sweetness in roast game, especially when accompanied by redcurrant jelly, bread sauce and such like.

■ Traditional flavourings include nutmeg, mace, butter, bacon, chestnuts, cream or gravy. Modern tastes include garlic, ginger and spring onion.

STIR-FRIED SPROUT TOPS WITH WATER CHESTNUTS

Around January each year, sprout tops are sold from market stalls across the land. Try making this simple, crunchy vegetable dish with them. It will make you feel virtuous on a winter's day.

SERVES 2

450g/1lb sprout tops
150g/5½ oz canned water chestnuts, drained
1 clove garlic

2 tablespoons sunflower oil
sea salt

1 Prepare all your ingredients: strip the sprout tops of their outer leaves, discarding all but their tender hearts. Wash in lots of water, then shake dry and slice into thick strips. Rinse the water chestnuts and cut in half, so you have 2 thin discs, then finely slice. Finely slice the garlic into strips.

2 Set a large non-stick frying pan (or wok) over a high heat. Once hot, add the oil and, when hot, add the garlic. Stir-fry for a second or two, until it smells fragrant, then immediately add the sliced sprout tops and water chestnuts with salt to taste. Stir-fry briskly as they sizzle and spit, but keep stirring and within a few seconds they will collapse. Serve immediately.

BRUSSELS SPROUTS WITH BACON AND CHESTNUTS

Every year, cookery writers try to think of new ways to present Brussels sprouts for Christmas dinner. This is a festive version I once wrote, but you can adapt it to your own taste. There are only so many things you can do with sprouts!

SERVES 6

680g/1½ lb Brussels sprouts
200g/7oz vacuum-packed sweet chestnuts
6 medium thick slices smoked back bacon,
    fat removed

3 tablespoons extra virgin olive oil
15g/½ oz unsalted butter (optional)
salt and freshly ground black pepper

1 Prepare the Brussels sprouts by trimming their stalks, peeling off any tough outer leaves and, if the sprouts are large, cutting a small cross in their base.

2 Bring a large saucepan of unsalted water to the boil. Add the sprouts, return to the boil and cook briskly for about 5 minutes, or until they're tender, depending on their size.

3 Meanwhile, place the chestnuts in a colander and rinse under the hot tap. Gently break into large chunks. Roughly dice the bacon.

4 Set a non-stick frying pan over a medium heat. Add the oil and, once hot, stir in the bacon. Fry for 5 minutes, or until crisp, then add the butter, followed by the chestnuts. Drain the sprouts and mix into the pan. Toss thoroughly, season to taste and serve.

PURÉE OF BRUSSELS SPROUTS

This is one of those recipes that you either love or hate. Strangely, Brussels sprout haters generally like this recipe, whereas those who prefer the textural crunch of a sprout tend to view it with suspicion.

SERVES 6

500g/1lb 2oz Brussels sprouts, trimmed
170ml/6fl oz double cream (or to taste)

salt and freshly ground black pepper
freshly grated nutmeg, to taste

1 Trim the sprouts and drop them into a saucepan of boiling unsalted water. Cook briskly for about 5 minutes or until just tender, then drain and cool under cold running water. Shake dry and tip into a food processor with the cream. Process until the sprouts turn into a bright green, roughly-textured purée. Transfer to a clean pan and season to taste with salt and freshly ground black pepper.

2 Reheat at the last minute, as over-cooking Brussels sprouts spoils both their colour and, more importantly, their flavour. Transfer to a serving dish and lightly dust with some freshly grated nutmeg.

SEE ALSO
■ Stir-fried greens with mustard seeds on page 29.

CABBAGE AND KALE

As the snow settles in soft drifts in the walled garden at Knightshayes Court in Devon, the bushy blue green leaves of the perennial Cottagers' kale soften into the outline of a substantial hedge. Once such plants grew in every cottage garden, yielding invaluable fresh green leaves even in the harshest of weather – now they are rare.

The European cabbage, *Brassica oleracea*, which includes kale in its extensive family, has always formed an essential part of our diet. No one knows when cabbage was first introduced into Britain, but it has grown wild here since Roman times. Over the centuries, we've dined on all manner of coleworts, from dimple-leafed Savoy cabbage to curly kale. We've pickled red cabbages, stuffed green cabbage leaves and stored hard white cabbages. Kale has been cooked in broths and loose-leafed cabbage tossed in butter with pepper and nutmeg.

In the last 200 years or so, we've become a little sniffy about the cabbage family. Its association with poverty and bad cooking has led many cooks to ignore it in favour of other vegetables. It takes a foreign name, such as cavolo nero (a dark-leafed kale), to lure us back into cooking it. Surely, the time has come to re-establish cabbages and kale as superlative home-grown vegetables.

PRACTICALITIES

■ Always look for succulent fresh cabbage leaves. Headed cabbages should feel heavy for their size. Hard white or red 'Dutch'-style cabbages keep well in a cool environment.

■ To prepare headed cabbages, discard tough outer leaves and, if slicing, quarter and cut out the core. To prepare loose-leafed cabbages, discard tough stems or damaged leaves.

■ Kale and curly kale are often sold ready-to-use in pillow-packets. To prepare whole kale leaves, wash thoroughly, then take a sharp knife and cut down each side of the main leaf vein. Discard the tough vein along with any stems.

CULINARY NOTES

■ Curly and plain kale have a strong cabbage flavour, so cook lightly and use in moderation in spring green recipes.

■ Cabbage tastes good in salads and stir-fries. Oriental flavourings, such as soy, ginger, garlic and sesame oil, enhance its flavour, as do lemon, orange, olive and nut oils.

■ Red cabbage is also excellent in pickles and slow-cooked sweet and sour dishes, especially when flavoured with spice and combined with apples, dried fruit, chestnuts or bacon.

■ The outer leaves of Savoy cabbage can be blanched and used to wrap foods for poaching, or you can blanch the entire cabbage and stuff and bake it whole.

CABBAGE WITH SPRING ONION AND BACON

This dish is gorgeous with seared duck breasts, roast game or venison, especially with roast potatoes or potato rösti.

SERVES 4

170g/6oz smoked back bacon
1 small green cabbage, such as Savoy
3 tablespoons extra virgin olive oil

1 clove garlic, finely chopped
5 spring onions, trimmed and finely sliced
salt and freshly ground black pepper

1 Cut the fat from the bacon and cut the lean meat into small lardons. Set aside. Remove the tough outer leaves of the cabbage, cut into quarters and wash thoroughly. Cut out the tough white core of each section and roughly slice each quarter.

2 When ready to serve, set a frying pan over a high heat. Add the olive oil and, once hot, add the bacon and fry briskly for 2 minutes, or until lightly coloured. Then add the garlic and spring onions, and fry for about 30 seconds, or until fragrant.

3 Add the cabbage, season lightly and stir-fry briskly for 3–5 minutes, or until the cabbage has wilted but still retains some crispness. Serve immediately.

SPICY GREEN CABBAGE COLESLAW

Traditional mayonnaise-dressed coleslaws can be quite heavy. This light, modern variation is utterly delicious and can be made in advance as it retains its crunch, even if it sits for a while. Take care, however, when adding the chilli, as its heat will infuse the salad and make it hotter the longer it sits.

SERVES 4

1 small pointed spring cabbage

3 carrots, peeled

4 celery sticks, finely sliced

4 spring onions, finely sliced

a handful of mint leaves, finely sliced

a handful of coriander leaves, roughly chopped

¼–½ Thai green chilli, depending on taste,
    finely sliced

2 tablespoons lime juice

3 tablespoons extra virgin olive oil

salt and freshly ground black pepper

1 To prepare the cabbage, remove the tough outer leaves and wash in cold water. Cut into quarters, and remove and discard the tough white core of each section. Finely slice the green leaves and place in a large mixing bowl.

2 Cut the carrots into fine matchsticks, about 5cm/2in in length. Mix into the cabbage with the finely sliced celery and spring onions. Mix in the herbs, chilli, lime juice and olive oil. Season to taste and serve when ready.

STIR-FRIED CABBAGE WITH PORK BALLS

This is a warming supper dish, served with steamed rice. You can make the pork balls in advance and chill until needed.

SERVES 4

60g/2¼ oz lean smoked back bacon

500g/1lb 2oz minced pork

6 spring onions, finely diced

2 teaspoons finely chopped peeled ginger

5 tablespoons naturally brewed soy sauce

3 tablespoons sake (or dry sherry)

1 medium egg white

7 tablespoons sunflower oil

2 teaspoons cornflour

225g/8oz shiitake mushrooms

1 clove garlic, finely chopped

½ teaspoon dried chilli flakes, or to taste

450g/1lb pointed spring cabbage, roughly diced

1 Trim the fat from the bacon and finely dice the bacon. Place in a food processor with the minced pork, spring onions, ginger, 2 tablespoons soy sauce, 1 tablespoon sake and the egg white. Process briefly and then tip into a bowl, making sure that everything is mixed in. Roll 40 walnut-sized balls between the palms of your hands – wetting your hands under cold running water as necessary.

2 Heat a large non-stick frying pan over a medium-high heat. Add 3 tablespoons oil and fry the pork balls in batches, for about 6 minutes per batch, turning them regularly. Add another tablespoon of oil, if necessary. Set aside.

3 In a bowl, mix together the cornflour, the remaining soy sauce and sake and 8 tablespoons water. Discard the mushroom stalks and rip their caps into chunks.

4 Wipe the pan clean, set over a high heat and add 3 tablespoons oil. Add the diced garlic and chilli and, as soon as it begins to sizzle, mix in the mushrooms and stir-fry briskly for 1 minute. Add the cabbage and keep stirring until it begins to wilt, then add the pork balls, any juices and the soy cornflour sauce. Boil briskly for 2 minutes, or until the mixture thickens. Serve immediately.

CHUNKY VEGETABLE SOUP

This is an intuitive soup, which can be adapted to whatever vegetables you have to hand. It benefits from long, gentle cooking. You can add leeks, courgettes, celery, potatoes, different types of cabbage or beans.

SERVES 4

3 tablespoons extra virgin olive oil
1 onion, diced
1 fat clove garlic, finely diced
2 carrots, peeled and diced
½ celeriac, peeled and diced
400g/14oz can chopped tomatoes

1 bay leaf
a piece of Parmesan rind
salt and freshly ground black pepper
85g/3oz curly kale or cavolo nero
freshly grated Parmesan, to taste

1 As you prepare your chosen vegetables, try to ensure that they are all roughly diced to the same size. Set a large saucepan over a medium-low heat and add the oil. Once hot, stir in the onion and garlic. As they cook, start to prepare your carrots.

2 Once the carrots are chopped, stir them into the onion. Leave to cook while you peel and dice the celeriac. Stir it into the pan and gently fry for 5 minutes, then mix in the chopped tomatoes. Fill the tomato can with water 3 times and pour it into the soup. Add the bay leaf and Parmesan rind, and lightly season to taste.

3 Increase the heat and bring to the boil before lowering it again, so that the soup gently bubbles, uncovered, for about 1¾ hours. As it cooks it will thicken, but you may need to add a little extra water.

4 Wash the curly kale or cavolo nero. Remove any tough stalks and roughly slice. Mix into the soup, return to the boil and simmer for 20 minutes. Remove the bay leaf and serve piping hot with lots of grated Parmesan and crusty bread. This soup tastes even better the following day.

SWEET AND SOUR RED CABBAGE

This is a variant on the slow-cooked sweet and sour red cabbage. It reheats well and tastes wonderful with rich-flavoured meat dishes, such as braised pig cheeks or roast duck or goose. For a richer flavour you can cook the cabbage and garlic in duck or goose fat, if wished.

SERVES 4

1 small red cabbage, quartered and finely sliced
3 tablespoons extra virgin olive oil
1 clove garlic, finely chopped
30g/1oz dried cranberries

3 tablespoons crème de cassis
2 tablespoons balsamic vinegar
salt and freshly ground black pepper

1 Quarter the cabbage. Remove any tough or damaged outer leaves, and then cut out the tough white core. Finely slice the red cabbage quarters.

2 Set a medium heavy-bottomed saucepan over a low heat. Once hot, add the oil, followed by the sliced cabbage, garlic and dried cranberries. Briskly stir-fry to prevent it from catching. As soon as the cabbage has collapsed, stir in the cassis, vinegar and seasoning.

3 Reduce the heat, cover the pan and gently cook for a further 15 minutes, or until soft. Taste and add more cassis or vinegar, if wished. Reheat when needed.

RED CABBAGE SALAD

Red cabbage makes a wonderful salad that keeps well, so it is an ideal dish for winter parties. It's worth shelling fresh walnuts, as they add a fragrant note to this simple dish. Perry (pear) vinegar is harder to find but adds a lovely flavour.

SERVES 4

1 tablespoon perry or cider vinegar

3 tablespoons walnut oil

1 teaspoon honey

salt and freshly ground black pepper

½ red cabbage

2 semi-dried pear halves, finely sliced

85g/3oz freshly shelled walnuts

1 Cox or Braeburn apple

3 tablespoons finely sliced chives

1 Measure the vinegar, walnut oil and honey into a large mixing bowl. Season to taste and whisk together.

2 Cut the halved cabbage in half. Cut out the tough white core and remove the outer leaves. Finely slice and toss into the dressing. Add the pears and walnuts.

3 Quarter, core and finely slice the apple. Mix into the salad, along with the chives, taking care that the apple slices are coated in the vinaigrette. If making the salad a few hours in advance, cover and chill but bring up to room temperature before serving.

SEE ALSO

- Mini-colcannon with buttermilk dip on page 298.
- Potato, bacon and greens cheesy bake on page 30.
- Stir-fried greens with mustard seeds on page 29.

POTATOES

The wonderful Dr Kitchener starts the vegetable section in his book *The Cook's Oracle* (1818) with *Fifteen ways of dressing Potatoes.* He writes: 'Although this most useful vegetable is dressed almost every day, in almost every family, it is very seldom well prepared; and for one plate of Potatoes that comes to table as it should, ten are spoiled'. He then proceeds to give heartfelt instructions on everything concerning potatoes, from how to choose them to how to make *The Gipsies Potatoe Pye.*

Since then, the potato has become an iconic British vegetable – something I have never quite understood, given its chequered history here. Even the poor rejected it at one time; and it has rivalled the cabbage in being badly cooked by the general population. Nevertheless, a well-prepared potato dish is food fit for the gods, from perfectly crisp chips to a fish pie topped with creamy mashed potato.

Today, there are literally hundreds of potato cultivars to choose from. Main crop potatoes are categorised by their skin colour, flesh colour and cooked texture. Don't be put off by deep-eyed or oddly shaped potatoes – some heritage varieties, such as Arran Victory, Fortyfold and Shetland Black taste amazing. The possibilities are infinite; there are further suggestions under new potatoes on pages 62–7.

PRACTICALITIES

■ Choose dry-textured potatoes, such as Golden Wonder, Kerr's Pink, King Edward, Rooster, Yukon Gold and Sante, for chips, roast and baked potatoes. Moist-textured potatoes, such as Kestrel, Maris Peer, Roseval and Nicola, are good for boiled potatoes or in cooked salads.

■ Medium-dry, all-purpose potatoes, such as Estima, Desiree, Lady Balfour, Maris Piper, Marfona, Wilja and Vivaldi, are useful as their flesh becomes fluffy without disintegrating once boiled. They are perfect for mash, gratins, chunky soups and sautéed potatoes.

■ As potatoes are stored, they convert their starch to sugar. By February and March this results in very sweet but less crisp chips or roast potatoes.

CULINARY NOTES

■ A mouli-legume or a potato ricer makes the fluffiest mashed potato. Never use a food processor or liquidiser to purée potatoes – they turn to glue.

■ For extra-fluffy roast or sautéed potatoes, par-boil (half-boil) them, so that they're still firm, then add to hot fat and roast or fry. Olive oil, beef dripping, goose or duck fat all add flavour.

■ Potatoes taste gorgeous with butter, cream, milk, various cheeses, nutmeg or mace. They are delicious in meaty stews, and dry and wet vegetable curries. They also taste good with paprika, cumin, caraway, Indian mustard seeds, turmeric, garam masala, ginger, chilli and garlic.

MINI-COLCANNON WITH BUTTERMILK DIP

Colcannon can be served as a vegetable, but it also makes lovely canapés, served with a buttermilk dip.

MAKES 50 PATTIES

500g/1lb 2oz floury potatoes, such as King Edwards
200g/7oz smoked back bacon
extra virgin olive oil
225g/8oz green cabbage, finely diced
1 bunch spring onions, finely sliced
1 tablespoon milk

15g/½ oz unsalted butter
salt and freshly ground black pepper
285ml/½ pint buttermilk
1 tablespoon finely snipped chives
1 small egg, beaten

1 Peel the potatoes and cut into large pieces. Place in a saucepan of unsalted cold water and boil for 30 minutes, or until tender. Drain and leave to steam in a colander.

2 Remove the fat from the bacon and finely dice. Heat one tablespoon olive oil in a non-stick frying pan and fry briskly for 3 minutes, or until just coloured.

3 Drop the diced cabbage and sliced spring onions into a saucepan of boiling water. Drain into a colander as soon as the water returns to a full boil. Cool slightly under cold running water, then pat dry on kitchen paper.

4 Vigorously mash the warm potato until smooth, then beat in the milk and butter, followed by the bacon, cabbage and spring onion. Season to taste. Shape into little patties by rolling into small walnut-sized balls between the palms of your hand, then gently flatten them slightly. Place on a clingfilm lined sheet, cover with clingfilm and chill until firm.

5 To make the dip, season the buttermilk with salt. Divide between 2 small serving bowls and sprinkle with the chives. Cover and chill until needed.

6 Heat a non-stick frying pan over a medium heat. Add 3 tablespoons olive oil to the pan. Dip one-third of the colcannan patties into the beaten egg, and fry for 2 minutes on each side, or until golden. Set aside. Wipe the pan clean and repeat the process until all the patties are cooked. Serve warm arranged around the bowls of buttermilk.

POTATO PUFFS

These are a delicious way to serve potatoes. They take a little time to make, but you can cook them at the last minute. If you don't have a steamer, you can boil the potatoes, cut into large pieces, but this will make them hold more water and, ideally, you want them as dry as possible. They will take nearer 30 minutes to cook.

SERVES 4

500g/1lb 2oz floury potatoes
55g/2oz plain flour + extra for dusting
a pinch of salt
55g/2oz unsalted butter

150ml/5fl oz water
2 eggs, roughly beaten
freshly ground black pepper
corn oil for deep-frying

1 Peel the potatoes and cut into even-sized medium pieces. Place in a single layer in a steamer, add enough boiling water underneath to steam and cook over a high heat for 15 minutes or until tender. Pass them through a medium-fine mouli or ricer – otherwise, push through a sieve. Line a baking sheet with greaseproof paper and spread out the mixture. Leave to cool and dry.

2 Sift the flour and salt into a small bowl. Put the butter and water in a small saucepan and bring to a brisk boil. As soon as the butter has melted, reduce the heat to low and tip in the flour. Beat vigorously with a wooden spoon for 3–4 minutes, until the mixture is smooth and glossy and leaves the sides of the saucepan.

3 Remove from the heat and gradually beat in the beaten eggs, adding a little at time until the dough is smooth and glossy but stiff enough to hold its shape. Tip into a bowl and, using a wooden spoon, beat in the potato to make a smooth paste. Season to taste and, once cool, cover with clingfilm and chill for 3 hours, or until firm.

4 Using floured hands, take small pieces of the mixture and roll into balls the size of walnuts. Place on a floured plate, lightly cover and store in the fridge until ready to fry. Preheat the oil in a deep-fat fryer to 170°C. If you don't have a deep-fat fryer, pour in enough oil to reach one-third of the way up the sides of a large, heavy-bottomed saucepan and clip a thermometer on to the side of the pan.

5 When ready, add a single layer of potato balls and fry for 5 minutes, until crisp and golden. Drain on some crumpled kitchen paper. Let the oil return to 170°C and fry the next batch, until all are cooked. If your pan is small, keep them warm in a low oven.

CREAMY FISH PIE

A well-made fish pie is a sublime creation. It is a dish that should use the very best ingredients you can lay your hands on, from the flavoursome local potatoes to superb butter.

SERVES 4

1kg/2lb 3oz floury potatoes, such as King Edwards
285ml/½ pint double cream
285ml/½ pint whole milk
5 black peppercorns
1 bay leaf
3 sprigs parsley
1kg/2lb 3oz undyed smoked haddock fillets

200g/7oz cooked, peeled North Atlantic prawns
a handful of finely chopped parsley
70g/2½ oz unsalted butter
200g/7oz button mushrooms, halved
1 tablespoon lemon juice
salt and freshly ground black pepper

1 Peel the potatoes and cut into large chunks. Place in a saucepan and cover with cold unsalted water. Bring up to the boil over a medium heat and boil for 20 minutes, or until the potatoes are tender when pierced with a knife. Drain into a colander, cover with a clean tea towel and leave to steam for 5 minutes.

2 Place the cream, milk, peppercorns, bay leaf and parsley sprigs in a wide non-corrosive saucepan. Arrange a single layer of fish fillets, skin-side down, in the milk. Set over a medium-low heat. Once the liquid begins to tremble, poach the fish for about 5 minutes, or until just cooked. Remove the fish to a plate and repeat the process with the remaining fillets.

3 Simmer the cooking liquid until it has reduced to the consistency of thick double cream and strain into a jug. Meanwhile, skin the fish and remove any bones. Flake the fish and mix into a bowl with the prawns and some of the chopped parsley.

4 Melt 30g/1oz butter in a frying pan over a medium heat. Add the mushrooms and fry for 2 minutes, or until just cooked. Add the lemon juice and tip into the fish.

5 Pass the potatoes through a mouli or a ricer, or mash as normal. Beat in 120ml/4fl oz strained cream along with the remaining butter. Season to taste. Add the remaining cream to the flaked fish and season to taste. Tip into a 22 x 22cm/8½ x 8½ in (5cm/2in deep) gratin dish. Cover with an even layer of mashed potato, fluffing it up with a fork. It can be chilled at this point.

6 Preheat the oven to fan 190°C/gas 6. Bake for 50 minutes from cold or 30 minutes from warm. Garnish with the remaining chopped parsley.

STUFFED PARATHAS

Parathas are an Indian flatbread that is cooked on a *tawa* – a small cast-iron flat pan. I use my battered old cast-iron omelette pan. They can be stuffed with potato, cauliflower, grated carrot or mouli and make a delicious brunch served with natural yoghurt and a tart mango pickle. They take some time to cook but reheat well under the grill.

MAKES 12

Dough

340g/12oz chapatti flour (use wholemeal if you can't find any) + extra for dusting

½ teaspoon salt

100g/3½ oz clarified butter (double the recipe on page 175) for cooking parathas

Filling

450g/1lb unpeeled potatoes

1 small onion, roughly grated and squeezed dry

½ tablespoon amchoor powder (see page 148) or 1 teaspoon lemon juice

1 teaspoon finely grated peeled ginger

2 tablespoons finely chopped fresh coriander

1 teaspoon garam masala

½ teaspoon (or to taste) chilli powder

400g/14oz cauliflower, roughly grated

salt

1 To make the dough, sift the flour and salt into a bowl. Add enough cold water (about 200ml/7fl oz) to make a soft, supple dough that springs back when you gently push it. Knead vigorously for 10 minutes to ensure a light bread. Cover with clingfilm and leave for 1 hour.

2 Prepare your fillings: if your potatoes are large, cut them into pieces; otherwise cook whole. Boil as usual and, once tender, drain, peel and place in a mixing bowl with the grated onion, amchoor powder or lemon juice and half the other spices.

3 Put the remaining half in another mixing bowl with the grated cauliflower. Season both bowls with salt and roughly mash the potato mixture – retain some lumps.

4 Re-knead the dough and divide into 12 equal-sized pieces. Cover with clingfilm. Set your pan over a medium-high heat – too cool and the parathas will be tough.

5 Shape the first piece of dough into a ball. Dust with some flour and roll into a thin round pancake. Heap one-sixth of the potato mixture in the centre and fold in all the edges so that the filling is encased in dough. Dust with flour once more, turn over and lightly roll into a pancake.

6 Liberally grease the pan with clarified butter and place the paratha, best-side down, in the pan. As soon as it is speckled golden brown, flip it over, adding a good smear of clarified butter as you do so. Continue cooking for a few more minutes. Keep warm under a cloth while you cook the remaining 5 potato parathas.

7 Squeeze any excess liquid out of the spiced cauliflower. Add one-sixth of the mixture to the centre of the next pancake. Continue as you would for the potato parathas. Seve warm.

CHIPS

Britons fall into two groups: chunky chip lovers and thin 'French fry' fans. I love the latter, so this is a recipe for thin chips, but you can adapt the method below to thicker-cut chips by allowing for longer cooking times. For fluffy chips, choose a floury-textured potato, such as King Edwards; otherwise, go for a firmer-textured variety with Maris Piper.

SERVES 4

4 large potatoes, preferably King Edwards
corn oil for deep-frying
fine sea salt

1 Peel the potatoes and cut into thin chip-sized batons. Place in a large bowl of cold water and leave to soak for 30 minutes to remove the excess starch.

2 Preheat the oil in a deep-fat fryer to 150°C. If you don't have a deep-fat fryer, pour in enough oil to reach one-third of the way up the sides of a large, heavy-bottomed saucepan and clip a thermometer on to the side of the pan.

3 Drain the chipped potatoes and pat dry on some kitchen paper. Cook in batches so that the oil retains its temperature as the potatoes 'blanch'. Fry the potatoes until they have a crisp uncoloured skin with a soft centre – this will take around 4 minutes. Remove from the oil and shake off any excess oil before spreading them out to cool on kitchen paper. Once cold, either set aside or, if you're prepping well ahead, chill until needed.

4 To serve, heat the oil to 180°C and cook the blanched chips in batches for about 3 minutes, or until golden and crisp. Drain on kitchen paper, tip into a mixing bowl and salt liberally before dropping a pile of chips on to each plate.

SEE ALSO

- New potatoes on pages 62–7.
- Celeriac and potato fluff on page 273.
- Celery soup with truffle oil on page 209.
- Crispy parsnip cakes (adapt to potatoes) on page 186.
- Lettuce soup on page 96.
- Potato, bacon and greens cheesy bake on page 30.
- Celeriac crisps on page 269.
- Scallop chowder on page 149.

IN A
PERFECT
KITCHEN

HOME-MADE STOCK

There are certain myths about making your own stock – one of which is the idea that you can put in any old trimmings or bones to make a stock. In reality, you will taste whatever you simmer in the water, so the better the quality of your ingredients, the more delicious the final taste. Forget peelings, cooked vegetables and the debris from a roast; and think instead about how to combine the most delicious flavours in your broth, such as by adding peppery celery, fresh-tasting parsley or sweet carrots. Do you want to add greater depth of flavour and sweetness by initially browning your vegetables or bones? Would wine make it too acidic?

Stock, like everything else in cooking, is a matter of personal taste. I am a great believer in simplicity and have gradually reduced the number of ingredients I add to my stock, as it seems to taste better with less. Some cookery writers advocate adding stock cubes to add extra oomph to their broth. In effect, this adds extra savouriness, which I feel is unnatural and unnecessary. Have you ever read the ingredients on a stock cube packet?

VEGETABLE STOCK

If you can't get hold of any celeriac, just add an extra stem of celery.

MAKES JUST OVER 1.5 litres/2½ pints

3 leeks

3 large carrots, peeled and roughly sliced

2 onions, roughly sliced

2 outer stems of celery, roughly sliced

½ celeriac, peeled and cut into large chunks

200g/7oz ripe tomatoes, halved

115g/4oz button mushrooms, cleaned

4 cloves garlic

a handful of parsley sprigs

1 bay leaf

3.5 litres/scant 6 pints cold water

3 black peppercorns

salt, to taste

1 Cut off and discard the roots and dark green tops of the leeks. Slice in half lengthways, discard the toughest outer leaves and wash thoroughly in cold water. Roughly slice and place in a large stainless steel saucepan. Add the remaining ingredients, apart from the peppercorns and salt.

2 Set the saucepan over a high heat and bring up to the boil. As it begins to bubble, the vegetables will throw up some froth. Skim this off the surface of the water and, as soon as the water starts to boil, reduce the heat to low, so that the liquid barely trembles. Add the peppercorns and simmer uncovered for 3 hours, or until the liquid has reduced by half.

3 Strain the stock through a fine sieve. Season to taste with salt but remember that your stock may be reduced further if it is added to a dish such as risotto, so it is wise to under-salt. Portion and label into freezer-containers. Once cool, chill and then freeze.

CHICKEN STOCK

For the best stock, use good-quality free-range or organic chicken. I've suggested here that you use chicken drumsticks or thighs for ease and speed, but I buy two chickens and use the raw carcasses for stock after I've removed their breasts and legs (which I freeze for later use).

MAKES 3 litres/5 pints

2 tablespoons sunflower oil

1kg/2lb 3oz chicken drumsticks

2 leeks, trimmed

3 large carrots, peeled

3 outer sticks celery

2 onions, peeled and halved

2 cloves garlic, peeled

1 bay leaf

a few parsley stalks

3 peppercorns

1 Place a large deep stainless steel saucepan over a medium-high heat. Add the oil and, once hot, add the chicken. Fry briskly, turning the chicken pieces regularly until they are flecked golden.

2 Cut off and discard the roots and dark green tops of the leeks. Slice in half lengthways, discard the toughest outer leaves and wash thoroughly in cold water. Cut each leek, carrot and celery stick into 3 or 4 pieces. Mix into the chicken with the onions and garlic. Continue to fry for about 5 minutes, or until the vegetables are lightly coloured, then add the bay leaf, parsley, peppercorns and enough cold water to come up to the top of the saucepan.

3 Turn the heat to high and skim off the fat and any froth as it floats up to the surface – it is crucial to keep skimming during this period. As the water heats up and comes to the boil, scum and fat will rise to the surface. Keep lightly skimming until the stock comes to the boil. This will take around 20 minutes, depending on the size of your pan.

4 As soon as the liquid starts to boil, reduce the heat to a low, trembling simmer. Cook very gently for 3 hours. If you let the liquid boil briskly, it will turn cloudy. The stock is ready when it tastes good.

5 Carefully strain the stock through a fine sieve into a large bowl. Ladle it into freezer containers, and label and date them. Once cool, chill and then freeze.

SHORTCRUST PASTRY

As with all pastry, choose a good-quality unsalted butter and, ideally, an organic local flour to ensure a wonderful flavour. I always use half the weight of butter to flour. The quantity of water will vary with different brands of flour.

MAKES 225g/8oz PASTRY (FLOUR WEIGHT)

225g/8oz plain flour
a pinch of salt

115g/4oz chilled unsalted butter, diced
about 3 tablespoons cold water

1 Put the flour and salt in a food processor. Add the butter and process in short bursts until the mixture forms fine crumbs. Don't over-process into a paste or the pastry will be too crumbly once cooked.

2 Tip the crumbs into a mixing bowl. Using a fork, mix in about 3 tablespoons of cold water. You want the crumbs to form themselves into larger balls of dough. If the dough is too dry, it will be crumbly when cooked. If it is too wet, it will shrink when it is baked and will have a more brittle texture.

3 Place the dough on a scantily floured surface and lightly knead into a ball. It can be frozen at this stage. Otherwise, roll out as needed. Loosely roll the pastry around the rolling pin, lift it over the tart tin or pie, and then carefully unroll.

4 Cover and chill for 30 minutes (or longer if you like) before baking.

PUFF PASTRY

Puff pastry doesn't take long to make, but it needs to be rested regularly in between rollings. The chilling times below are the minimum period of time you should leave the dough, but you can rest it for several hours if you like.

MAKES 225g/8oz (FLOUR WEIGHT)

225g/8oz plain flour
a pinch of salt

225g/8oz cold unsalted butter
120ml/4fl oz cold water

1 Mix together the flour and salt in a food processor. Add 30g/1oz diced cold butter and whizz until it forms fine crumbs. Tip into a bowl and mix in about 120ml/4fl oz cold water or enough to form a rough dough. Lightly knead into a ball and wrap in a polythene bag. Chill for 30 minutes.

2 Fifteen minutes before you are ready to roll, take the remaining 200g/7oz butter out of the fridge and let it soften slightly. Place the butter between 2 sheets of clingfilm and use a rolling pin to flatten it into a 2.5cm/1in thick rectangle.

3 On a floured surface, roll out the dough into a rectangle that is three times the length of the butter and about 2.5cm/1in wider than the butter. Place the butter in the centre of the dough and then fold over the top and bottom flaps of dough, so that the butter is completely covered. Using the rolling pin, lightly press down on each edge so that the butter is sealed in. Give the dough a half-turn clockwise.

4 Using short sharp strokes, roll out the dough so that it returns to its original length (three times that of the butter) but retains the same thickness. Then fold in the top and bottom ends, press the edges with the rolling pin and give a further half-turn clockwise. If the butter is breaking through the pastry or the pastry is becoming warm, stop, wrap and chill for 30 minutes. If not, you can repeat the rolling process one more time before resting the dough. Make a note of which way the dough is facing before chilling, as you will need to continue with the clockwise half-turns.

5 After 30 minutes of chilling, replace the pastry on the floured surface in the position that you left off and continue with a further two rolls and half-turns. Wrap and chill until needed or cut in half and freeze.

PIZZA DOUGH

Uncooked pizza dough freezes very well. This is a classic recipe, but you can blend different flours into the white flour, such as one-quarter rye or wholemeal flour to add different flavours.

SERVES 4

225ml/8fl oz lukewarm water + 3 tablespoons
2 teaspoons fast-action dried yeast

400g/14oz unbleached strong flour
1 teaspoon salt

1 Place 3 tablespoons of lukewarm water into a small bowl. Sprinkle the yeast over the water and gently mix with your finger. Measure the flour into a large mixing bowl. Once the yeast has dissolved and looks frothy, mix thoroughly. Add 2 tablespoons of the measured flour and stir until it forms a smooth paste. Leave to rise for 30 minutes – it will puff up and double its volume.

2 Mix the salt into the remaining flour, and pour in the yeast mixture. Add 225ml/8fl oz lukewarm water to the empty yeast bowl and then tip into the flour and yeast mixture. Using your hands, mix together until it forms a dough, then turn on to a clean surface.

3 Knead thoroughly for 10 minutes. Once the dough is silky smooth and elastic, divide into 4 evenly-sized balls. Place on a floured sheet and, if possible, encase the baking sheet in an inflated clean plastic bag; otherwise, cover with a clean tea towel. Leave in a warm, draught-free place for 2 hours, or until the dough balls have doubled in size.

4 Preheat the oven to its highest setting, which is usually around fan 230°C/gas 9. Taking one ball of dough at a time, knead for 2 minutes and then, using the palm of your hand, press out and flatten into a thin circle. You can use a small rolling pin to make it really thin, but press your knuckles just inside the edge to create a raised edge. If you're making a calzone, the edge should be slightly thicker.

5 Top the pizza or fill the calzone as suggested in your chosen recipe.

PITTA BREAD

It might seem strange to include a recipe for pitta bread in a book about British cooking, but over the centuries we've embraced countless foreign introductions from potatoes to pasta, so why not pitta bread? There is a world of difference between home-made and shop-bought pitta bread. Once tried, it's hard to go back. These fragrant pitta bread are really fluffy and luckily they freeze well.

MAKES 10 PITTA BREADS

285ml/½ pint tepid water
2 teaspoons fast-action dried yeast
450g/1lb strong white flour

¾ teaspoon salt
1 tablespoon olive oil

1 Place about 120ml/4fl oz tepid water in a small bowl. Sprinkle the yeast over the water and gently mix with your finger. Sift the flour and salt into a large mixing bowl. Once the yeast has dissolved and looks frothy, mix thoroughly and pour into the flour. Rinse the yeast bowl with the remaining water and tip into the flour. Mix with your hands until it forms a soft dough – you may need to add another 55ml/2fl oz tepid water.

2 Turn out onto a clean surface and knead vigorously for 10 minutes. Flatten the dough, making several indentations with your fingers. Add the oil, then fold and knead the squelchy dough until it becomes a smooth, elastic ball.

3 Return the dough to a large bowl. Rub it with extra oil, cover and leave in a warm place for 2 hours. When the dough has doubled in size, turn it out, punch it down and knead for 5 minutes.

4 Place 2 large baking sheets in the oven and preheat to fan 220°C/gas 8. Meanwhile, lay out a large sheet of baking paper and sprinkle with flour.

5 Divide the dough into 10 equal lumps. Lightly flour your work surface and roughly shape the first lump into a ball. Using a rolling pin, press flat and quickly roll into a 5mm/¼ in thick oval. Place on the greaseproof paper. Repeat until all the balls are rolled, then cover with a clean cloth and leave for 20 minutes.

6 When the pitta breads look puffy, brush each one with water and quickly transfer from the greaseproof paper to the hot baking sheets. Bake for 6–10 minutes. Do not open the oven door while cooking. The bread will puff up and lightly colour but must not brown. It will smell bready. It should be soft and easily parted into a pouch if split open. Remove from the oven and cool on a wire rack.

CLYSTON MILL BREAD

The National Trust's Clyston Mill in Devon stone-grinds local wheat into wholemeal flour, much of which is then used by nearby Trust properties, such as the Killerton Estate, where it is turned into bread.

MAKES THREE 450g/1lb LOAVES

¼ teaspoon runny honey
500ml/17fl oz tepid water
2 teaspoons fast-action dried yeast
375g/13oz stone-ground wholemeal flour

375g/13oz strong white flour
2 teaspoons fine sea salt
sunflower oil for greasing

1 Put the honey in a small bowl. Stir in 100ml/3½ fl oz tepid water. Sprinkle the yeast over the water, mix and leave for 5 minutes, or until it smells of fresh yeast and looks frothy.

2 In a large bowl, mix together the wholemeal and white flours and salt. Add the frothy yeast. Rinse the yeast bowl with a scant 400ml/14fl oz water and gradually mix into the flour to form a supple dough. Different flours absorb different amounts of water.

3 Tip the dough on to a clean surface and knead for 10 minutes, until smooth and elastic. Place the dough in a mixing bowl. Cover with clingfilm and leave in a warm, draught-free place for a good hour, or until the dough has doubled in size.

4 Lighly oil three 450g/1lb loaf tins. Turn the dough out on to a clean surface and knock back by briefly kneading, then shape into 3 loaves and place in the loaf tins. Place in a large inflated plastic bag and leave to rise for 1 hour, or until the loaves have doubled in size.

5 Preheat the oven to fan 190°C/gas 6. When you are ready to bake, drop 10 ice cubes into a wide roasting tray, placed on the floor of the preheated oven. Arrange the bread tins on the same rack and bake for 25 minutes, or until cooked. You can check by tapping the bottom of the loaf: if it sounds hollow, it is cooked. Leave to cool on a wire rack.

HOME-MADE PASTA

Pasta is very easy to make but it does require time and a pasta machine. Although you can make it with a rolling pin, it's quite a daunting task for British cooks, such as myself. One of the benefits of making your own pasta is that you can control the thickness, which means you can make very delicate ravioli and incredibly light lasagne.

SERVES 6

300g/10½ oz Italian 00 flour
3 large eggs

1 To make the pasta, put the flour and eggs in a food processor. Whizz until the mixture forms a dough. Turn out, lightly knead into a ball and wrap in clingfilm. Chill for 30 minutes.

2 Divide the dough into 3 pieces. Roll the first third into a rectangle on a floured surface and roll through the widest setting of your pasta machine. Refold it into 3 layers and re-roll. Repeat the process, then narrow the pasta machine setting, and keep rolling the pasta into long lengths. Gradually pass the pasta sheets through ever-narrower settings until it feels silky and thin. Repeat the process with the remaining two-thirds.

3 Cut the pasta sheets into easy-to-work lengths. You can now cut it as you wish, according to your recipe instructions. If making pappardelle, cut by hand; if making tagliatelle or fettuccine, pass through your pasta machine. Lightly toss each portion in flour or semolina and loosely arrange on a lightly floured or semolina dusted tray. Cover with a clean tea towel and chill until you are ready to serve.

CONVERSION TABLES

Weights

7.5g	¼ oz
15g	½ oz
20g	¾ oz
30g	1oz
35g	1¼ oz
40g	1½ oz
50g	1¾ oz
55g	2oz
60g	2¼ oz
70g	2½ oz
80g	2¾ oz
85g	3oz
90g	3¼ oz
100g	3½ oz
115g	4oz
125g	4½ oz
140g	5oz
150g	5½ oz
170g	6oz
185g	6½ oz
200g	7oz
225g	8oz
250g	9oz
285g	10oz
300g	10½ oz
310g	11oz
340g	12oz
370g	13oz
400g	14oz
425g	15oz
450g	1lb
500g	1lb 2oz
565g	1¼ lb
680g	1½ lb
700g	1lb 9oz
750g	1lb 10oz
800g	1¾ lb
900g	2lb
1kg	2lb 3oz
1.1kg	2lb 7oz
1.4kg	3lb
1.5kg	3½ lb
1.8kg	4lb
2kg	4½ lb
2.3kg	5lb
2.7kg	6lb
3.1kg	7lb
3.6kg	8lb
4.5kg	10lb

Oven temperatures

Oven temperatures	Fan	Conventional	Gas
Very cool	100°C	110°C/225°F	Gas ¼
Very cool	120°C	130°C/250°F	Gas ½
Cool	130°C	140°C/275°F	Gas 1
Slow	140°C	150°C/300°F	Gas 2
Moderately slow	160°C	170°C/325°F	Gas 3
Moderate	170°C	180°C/350°F	Gas 4
Moderately hot	180°C	190°C/375°F	Gas 5
Hot	190°C	200°C/400°F	Gas 6
Very hot	200°C	220°C/425°F	Gas 7
Very hot	220°C	230°C/450°F	Gas 8
Hottest	230°C	240°C/475°F	Gas 9

Volume

5ml	1 teaspoon	
10ml	1 dessertspoon	
15ml	1 tablespoon	
30ml	1fl oz	
40ml	1½ fl oz	
55ml	2fl oz	
70ml	2½ fl oz	
85ml	3fl oz	
100ml	3½ fl oz	
120ml	4fl oz	
130ml	4½ fl oz	
150ml	5fl oz	
170ml	6fl oz	
185ml	6½ fl oz	
200ml	7fl oz	
225ml	8fl oz	
250ml	9fl oz	
270ml	9½ fl oz	
285ml	10fl oz	½ pint
300ml	10½ fl oz	
345ml	12fl oz	
400ml	14fl oz	
425ml	15fl oz	¾ pint
450ml	16fl oz	
465ml	16½ fl oz	
565ml	20fl oz	1 pint
700ml	25fl oz	1¼ pints
750ml	26fl oz	
850ml	30fl oz	1½ pints
1 litre	35fl oz	1¾ pints
1.5 litres	53fl oz	2½ pints

Length

3mm	⅛ in
5mm	¼ in
1cm	½ in
2cm	¾ in
2.5cm	1in
6cm	2½ in
7cm	2¾ in
7.5cm	3in
9cm	3½ in
10cm	4in
18cm	7in
20cm	8in
22cm	8½ in
23cm	9in
25cm	10in
27cm	11in
30cm	12in
35cm	14in
38cm	15in

BIBLIOGRAPHY

Eliza Acton, *Modern Cookery for Private Families* (1855), Southover Press, 1993.

Lindsey Bareham, *Onions Without Tears*, Michael Joseph, 1995.

Isabella Beeton, *Beeton's Book of Household Management* (1861), Chancellor Press, 1994.

Antonio Carluccio, *Complete Mushroom Book: The Quiet Hunt*, Quadrille, 2003.

Robert Carrier, *The Robert Carrier Cookery Course*, W.H. Allen & Co., 1974.

Margaret Costa, *Margaret Costa's Four Seasons Cookery Book*, Thomas Nelson and Sons Ltd., 1970.

E.S. Dallas, *Kettner's Book of the Table* (1877), Centaur Press, 2008.

Elizabeth David, *A Book of Mediterranean Food* (1950), Penguin, 1983.

Alan Davidson, *The Oxford Companion to Food*, Oxford University Press, 1999.

Maria Elia, *The Modern Vegetarian*, Kyle Cathie Ltd., 2009.

William Ellis, *The Country Housewife's Family Companion (1750)*, Prospect Books, 2000.

A. Escoffier, *The Complete Guide to the Art of Modern Cookery*; The first translation into English in its entirety of Le Guide Culinaire (1921), Heinemann, London, 1986.

John Evelyn, *Acetaria: A Discourse of Sallets* (1690), Prospect Books, 1996.

Hugh Fearnley-Whittingstall, *River Cottage Veg Everyday!*, Bloomsbury, 2011.

Hugh Fearnley-Whittingstall, *The River Cottage Year*, Hodder and Stoughton, 2003.

Helen Gammack, *Kitchen Garden Estate*, National Trust Books, 2012.

Hannah Glasse, *The Art of Cookery Made Plain and Easy* (1747), Prospect Books, 1983.

Jane Grigson, *English Food* (1974), Penguin Books, 1977.

Jane Grigson, *Jane Grigson's Vegetable Book* (1978), Penguin Books, 1983.

Dorothy Hartley, *Food in England* (1954), MacDonald & Co., 1964.

Shaun Hill, *How to Cook Better*, Mitchell Beazley, 2004.

Simon Hopkinson, *The Vegetarian Option*, Quadrille Publishing, 2009.

Miles Irving, *The Forager Handbook*, Ebury Press, 2009.

Sybil Kapoor, *Citrus and Spice, A Year of Flavour*, Simon & Schuster, 2008.

Sybil Kapoor, *Modern British Food*, Penguin, 1996.

Sybil Kapoor, *National Trust Simply Baking*, National Trust Books, 2012.

Sybil Kapoor, *Simply British*, Penguin, 1998.

Sybil Kapoor, *Taste, A New Way to Cook*, Mitchell Beazley, 2003.

William Kitchener, *Apicus Redivivius or the Cook's Oracle* (1818), John Hatchard.

Joy Larkcom, *Oriental Vegetables, The Complete Guide for Garden and Kitchen*, John Murray, 1991.

Mrs C.F. Leyel and Miss Olga Hartley, *The Gentle Art of Cookery* (1929 rev. edition), Graham Watson, 1947.

Christopher Lloyd, *Gardener Cook*, Frances Lincoln, 1997.

Richard Mabey, *Food for Free* (1972), Harper Collins, 1992.

Laura Mason with Catherine Brown, *Traditional Foods of Britain*, Prospect Books, 2004.

Christine McFadden and Michael Michaud, *Cool Green Leaves & Red Hot Peppers*, Frances Lincoln Ltd., 1998.

Harold McGee, *McGee on Food and Cooking*, Hodder & Stoughton, 2004

Toby Musgrave, *Heritage Fruits & Vegetables*, Thames & Hudson, 2012.

Roger Phillips, *Wild Food*, Pan Books, 1983.

Sara Paston-Williams, *The Art of Dining* (1993), National Trust Books, 2012.

Sara Paston-Williams, *National Trust Good Old-Fashioned Jams, Preserves and Chutneys*, National Trust Books, 1999.

Elizabeth Raffald, *The Experienced English Housekeeper* (1769), Southover Press, 1997.

Nigel Slater, *Tender, Volume I*, Fourth Estate, 2009.

Christopher Stocks, *Forgotten Fruits: The stories behind Britain's traditional fruit and vegetables*, Windmill Books, 2009.

Thomas Tusser, *His Good Points of Husbandry*, Country Life Ltd., 1931.

J.G. Vaughan and C.A. Geissler, *The New Oxford Book of Food Plants*, Oxford University Press, 1997.

Alice Waters, *Chez Panisse Vegetables*, Harper Collins Publishers, 1996.

Robin Weir, Peter Brears, John Deith and Peter Barham, *Mrs Marshall The Greatest Victorian Ice Cream Maker*, Smith Settle, 1998.

Florence White, *Good Things in England* (1932), Jonathan Cape, 1951.

Alan Wilson, *The Story of the Potato*, Alan Wilson, 1993.

C. Anne Wilson, *Food and Drink in Britain* (1973), Constable, 1991.

INDEX

ACKNOWLEDGEMENTS

This book has come about through the hard work and support of many people. In particular, I would like to thank John Stachiewicz, Grant Berry and Jeannette Heard at the National Trust, for their enthusiastic support and sound advice throughout. I would also like to thank everyone at Anova Books especially Polly Powell and my long-suffering editor Cathy Gosling, as well as Lucy Smith, Lee-May Lim, Heather Thomas and Katie Hewett – all of whom have had to work very hard within a dauntingly tight schedule.

A special thank you to Helene Gammack who generously provided an incredible amount of invaluable information out of the kindness of her heart, and to Sara Paston-Williams for allowing me to use another one of her delicious recipes.

Working on the recipe shoots was an absolute pleasure with such a creative team. Karen Thomas not only took beautiful photographs, she managed to keep everyone relaxed and happy, while her assistant Laura Urschel fed us delicious home-made sweeties and endless cups of coffee, the perfect antidote to a diet of 'healthy' vegetables! Cynthia Inions once again sourced exquisite props, and Bridget Sargeson and Jack Sargeson cooked everything to perfection.

A big thank you to the many people who have so generously helped me within the National Trust, including Kate Nicoll, head gardener at Attingham Park, Shropshire; Jon Smye, director and horticulture lead at Broadclyst Community Farm, Devon; Chris Margrave, head gardener at Clumber Park, Nottinghamshire; Rachel Edwards, head gardener at Greys Court, Oxfordshire; the entire gardening team at Ham House, Surrey, namely, Samantha Green, Patrick Kelly, Jenni Wright and Dave Howard, who not only gave up their time to talk to me but also dug up a great deal of scorzonera for me to experiment on and later shoot. Sadly, the skirret didn't make it into this book, but maybe next time! Thank you too to Sue Lown, volunteer cookery demonstrator, Ham House for giving your recipe for beetroot soup; Neil Cook, head gardener and Liz Bartlett, catering manager at Hanbury Hall, Worcestershire; Lorraine Colebrook, head gardener at Knightshayes Court, Devon, and last, but by no means least, Jade Arnold, Catering Manager at Killerton House in Devon, who was a mine of information and recipes. I am also very grateful for everyone within the National Trust who has sent in recipes from their archives and photographs of the gardens.

Finally, I would like to thank my husband for his constant love, care and sound advice, even when presented with curly kale and Brussels sprouts!

PICTURE CREDITS